ANTITRUST

§1 Sherman Act
- Every K with restraint of trade is illegal
- rule of reason applied
- look to purpose and effect of ag. j if either is a restraint of trade, violation occurred (course of conduct)
- Variable R.R. may be violations, but not usually
- solid show. of dama. required

§2
- Unilateral activity of P.O.
- Monopoly or dominant position
  - requires 50% of relevant market
  - what happens if P.O. raises prices does demand stay the same
  - 50-60% of R. Mark. to be a violation
  - Most cts. require finding of probable success for liability

<u>MARKET POWER</u> - Power to set price w/o concern for competition

§3 Clayton Act
- Only have to show like possibility for reduction of competition
- Tie ins and Tie outs covered

§7 TRANSFER of Assets covered

Tying (Perse) - Factors

1) Tying product
2) Tyed product
3) Coersion - conditioning of sale
4) Sufficient economic power in product
5) To effect substantial amount of economics in tied product
- Must determine if a separated demand exists b/w tied and tying product

<u>Misuse (Perse)</u> 271 (d)

1. Tying
2. Unlawful extent of royalty bly patent term
3. Unlawful packaging agreement

Verticle relationship

restraints may foreclose access t or increases comp. costs of obtaining importing inputs.
- Preventing use of any other tech.

1)
2.
inf. has occurred.
- obj. baseless

HART - Scott - Rudino
Reporting req. for trans of ≥15 mill

Rules of Reason:

<u>Patent R of R.</u>
"Conveying less than title of patent or part of it, patentee may grant a license to make, use, and sell for any royalty or upon any condition the pet of which is reasonable w/in the reward which the patentee is entitled

1) Conduct of licensee being restricted
   - Could P.O. prohibit by inf.

2) Does conveying less than full title enhance monetary standing. of licensor and P.O. is manufacturer (than passes)
   Can always argue smaller grant enhances monetary interest.

<u>ANTITRUST R. of R:</u>
1. Restriction or limitation must be ancillary to the lawful main purpose of a K. [F. of Use - Just. - Tie in - UN Just.)
2. Scope and duration of limitation must not be sub. greater than necessary to achieve purpose
3. Limitation must be otherwise reasonable in the circumstances

<u>Balancing Test - R of R.</u>
whether on balance, considering procompetitive and anticompetitive effects on comp. inthe relevant market affected, the agreenet unreasonably restricts competition.

<u>Reasonable</u>
- Consider chain of relationship verticle or horizontal
- more restrictions may be seen as less reasonable

Drafting
Patent License
Agreements

Third Edition

Drafting Patent License Agreements

Third Edition

Harry R. Mayers

Brian G. Brunsvold

*Partner: Finnegan, Henderson,
Farabow, Garret & Dunner*

The Bureau of National Affairs, Inc., Washington, D.C.

Copyright © 1971, 1984, 1991

The Bureau of National Affairs, Inc.
Washington, D.C. 20037

Second Printing, October 1992
Third Printing, September 1994

Library of Congress Cataloging-in-Publication Data

Mayers, Harry R., 1909–
 Drafting patent license agreements / Harry R. Mayers, Brian G.
Brusvold.—3rd ed.
  p. cm.
 Includes bibliographical references and index.
 ISBN 0-87179-674-0
 1. Patent licenses—United States. 2. Trade secrets—United
States. I. Brunsvold, Brian G., 1938– . II. Title.
KF3145.M35 1990
346.7304'86—dc20
[347.306486]   90-48874
                                                                        CIP

Published by BNA Books
1250 23rd St. NW, Washington, D.C. 20037

Printed in the United States of America
International Standard Book Number: ISBN 0-87179-674-0

Contents

Contents

vii

Contents

Preface

The third edition of this book incorporates legal developments that have occurred since publication of the second edition in 1984. An effort was made to preserve the concise nature of the first and second editions.

Particularly significant developments took place in the following areas: patent misuse problems (Chapter 10), and the effect of bankruptcy law on termination (Chapter 12).

Two sample license agreements have been added as Appendix E and Appendix F. These added license agreements, along with Appendices C and D, concretely illustrate a broad spectrum of drafting practices discussed in the text and are tied to the text by footnote references.

A Table of Authorities (page 263) has been added to provide another technique for locating license drafting information related to specific legal issues, in addition to the Table of Contents (page v) and Topical Index (page 273).

The use of "he" and "his" in general discussions in this book should be understood to be a shortened form of "he or she" and "his or her." Obviously individuals of both sexes are involved in all aspects of the subject dealt with here.

It is my hope that the third edition will prove to be useful to contract drafters in eliminating the uncertainty that leads to litigation.

BRIAN G. BRUNSVOLD

November 1990

Preface to the First Edition*

> "To hunt after truth is properly our business, and we are inexcusable if we carry on the chase impertinently and ill; to fail of seizing it is another thing, for we are born to inquire after truth: it belongs to another power to possess it."
>
> Montaigne, *Essays*,
> Ill, 8.

> "Certainty is generally illusion, and repose is not the destiny of man."
>
> O.W. Holmes, *The Path of the Law*, 10 Harvard Law Review 457 (1897)

The viewpoints and practices of much twentieth century legal drafting derive from the experiences of able lawyers working in the thought context of the late nineteenth century. The spirit of that era was one of relative stability and belief in the possibility of firm solutions for even the most difficult problems. The apparent solidity of the Victorian empire and the seeming convergence of science toward a comprehensive explanation of the physical universe[1] surely encouraged the idea that, by due care and diligence, mere tasks of legal drafting could be brought to perfect resolution. The thought that residual uncertainty might remain even after the most Herculean efforts of lawyers must have been generally unacceptable—if not to the true philosophers of the trade, such as Holmes, at least to the commonality of solid practitioners. The elaborated and repetitious style of much contract and testimonial draftsmanship of the turn-of-century period—with surviving vestiges even today—can suitably be viewed as evidence of an exhaustive search for semantic certainty, undertaken in expectation of its eventual attainment.

---

*Originally entitled "The Certainty of Uncertainty—A Philosophical Preface."—Ed.

[1]"We supposed that nearly everything of importance about physics was known. Yes, there were a few obscure spots, strange anomalies having to do with the phenomena of radiation which physicists expected to be cleared up by 1900." DIALOGUES OF ALFRED NORTH WHITEHEAD, as recorded by Lucien Price (New York: Mentor, 1956).

The twentieth century, on the other hand, has specialized in the discovery of uncertainty. From Heisenberg's announcement of a principle of indeterminancy in the field of quantum physics, through various disillusioning analyses of the "meaning of meaning," to Bertrand Russell's observation that: "Mathematics is the subject in which we do not know what we are talking about, nor whether what we are saying is true," the trend of the century has been toward a general disclaimer of all certainty. Indeed, consistent with Russell's dictum, just quoted, one of the key contributions of the "Modern Math" has been to bring into the open the fact that even mathematics, that most precise of the various modes of thought, is merely a "hypothetico-deductive" system, with its roots in a set of *undefined* terms and a collection of hypotheses or postulates which are accepted as true without proof. The logic of the system may be rigorous, but the system as a whole never escapes from the indeterminacy and arbitrariness of its foundations.

For present purposes, the relevance of these contemporary mathematical insights is their unavoidable implication that all definitional systems share the limitations of mathematical systems. That is to say, every new defined term in any system of discourse specifies either (i) relationships among "primitive" (meaning "undefined") terms, or (ii) relationships among terms which have themselves been created from combinations of "primitive" terms. Hence the definitional procedure, where it does not fall into the vice of circularity, eventually takes us back to terms which we must accept as "undefined" and as incapable of definition in any conventional sense.

This inevitable prescence of undefined terms obviously applies even in the world of legal draftsmanship and introduces into that world an element of uncertainty which it might like to deny, but cannot. The draftsman may take up his task dedicated to excellence, but he is obliged to forswear the expectancy of absolute certainty in his product. This burden he must, of course, bear while still serving practical ends. "To teach how to live without certainty, and yet without being paralyzed by hesitation, is perhaps the chief thing that philosophy, in our age, can still do for those who study it."[2]

In the sense suggested by the sentence last quoted, the present writing is in part a philosophical venture.

HARRY R. MAYERS

July 1971

---

[2]B. Russell, *Introductory* to A HISTORY OF WESTERN PHILOSOPHY (New York: Simon and Schuster, 1945).

1

Some Premises and Limitations; Commentary on Principal Causes of Uncertainty in Contract Language

1.00 Orientation and a Disclaimer of Legal Completeness

This work concerns mainly the structure and technical aspects of the draftsmanship of patent license agreements and related documents. It is not, beyond what is essential to understanding, an exhaustive treatise on the law of its subject, as to which useful sources already exist. While it provides sample forms, it does not emphasize them, but attempts to provide systematic guidelines upon which sound forms may be based.

In particular, the materials provided do not, beyond the insertion of necessary caveats, attempt to advise the reader on the antitrust law pertaining to patent licensing, nor do they undertake to give definite tax advice. In both these fields of law, the ground rules are so subject to sudden change through either decisional or legislative developments that continuing reference to current law sources is the only safe means of guidance. Accordingly, the present text limits itself to noting areas in which antitrust and tax advice may be called for, with appropriate reference to source materials which are believed relevant to points being highlighted. It may be assumed, of course, that all specific recommendations of the authors are, in their judgment, consistent with law as of the date of writing.

The preparation of license agreements is obviously a direct branch of the more general discipline of contract drafting.[1] Accordingly, many of the principles to be argued for in this work require discussion in terms of the broader subject. The beginning discussion will be almost entirely in such terms, although an effort will be made to use illustrations which point toward the patent specialty. Later chapters will focus more specifically on the infield area of patent licensing.

1.01 A Pessimistic Prognosis Concerning Certainty of Draftsmanship

The object of the contract drafter is to record the transaction which is to be undertaken by the parties. In some cases he will have played a role in shaping the transaction, either by advising one of the negotiators or by participating directly in the negotiations. Even where neither has been done, the drafter may still make contributions of substance by suggesting, as an incident to his drafting effort, additions and special provisions which ought to be included for protective purposes before the contract is regarded as final. But in the end, the drafter's job is, in theory, to record exactly the transaction which the parties wish to undertake—a simply stated assignment, but a task laden with pitfalls and tending geometrically toward the impossible as the complexity of the transaction increases. The purpose of this section is to discuss some of the reasons for this ominous prognosis.

The Preface to this work introduces the authors' acceptance of an inescapable uncertainty principle in contract drafting. While the acceptance is based on experience, the reasons for the principle itself can be derived from two elementary facts of existence. These are (1) the semantic dilemma and (2) the imperfection of human intelligence and attentiveness. The semantic problem will be examined first.

A. The Semantic Problem

As the Preface suggests, we live in a world which has come to recognize the ultimate incompleteness of definitional approaches. Every definition pursued to its definitional roots ends in vacuity, that is, in an ambience of defining terms which are themselves indefinable—

---

[1]And contract drafting is in turn a branch of "legal drafting." For those who prefer to begin at the higher level of generality and work toward the more specific (as exemplified by the present writing), no starting point can be more highly recommended than R. Dickerson's THE FUNDAMENTALS OF LEGAL DRAFTING (Boston: Little, Brown & Co., 1965), published for the American Bar Foundation.

unless we permit circularity. We all know this abstractly, but decline, at least too often decline, to recognize it in practice. It takes courage and insight to say, as at times we surely ought to say, "I use this word for lack of a better, but I really cannot know for certain what it means." It is the aim of this part of Chapter 1, however, to suggest that contract drafters may frequently mislead both themselves and their clients if they shrink from this admission. Some examples may strengthen the argument.

Example 1

The following paraphrase and quotation are extracted from a 1969 regulation of the Securities and Exchange Commission. While it obviously does not directly concern contract drafting it illustrates, in an interesting way and in a situation analogous to contract drafting, a deliberate recognition by the drafter that he is leaving indeterminate in content an extremely important term in the universe of discourse which is being created.

1. A registrant is required to disclose "the approximate amount or percentage of total sales and operating revenue . . . attributable to *each line of business*" which contributed at least 10% of the total.

Various suggestions were made for more specific indications of the meaning of "line of business." However, in view of the numerous ways in which companies are organized to do business, the variety of products and services, . . . and the diversity of operating characteristics, . . . it is not deemed feasible or desirable to be more specific in defining a "line of business."

SEC; Rules and Regulations Amended,
7/14/69 (Quoted in part)

Contract drafters often find themselves in essentially this position, but all too frequently they fail to appreciate or to communicate to their clients the fact that an area of recognizable vagueness is being left for post-contract resolution because no better solution can be reached.

Example 2

The temptation in these situations (i.e., situations in which language may have reached the practical limit of precision) is to seek escape through further definitional effort and to find comfort in the illusion that every such effort succeeds. Consider the following:

"Astronomical apparatus" means any aggregate of *instrumentalities* of a design primarily adapted for astronomical purposes.

> Here the drafter (or one of the parties instructing the drafter) has recognized the considerable indefiniteness in the word "apparatus" and has attempted to remedy it by adoption of a formal definition. But how successful is the effort? Must "instrumentalities" now be defined, or does one assume that this is a term so fundamental in the language as to be universally understood to have a single meaning. If the latter, we may pose the question, "Does 'instrumentalities' include or not include 'computer programs'?"

Many definitions to be found in license agreements are of a quality similar to that just discussed. That is to say, when a certain vagueness is recognized in a particular term, a cure is sought through the process of definition, out of a misplaced faith in the efficacy of that process. The result is that more words are added, with the outcome being only the substitution of one uncertainty for another.

It is, of course, not the authors' position that the process of definition should be forsworn. On the contrary, definition is essential to the drafter's art and may be his sharpest tool for simplifying contract structures. Some completely affirmative things will be said about definitional procedure at a later point.[2] Here, the intention is simply to emphasize that any process of definition eventually comes to an end with undefined terms and thus with certain questions unanswered. At that point, an irreducible measure of uncertainty must be accepted on the ground that an effort toward greater certainty would cost more than it is worth. This is what is done in every agreement to a greater or lesser degree, and the drafter's creed must admit it on pain of encouraging a hopeless quest for unattainable perfection. The practical question to be asked at any given point is whether the level of precision that has been attained is sufficient reasonably to serve the business needs of the parties insofar as these can be foreseen.

B. Uncertainty Through Human Frailty

Definitional inconclusiveness is inevitable for reasons just given. Other causes of drafting inadequacy spring from human frailty and therefore have the possibility of mitigation. Three principal frailty-caused defects are "ambiguity," "excessive vagueness," and "the modifier whose reference word is unclear." Each of these deserves systematic attention by the drafter seeking excellence. They will be considered *seriatim* in the following.

(1) *Ambiguity*. To the student of drafting theory, the distinction between "ambiguity" and "vagueness" (to be discussed in detail be-

---

[2]*See* Chapter 3.

low) is of considerable interest. "Ambiguity" is that quality of a word or phrase which gives it at least two possible meanings, each of which may be quite definite, but only one of which is the meaning intended in the given context. "Vagueness" is that fuzziness which arises because the boundaries of meaning of a word or phrase are imprecise.

In law, a favorite example of ambiguity is the word "residence," which, unless context resolves the doubt, can refer either (1) to the place where a person has his abode at a particular time or (2) to the place which the individual and the law consider to be his permanent home, though he may not at the moment live there.

For a second example, consider the phrase "a person who is divorced on June 1, 1967." Does this include (or not include) a person who became divorced on January 1, 1967 and continued divorced through 1967?

Or for an example closer to the field of patent licensing, does "the period from June 15, 1963 to January 1, 1964" include or exclude the 15th day of June 1963? (This kind of uncertainty can be especially important in license agreements of such character that one day's royalties may be important.)

All questions of this kind are avoidable by sufficient insight and diligence on the part of the contract drafter. Choice of a different word or use of additional words can always eliminate ambiguity. But every drafter will eventually have the experience of discovering long after the fact that in preparing a particular contract he failed to discover and correct a consequential duplicity of meaning. The discovery will be distressing to his ego but good for his soul.

(2) *Vagueness.* The problem of vagueness is different. As has been said above, a word is vague insofar as its boundaries of meaning are imprecise. But it has also been pointed out that every word is "vague" because of our inability to give it an ultimately dispositive definition. We must therefore accept and accommodate vagueness. Our only legitimate concern is with the avoidance of "excessive" vagueness, by which is meant generally a penumbra of imprecision too great for the parties to live with.

As an example of vagueness close to the field of patent licensing, consider the word "indivisible" as used, for instance, in the often encountered phrase "a nonexclusive, indivisible, irrevocable license." The meaning of this term is, in the judgment of the writer, so uncertain as to make its unqualified and undefined use frequently undesirable from the standpoint of either the licensor or the licensee. For reasons for this viewpoint, reference is had to the 1948 decision of the 8th Circuit Court of Appeals in *Rock-Ola Manufacturing Corporation* v. *Filben Manufacturing Co.*[3]

---

[3]168 F.2d 919, 78 USPQ 175 (8th Cir. 1948).

In this case there was granted an "indivisible" license "to manufacture phonographs . . . and to use and sell such phonographs." In a somewhat complicated fact situation the court appears to have held that this language precluded the licensee from having the patented phonographs manufactured for it, as distinguished from manufacturing them itself. This may have been the effect intended for the word "indivisible" by the licensors, but that it was not the meaning as understood by the licensee is indicated by the fact that the issue was contested in a long and bitter lawsuit. From the licensee's viewpoint, at least, the word "indivisible" proved to be "excessively vague."

(3) *The Modifier Whose Reference Word Is Unclear.* The use of a modifier whose reference word is unclear is by all odds the commonest and most dangerous of all faults attributable to unskilled drafting— or to skilled drafting in a moment of inadvertence.

Example 1

The following is the license-granting provision in an agreement presented for construction:

5. The Licensor hereby grants and agrees to grant to the Licensee an exclusive license to make, use, and sell in all fields under all patents owned or controlled by the Licensor during the life of this agreement, such license to be subject, however, to a nonexclusive license to make, use, and sell in all fields reserved to the Licensor.

What shall we make of the concluding phrase, "in all fields reserved to the Licensor"? If the total provision quoted above is the only license grant in the agreement, we may eventually come to the conclusion that the answer is "nothing"—because there is no such phrase. The provision as a whole makes sense only if we conclude that the words "reserved to the Licensor" are intended to modify not the word "fields," which immediately precedes them, but the word "license" from which they have improvidently been separated. In other words, in the absence of other relevant language in the agreement, it becomes quite certain that the last lines of the quoted provision are to be interpreted as though they read

subject, however, to a nonexclusive license reserved to the Licensor to make, use, and sell in all fields.

Our question then becomes, "Why was the provision written as it was?" And the answer—"drafting inadvertence."

Example 2

Expressions of the following kind are often encountered in license grants:

a license under patent applications other than design patent applications filed before July 1, 1964.

Is this or is it not to be interpreted as though it read

a license under patent applications (other than design patent applications) filed before July 1, 1964?

Example 3

The following kind of expression is also common:

agrees to pay on devices sold by Licensee in the United States or Otherwise Disposed Of (as herein defined) during the preceding three calendar months.

Is this or is it not to be interpreted as though it read

agrees to pay on devices sold by Licensee in the United States during the preceding three calendar months or Otherwise Disposed Of (as herein defined) during the same period?

We suspect that in both Examples 2 and 3 the answer to our rhetorical question is in the affirmative. Please note, however, that reaching this result requires us to ignore the well-recognized semantic presumption that a modifier attaches preferentially to the word it follows most closely. Moreover, it is easy to imagine economically important situations in which one party will not accept, short of litigation, the answer which the other party argues is logically indicated by context, although not by the rules of grammar.

In respect to the selection and placement of modifiers, eternal vigilance is the price of clarity, as in another sphere it is the price of liberty. The absolute avoidance of error in this regard may well signify attainment of the highest achievable level of drafting excellence.

2

The Opening Part of the Agreement

It is conventional and convenient to provide at the outset of any agreement a paragraph or "heading" which assigns a date to the agreement, identifies the parties, and serves generally as an opening for the agreement. While, as will appear in later comment, the author does not favor the style employed, the following is a common format for such an opening:

> THIS AGREEMENT, effective _____, 1983, by and between ABC Company, a corporation of the State of New York, having a principal place of business at 20 Church Street, New York, N.Y. (hereinafter referred to as ABC), and the XYZ Company, a corporation of the State of New Jersey, having a principal place of business at 7 Wall Street, Elizabeth, N.J. (hereinafter referred to as XYZ),
> WITNESSETH
> 1. WHEREAS . . . .
> 2. WHEREAS . . . .
> 3. WHEREAS . . . .
> NOW, THEREFORE, the parties agree as follows:

Some analysis of the elements of this kind of opening will be helpful.

2.00 Date

The general rule of contract law is, of course, that, in the absence of contrary provisions, an agreement becomes effective on the date on which it is signed by the last of the parties required to execute it, provided such signing is with intent to be bound and is not contingent upon some other event, such as delivery of the agreement to the other party.

The phrase, "effective _____, 1983," used in the context above, is intended to indicate that, regardless of when the agreement

9

is actually executed, its principal operative provisions are to take effect as of the date written in the agreement heading. This is generally confirmed in the body of the agreement by having the affected operative provisions refer specifically to the "effective date" of the agreement, which term is given to a specific antecedent by the opening language under consideration.

Where the discrepancy between the execution date and the intended effective date is substantial, as where the agreement is intended to become fully operative several months (or years) after or before the execution date, this intention is sometimes emphasized by using in the agreement heading the phrase "effective *as of* _____, 19____." The "as of" phraseology (like all stock words or phrases used in contract drafting) should be employed, however, only with full recognition of its potency. This point is well illustrated by the 1954 decision of the New York Supreme Court in *Matthews* v. *Jeremiah Burns, Inc.*[1] In this case it was held that a 1949 labor contract change covering, among other things, payments by the employer into an employee welfare fund required such payments to be made *back to 1946*, the date of the original agreement, because the amendment document purported to be made "as of" 1946. It is probable that the union had intended this result, or at least hoped for it. It is less certain whether the employer had the same intention. But, as the opinion in the case states, ". . . it is fundamental that where parties to an agreement expressly provide that a written contract be entered into 'as of' an earlier date than that on which it was executed, the agreement is effective retroactively 'as of' the earlier date, and the parties are bound thereby accordingly."

2.01 Description of Contracting Parties

The basic objective in describing the contracting parties is to identify each of them with sufficient certainty that identity cannot later become a subject of controversy. In the case of individuals, careful spelling of names, distinction between junior and senior family members of the same name, and precise specification of address usually serve. In respect to corporations, recognizing that identically titled corporations may exist in different states by virtue of state laws to this effect, but not legally in the same state, it is customary to couple the corporate name with a showing of the state (or "commonwealth") or other principal national subdivision of incorporation. Still greater security of identification is added by describing the location of "a principal place of business" where this is in fact a sig-

---

[1] 129 N.Y.S.2d 841.

nificant reference point for the particular company. A partnership or other noncorporate form of business entity will, of course, require its own kind of careful and precise identification.

For those who may at some time be concerned with the preparation of agreements for multidivisional companies in which the divisions are not themselves separately organized corporations, it may be useful to mention a point that is not always understood. Particularly where the organization is somewhat decentralized, there is occasionally a disposition on the part of individual divisions to feel that they can execute contracts without binding the remainder of the company. It is essential to keep in mind, however, that contracts entered into by company components are binding upon the company as a whole, and that the contracting party, in legal contemplation, is the company itself, regardless of purported limitations to a particular department or division which may appear in the recital of parties or in the signatory clause.

On the other hand, it is perfectly possible and frequently desirable that the only products or facilities *affected* by particular terms of an agreement be those of a specified company component. The principal problem in undertaking this kind of limitation is that of appropriately defining the component in question, having in mind the likelihood that changes in company organization and nomenclature will occur after the contract is executed. For those confronted with this problem the following clause is suggestive of an approach that may be explored. It should be borne in mind, however, that this clause was prepared for a particular purpose and might not be appropriate for all situations of the kind under consideration. (This caveat applies, of course, to all "forms" used in this work by way of exemplification.)

> The term "Engine Department" as used herein shall mean the plants, shops, and facilities now or in the future during the term of this agreement administered by the management of the Engine Department of AG as established in the AG organization as of the effective date of this agreement. Change in name of the Engine Department at any time shall not for purposes of this agreement affect the identity of the Engine Department as herein defined.
>
> In the event of any reorganization resulting in substantial change in the character of the Engine Department, as by its subdivision or its aggregation with other major components of AG, the term "Engine Department" shall, as to the plants, shops, and facilities affected, on and after the date of such reorganization mean the plants, shops, and facilities administered by the management of the Engine Department on the day prior to such reorganization.

To one who has adopted a clause such as that just given to define an "Engine Department" or other company subdivision, it needs to be emphasized again that the defined term is *not* suggested for use in the heading of the agreement, or as a purported description of the signing entity, as, for example

Signed:

    Engine Department,
        XYZ Company
    By
        Manager

Its only proper use is in some such operative context as the following:

> 10. This license extends only to the products of the Engine Department (as defined) and covers only such products as are manufactured in the plants, shops, and facilities pertaining to that Department. No licenses are granted to the AG Company other than in respect to products of its Engine Department and, conversely, no commitments for the payment of royalties or otherwise are made by the AG Company in respect to products of any other component of the Company than its Engine Department.

2.02 Recitals

The agreement heading presented at the opening of this chapter may seem to suggest that the inclusion of "Whereas" clauses (generally called "recitals") is an essential element of the agreement. This suggestion is by no means valid, and there is no reason in any agreement to include recitals except as they may serve a useful purpose in a particular case. However, the very common use of recitals in patent license agreements (with or without the largely archaic "Whereas") attests that they have certain values, and it may be useful to identify some of these. Consider, for example, the following fairly typical set of recitals.

RECITALS

1. Licensor and Licensee entered into an Agreement dated April 1, 1980 extending certain licenses to Licensee under identified patents of Licensor relating to electric bedwarmers.
2. Licensor is now the owner of the following patents on electric bedwarmers, which are in addition to those identified in the Agreement of April 1, 1980.

    U.S. Patent No. _____ Issued _____

    U.S. Patent No. _____ Issued _____

3. Licensee wishes to extend the agreement of April 1, 1980 to include rights under the two additional patents referred to, and Licensor is willing to join in such an extension on the terms and conditions set forth below.

THEREFORE, the parties agree as follows:

These recitals acquaint the reader not previously informed on the subject with the nature of the transaction which is to be or which has been entered into.

Particularly in a company having many license agreements of widely varying subject matter which, over a period of time, may need to be reviewed and understood by persons not participants in the negotiation of the agreements, front page identification of subject matter may be extremely useful. Therefore, if this can be done without getting into complex definitional matters better left for the body of the agreement, it may be helpful to provide background paragraphs that identify concisely the *technical subject matter* of the license (or other rights granted). Secondly, and for similar reasons of later information retrieval, it may be helpful to identify at the very outset the *patent rights* involved in the agreement to the extent these are capable of simple description, either by reference to particular patent or application numbers and titles or by brief generic reference. Finally, so far as it is possible to do this without risk of inadvertently importing unintended limitations or extensions into the granting clause itself, it will frequently be useful for purposes of reader orientation to indicate at the outset the nature of the rights to be granted in the agreement as a whole.

Recitals, then, have value in some contexts. However, they are not the only scheme of advance orientation that can be employed and, as will be suggested in the succeeding section, their use may well be avoided in favor of more direct contractual approaches in agreements of such complexity that the careful interrelating of all parts is of crucial importance.

2.03 A "Modern" Style of Contract Opening

As has been developed in the immediately preceding sections, a fairly traditional scheme for introducing a license agreement involves (1) a heading which identifies the parties and assigns the agreement an effective date, (2) a set of "recitals," and (3) a formalistic transition clause such as "NOW, THEREFORE, the parties agree as follows:"

Many drafters now find it more direct and more natural to introduce their agreements by the different kind of language suggested by the following:

AGREEMENT

Effective January 1, 1979, ABC Corporation, a New York corporation (hereafter ABC), having a principal place of business at 20 Church

Street, New York, New York 10020, and XYZ Corporation, a New Jersey corporation (hereafter XYZ), having a principal place of business at 7 Wall Street, Elizabeth, New Jersey 90832, agree as follows:

ARTICLE I

BACKGROUND

1.00 . . . .

In this format, the heading paragraph, which ends with the words "agree as follows," becomes directly and immediately an operative element of the agreement. "Whereas" clauses as such are omitted, and there is no need for a "Now, therefore" clause. To the extent that background information comparable to that conventionally included in recitals is required, it can be put in a "Background Article," identified as such. This article may, for example, include any historical items (e.g., reference to prior agreements) necessary to relate the agreement to essential antecedent matters and any representations of either party concerning its ownership of properties proposed to be dealt with. If not needed, it will, of course, be omitted in favor of an immediate introduction of operative provisions of the agreement.

It seems likely that the trend of the future in contract drafting will favor this simplified, more streamlined approach.

2.04 Formal Structure of the Body of the Agreement

In an agreement which is short and simple, say a matter of a few pages, formal structure is of little consequence. Whether or not major subdivisions bear titles, and whether they are numbered or lettered makes little difference. A quick scanning of the entire document reveals its scheme.

On the other hand, as soon as a transaction assumes some degree of complexity, careful and systematic organization of the contracting documents will not only facilitate comprehension by a subsequent reader but will equally assist the contract drafter in determining when his descriptive task has been fully accomplished. There are several formalistic devices which may be considered for use in this connection. These include:

(1) Use of carefully designed titles for major subdivisions.
(2) Adoption of decimal numbering of secondary subdivisions.
(3) Uniform indentation and tabulation of dependent clauses and substantive categories which have equal rank in the descriptive scheme being developed.

All of these devices are illustrated by the selected excerpts from an imagined agreement which are set forth in skeletonized outline immediately below. (These excerpts are assumed to follow an agreement heading of the kind offered in Section 2.03, above.)

ARTICLE I

BACKGROUND

1.00 ABC represents that it has certain patents pertaining to the processing of petrochemicals in respect to which it is prepared to grant nonexclusive licenses on established terms to all financially responsible applicants.

1.01 XYZ wishes to acquire a license under selected patents of ABC for purposes of producing DYE-STUFFS.

ARTICLE II

GENERAL DEFINITIONS AND RELATIONSHIPS AMONG DEFINITIONS

2.00 ABC and XYZ are hereunder commonly referred to as "parties" (in singular and plural usage, as required by the context).

2.01 Terms in this agreement (other than names of parties and Article headings) which are set forth in upper case letters have the meanings established for such terms in the succeeding paragraphs of this ARTICLE II and in ARTICLE VI (ANCILLARY TECHNICAL DEFINITIONS).

2.02 LICENSED PATENTS means. . . .

2.03 DYE-STUFFS means. . . .

ARTICLE V

GENERAL

5.00 . . . .

5.01 . . . .

5.02 Nothing in this Agreement shall be construed as
   (a) a warranty or representation by any grantor as to the validity or scope of any patent; or
   (b) a warranty or representation that any manufacture, use, lease, or sale will be free from infringements of patents other than LICENSED PATENTS; or
   (c) . . . .
   (d) . . . .

Attention is particularly invited to Article II of the outline just given. The definitional scheme which it describes reminds the reader that a term which he finds to be in full caps (e.g., LICENSED PATENTS as encountered in Article V) is a defined term and that the reader may need to refer to its definition for full understanding of its meaning. There is frequently virtue also in dividing the definitional lexicon between an article which appears early in the agreement and a second article near the end of the agreement, as paragraph 2.01 of Article II indicates is to be done in the agreement to which it pertains. Doing this permits immediate definition of terms which are going to be encountered frequently in the agreement, thus enabling the reader to focus selectively on their significance at the outset. On the other hand, the definitions of technical terms which may be encountered only once or twice in the agreement are placed where they need not be considered until they actually appear in the text—perhaps quite late in the agreement. Whether such terms are defined one by one as they appear, or are collected in a compendium of technical definitions at the end of the agreement is a matter of artistic choice. (See Chapter 3.)

3

Definitions

Chapter 1 of this work may appear to have belittled the definitional process by noting that it is a road which, pursued to the ultimate, ends in terms which are themselves undefined and indefinable. But this was a warning against misplaced reliance on definitions as a path to drafting certainty and not an advice against their proper use when undertaken with due recognition of their inescapable limitations. This chapter attempts to explore the subject of "proper use."

3.00 The Location of Definitions

A given definition should obviously be placed where it will best serve the interpretive problem of the reader. In a simple agreement in which only one or two terms require definition and where these terms do not recur at locations so remote from the point of definition that rediscovering the definition will be a problem, coupling the definition in each case with the first occurrence of the defined term may be the indicated procedure. On the other hand, in a complex agreement, involving relatively many definitions, a more systematic arrangement is to be preferred.

Section 2.04 of the preceding chapter has suggested a scheme of introducing general definitions (i.e., definitions of terms which are basic to the agreement) at the very outset, so that their content is immediately disclosed to the reader. As a generality, this plan is recommended, particularly if coupled with the device of fully capitalizing the defined terms to remind the reader repeatedly of their special content and of the availability of definitions which elucidate this. Technical terms which are exceptional in being basic may be located with general terms in the agreement opening. Whether the general terms should be arranged alphabetically or otherwise de-

17

pends on their relationship to one another. For example, terms that are hierarchical, some defined terms depending on one or more others, should ordinarily be arranged in order of increasing complexity.

The plan argued for in the immediately preceding paragraph insofar as it recommends (1) an introductory definitional article, (2) full capitalization of defined terms, and (3) a hierarchical order of related definitions, may be illustrated as follows:

ARTICLE I

DEFINITIONS

1.00 Terms in this agreement (other than names of parties and Article headings) which are set forth in upper case letters have the meanings established for such terms in the succeeding paragraphs of this ARTICLE I,

1.01 LICENSED PATENTS means the United States Patents listed in Appendix Z attached to this Agreement.

1.02 ELECTRIC BEDCOVER means an electrically heated blanket or cover designed to encompass the whole or substantially the whole of the sleeping surface of a bed or other sleeping facility. It does not mean or include a partial coverlet, such as, for example, a heated foot warmer.

1.03 ROYALTY-BEARING PRODUCT means any ELECTRIC BEDCOVER which comes within the scope of any unexpired claim of any of the LICENSED PATENTS.

In agreements which differ from the case suggested directly above in containing a substantial number of nonbasic technical or other terms which require definition, the introduction of all of such terms at the beginning of the agreement in direct conjunction with the more essential general terms may be more confusing than helpful. In such a situation, the definitions of these less fundamental terms may conveniently be placed at or near the end of the agreement, preferably in a tabulation which is alphabetically arranged to facilitate their convenient location. There should, of course, be some reference to this arrangement in whatever definitional article is used to correspond to Article I, above. (See, for example, the forms suggested in Section 2.04.)

3.01 The Several Kinds of Definitions

Professor Irving Copi, a contemporary authority on formal logic,[1] has identified five types of "definition" and has discussed five purposes for which the process of definition may be used. The types which

---

[1] I. M. Copi, INTRODUCTION TO LOGIC, 2nd ed. (New York: Macmillan, 1961). *See* particularly pages 89 to 127. *See also* the excellent paper on "Definitions in Legal Instruments" by F. R. Dickerson in THE PRACTICAL LAWYER, vol. 12, at 45 (1966).

appear to be of special interest to the contract drafter are those designated by Copi as "precising" and "stipulative."

A. The Precising Definition

A "precising definition" is, as its name suggests, a definition which attempts to improve the precision of meaning of a term whose general significance is known but which has some peripheral vagueness, the elimination or minimization of which is desirable. This is an extremely common problem in patent license drafting, where almost every important term is apt to have an objectional penumbra of uncertain meaning. A common device for improving the situation is to provide a definition of each questioned term to specify that its meaning either includes or does not include critical features as to the inclusion or exclusion of which the parties agree. Examples of this definitional approach include the following:

(Emphasis on Omissions)

(a) COCKPIT DISPLAY EQUIPMENT means airborne apparatus primarily designed to display in an aircraft cockpit aircraft information (such as speed, height, and headings) disposed between the pilot and his direct optical view of the real world. "Direct optical view," as used in this Section (a), does not include an electronically reproduced view.

(b) MOTOR means an integral device of the continuously rotatable type for converting electrical power into mechanical power. The term does not include any apparatus for controlling the application of electric power to the converting device, such as switchgear, fuses, or amplifiers, nor any apparatus for controlling the mechanical power, such as a clutch or mechanical variable speed drive.

(Emphasis on Inclusions)

(c) PRIME MOVER means an engine or other device or apparatus by which a natural source of energy is converted into mechanical power. By way of example, but not limitation, PRIME MOVER includes gas engines, gas turbines, internal-combustion engines, oil engines, petrol engines, steam engines and turbines, water turbines, and mechanical reaction engines.

(d) VARISTOR means a semiconductive device consisting of a body of semiconductive material and electrodes associated therewith, the device being of a design primarily adapted to have a nonlinear volt-ampere characteristic and in which the electrical resistance is a function of the magnitude or the polarity of the voltage across the electrodes; such device includes, if supplied therewith, instrumentalities for holding or supporting the device.

(Emphasis on Both Inclusions and Omissions)

(e) SUBSIDIARY shall mean any business organization with respect to which the parent organization has or shall have the right or power, directly or indirectly, to cast or control the casting of more than one-half the votes qualified for consideration in the designation of the members of the governing body of such business organization. An organization shall be a SUBSIDIARY of a parent only so long as such right or power exists.

(f) RADIO BROADCAST SYSTEM means (i) a radio broadcast transmission system; or (ii) a radio broadcast reception system; or (iii) any combination of (i) or (ii); but the term does not mean nor does it include a system for radio relaying. The term also means (iv) any part of which is of a design primarily adapted for use in (i), (ii), or (iii).

The importance of "precising definitions" of this kind is amplified when they concern subject matter which is to be (1) considered as covered by the license granted or (2) included in the base on which percentage royalties are to be calculated.

Thus, in *Ben Pearson Inc.* v. *Rust,*[2] the court had occasion to construe the following agreement language:

> It is . . . agreed that on each and every cotton picking machine and all cotton picker parts and equipment embodying the invention or inventions of said Letters Patent, manufactured in whole or in part and sold by Pearson, said Pearson shall pay . . . a royalty as follows: (royalty schedule based upon a percentage of retail prices).

As originally sold, the licensed cotton picker was in the form of a trailer adapted to be pulled by a conventional tractor. Later the tractor and picker were built integrally, with certain additional equipment also attached. The court held the licensee to be obligated to pay royalties on the tractor and attachments, reasoning that while the agreement does not require payment of royalties on unpatented separate parts when sold separately, it does require payment on cotton pickers sold as complete machines, even though the machines as so sold contain unpatented parts.

With this case may be compared *Farmland Irrigation Company, Inc.* v. *Dopplmaier.*[3] In this case royalties were to be paid on "sums received . . . from sales . . . of apparatus and parts thereof . . . the manufacture of which . . . would infringe any patent right of M." The claims of the licensed patent purported to cover sprinkling apparatus comprising pipe sections joined by wheel-like coupling units that enabled the assembly to be rolled from place to place. The licensor eventually rejected the licensee's proffer of royalty payments on the ground that they were computed on the basis of sales of wheel and coupling units only rather than on the basis of sales of complete sprinkling apparatus. In spite of the comprehensive language of the patent claims, the court concluded that the distinguishing feature of the patented invention was in the improved wheel and coupling unit and that, accordingly, all other parts could be sold free of royalty burdens.

---

[2] 268 S.W.2d 893, 101 USPQ 424 (Ark. 1954).

[3] 308 P.2d 732, 113 USPQ 88 (Cal. 1957).

Had there been any hint in either of these cases during the negotiating period of lack of agreement concerning the scope of royalty obligations, "precising definitions" adequate to avoid future controversy could readily have been hammered out. It is the obligation of the drafter to recognize these areas of potentially harmful vagueness in such cases and to recommend a curative approach.

B. The Stipulative Definition

A "precising definition" of a word as discussed in Section 3.01 (a), above, normally tends to follow as far as possible the conventional or public definition of the word and, where the word is to be found in a general dictionary, may be expected to resemble the dictionary definition of first choice. Although this norm is inapplicable where the subject matter dealt with is so technical as not to be in general use, the core of any "precising definition" of a technical term will still ordinarily follow the prevalent usage of the field of technology to which it pertains.

The "stipulative definition," on the other hand, is of quite different quality. The adoption of such a definition, at least in contract drafting, represents a decision of the parties to replace the awkwardness of an extended collection of words (or other symbols) by the simplicity of a single (or at least a simplified) symbolism of equivalent meaning.[4]

All of the following may be recognized as "stipulative definitions":

(a) LICENSED PATENTS means the United States patents enumerated in Appendix A attached to this Agreement.

(b) LICENSED PATENTS of a party shall mean all patents throughout the world (including patents of importation, improvement patents, patents and certificates of addition and utility models, as well as divisions,

---

[4]The stipulative technique has wide use in mathematical exposition, and its theory has probably never been better stated than in the Introduction to the PRINCIPIA MATHEMATICA of A. N. Whitehead and B. Russell (New York: Cambridge University Press, 1913). This statement, considerably abbreviated for present purposes, follows:

A definition is a declaration that a certain newly-introduced symbol or combination of symbols is to mean the same as a certain other combination of symbols of which the meaning is already known. . . . We will give the names *definiendum* and *definiens* respectively to what is defined and to that which it is defined as meaning. . . .

Theoretically, it is unnecessary ever to give a definition: we might always use the *definiens* instead, and thus wholly dispense with the *definiendum*. . . . Practically, of course, if we introduced no definitions, our formulae would very soon become so lengthy as to be unmanageable; but theoretically, all definitions are superfluous.

reissues, continuations, renewals, and extensions of the foregoing), applications therefor, and patents which may issue upon such applications

(i) As to which patents or applications the party has at any time during the TERM OF THIS AGREEMENT the right to grant licenses of or within the scope of the licenses granted in this Agreement, and,

(ii) Which cover inventions or designs applicable to LICENSED PRODUCTS.

(c) TYPE I MEASURING SYSTEM means an aggregate of instrumentalities of a design primarily adopted for use in the examination, recording, reproduction, simulation, or indication of the characteristics, conditions, or properties of systems, apparatus _____, lines materials, or biological, geophysical, meteorological, or extraterritorial phenomena.

(d) TYPE II CARRIER CURRENT SYSTEM means a carrier current system so designed that the transmitted waves representing signals occupy an effective band width not exceeding 7 megacycles per second.

It will be apparent that none of the terms covered by the four definitions set forth above has a "public meaning" which is in any sense comparable to that which it is given for agreement purposes. While clarity of meaning is obviously of just as much concern in reference to these "stipulated definitions" as it is in the "precising definitions" presented in Section 3.01(a), the central object of each of the former is to shorten and simplify the text of the main body of the agreement. Their possible usefulness for this purpose may be judged from the observation that a certain agreement from which definition (b), "LICENSED PATENTS," has been paraphrased employs this term 11 times in the text of the agreement. The compression of text realized by making "LICENSED PATENTS" a stipulatively defined term is obviously enormous.

3.02 Strategy in the Choice and Design of Definitions

Work devoted to the designing of "precising definitions" is, on the part of the legal drafter, an obeisance to the gods of humility. If, in the words of Holmes, it is the mark of an educated man to have questioned his own first principles, it is equally the mark of the perceptive drafter to have questioned the semantic adequacy of each of the crucial terms of his work piece. Vagueness and ambiguity must be sought out with craft and guile, and, where discovered, eliminated or minimized by choice of new words, rearrangement of the preselected words, or, as a final resort, by adoption of definitions. Then the terms of the *definiens* of the definitions must be studied for their own degree of indeterminacy and the process continued until the residuum of uncertainty is thought to be small enough for the parties to live with.

On the other hand, the adoption and handling of "stipulative definitions" is largely an esthetic enterprise. The objective is to produce an agreement which is as compact, as readable, and as understandable as skill can make it. The choice and orderly arrangement of convenient symbols of communication are the fine brush strokes of the artist. Proper choice of stipulative definitions contributes to artistry.

4

Reservations and Exceptions

The patent owner who is granting his first license may have little or no interest in the problem of "reservations and exceptions." This problem grows, however, with the magnitude and complexity of a company's licensing program, and at a certain point of complexity may reach a level of serious concern. It is not necessary, and in many cases may not even be appropriate, that the problem be treated in an isolated part of the license agreement. It is, however, worthwhile to give it such consideration as it requires early in the agreement-drafting process so that it will not be inadvertently overlooked when the financially more significant parts of the agreement are the principal subjects in focus. This chapter undertakes to collect some of the questions which ought to be weighed in this connection.

The party who proposes to grant an exclusive license must, of course, consider whether any reservation needs to be made in recognition of prior nonexclusive licenses granted in reference to the same rights. He must also question whether he wishes to reserve for himself a nonexclusive license to practice the licensable invention, either generally or in some particular field of use peculiar to his interests. Conversely, one who offers a nonexclusive license must search his mind as to whether there are any outstanding exclusive grants, for example, in the form of field licenses, with which the proposed nonexclusive grant would be in conflict. Particularly for the holder of a large and actively administered patent portfolio, these issues can be material and, depending on the facts, may require contract clauses which are meticulously drawn to avoid later charges of bad faith or deceit. Several imaginable situations are explored in the following.

4.00 Reservations in Respect to Exclusive Grants or Sales of Patents

A. Reservation of Rights in the Grantor

It is quite common for the patent owner (say a corporation) which sells a patent or grants an exclusive license under it to wish to reserve for itself some rights of continued use of the transferred invention. No such rights are implied in an unequivocally exclusive grant, and they must, therefore, be expressed. Some commonly encountered reservations are the following:

> The license granted in Article ___ of this Agreement is subject to a reserved nonexclusive license in the Licensor to make, use and sell LICENSED PRODUCTS.

> The license granted in Article ___ of this Agreement is subject to a reserved nonexclusive license in the Licensor to make LICENSED PRODUCTS and to use and sell such LICENSED PRODUCTS as components incorporated in communication equipment of its manufacture, but not otherwise.

> The license granted in Article ___ of this Agreement is subject to a reserved nonexclusive license in the Licensor to use the LICENSED PROCESS in its manufacturing facilities for the production of communication equipment, but not otherwise.

B. Reservations Made Necessary by the Existence of Prior Licenses

It occasionally happens that a company has licensed "all of its patents" insofar as and to the extent that they apply to a particular field of use, for example, the field of "communications products." It may later be desired to license exclusively specifically identified patents, the inventions of which, according to their description, apply, say, only to the field of "geophysical surveying." It may be impossible to guarantee, however, that these inventions have *no* conceivable application to "communications products."

Candor and good practice seem to demand that the prospective exclusive licensee (or purchaser) of the patent rights in question be acquainted with the existing situation and be asked to accept a contract provision such as the following:

> Notwithstanding anything to the contrary in this Agreement, Purchaser (or Licensee), his successors, and assigns shall take the aforesaid United States Patent No. ___ (or the aforesaid license) subject to any outstanding licenses, options to acquire licenses, or other rights existing in third parties under agreements executed by ABC Company prior to the effective date of this agreement.

It will occasionally be true, of course, that language of the foregoing type will not satisfy the prospective purchaser or exclusive licensee, in which case more elaborate wording such as the following may be considered.

> (1) Notwithstanding the exclusive character of certain licenses granted in this Agreement, licensee shall take such licenses subject to any rights in third parties established by agreements entered into by ABC prior to the date of the Agreement. In this connection ABC represents that no rights have been granted to others in specific reference to the patents which are the subject matter of this Agreement and that no licenses have been granted affecting the subject matter of such patents which would in its judgment significantly diminish the value of the rights herein conveyed. These patents are, however, subject to certain comprehensively defined nonexclusive rights which have been granted by ABC in reference to particular fields of use, e.g., under all ABC patents insofar as these apply to inventions useful in public service communication.

In especially complex situations where the possibility of partially overlapping agreements must also be anticipated, additional protective clauses of the following kind may be useful:

> (2) While ABC recognizes that its grant of exclusive rights to licensee in the present Agreement involves a commitment on its part not to grant other licenses in derogation of these rights, licensee on its part recognizes the extraordinary diversity of ABC's business activities and patent licensing arrangements and agrees that inadvertent inclusion by ABC of limited rights in the patents exclusively licensed hereunder in any future grant by ABC to others of general or field licenses shall not be deemed to be in derogation of licensee's rights or a breach of this Agreement provided such limited rights:
>
> (a) Do not impinge directly on the field of this Agreement and
>
> (b) Do not tend in any substantial way to diminish the value of the rights extended to licensee under the terms of this Agreement.
>
> (3)(a) Notwithstanding paragraph 2, above, if future rights granted by ABC to others than licensee are considered by licensee to diminish in any substantial way the value of the rights extended to licensee under the terms of this Agreement, ABC agrees to negotiate in good faith with licensee respecting the substantiality of such diminution and the appropriateness of reducing the compensation paid to ABC under this Agreement in order to reflect the magnitude of the diminution.
>
> (b) In event of the failure of the parties to agree in respect to the matters referred to in paragraph 3(a), above, the issues in dispute shall be submitted to arbitration, either under the rules and procedures of the American Arbitration Association or as otherwise may be mutually determined by the parties at the time.

Regardless of negotiating difficulties, the problem of potential conflict in respect to rights granted and to be granted exists and must be evaluated and dealt with in some appropriate way in each new license agreement entered into. The suggestions made in this Section are obviously starting points only and may be refined and developed as indicated by the requirements of the particular situation.

4.01 Reservations in Nonexclusive Grants

The problem of reservations in connection with nonexclusive grants is obviously far simpler than in the exclusive grant case. If it is to arise, this will probably be in connection with nonexclusive grants which purport to extend rights under all of the licensor's patents relevant to a designated technical field.

In such a situation difficulties exist only if there is a chance that exclusive rights may have been previously granted in respect to some of licensee's patents which are contingently, although remotely, applicable to the field now proposed to be nonexclusively (but comprehensively) licensed. If such prior situations are identifiable with certainty, they should, of course, be cataloged and brought to the attention of the prospective licensee in a document providing for his written acceptance of their existence. However, if the situation is too complicated to make this solution possible, a catch-all provision, such as the following, may provide protection against controversy based upon a purely technical breach of the agreement (i.e., through failure to identify an arguably relevant but clearly immaterial conflict established by an unnoted prior agreement):

> Licensor has noted and Licensee recognizes and accepts the possible existence, in reference to particular patents or situations, of prior commitments of the Licensor which may be inconsistent in some respect with the commitments of this Agreement, but Licensor represents and warrants that it has accepted no commitments or restrictions which will materially affect the value of the licenses and rights granted by it in this Agreement.

5

Nonexclusive Licenses and Nonassertions; Assignments and Exclusive Licenses; Cross-Licenses and Grantbacks

"License" is from the Latin "licentia," meaning "freedom" or "liberty." Consistent with this derivation, it has been defined in the law of real property as follows:

> A license in the law of land is ordinarily a permission merely to do something on or to the detriment of the land of the giver of the licensee. . . . It creates a privilege in favor of the licensee.[1]

Similarly, in the field of municipal law a license has been described as "a permit to do what otherwise would be unlawful,"[2] or as "merely permission granted by the sovereign, to do an act which without the license would not be permissible."[3]

In general legal usage, therefore, a license is merely a waiver of a right to sue the licensee for conduct which, absent the license, would be actionable.

5.00 The Nonexclusive Patent License

The term "license" undergoes no significant inflection in meaning when used in context of a patent licensing grant that confers

---

[1]Tiffany, REAL PROPERTY §829 (3rd ed., Chicago: Callaghan & Co., 1939).
[2]LaPlante v. State Bd. of Pub. Rds., 131 A. 641 (R.I. 1926).
[3]City of Shreveport v. Brister, 194 La. 615, 194 So. 566 (1939).

upon the licensee no rights of exclusion that he may assert against others—although the giving of consideration for the grant destroys the revocability which is the asserted hallmark of the license respecting land. The "nonexclusive license," so called, is, in essence, only an assurance of immunity from suit in respect to acts done within the scope of the license. Subject to various possibilities of elaboration or limitation which will be discussed in Chapter 7, the conventional words of conveyance of a nonexclusive license are essentially the following:

> LICENSOR grants to LICENSEE a nonexclusive license to make, use, and sell products embodying or made in accordance with the inventions of the LICENSED PATENTS.

It is hornbook law that, in the absence of supplementary covenants by the licensor, the nonexclusive licensee acquires no affirmative rights in respect to the enforcement of the licensed patents.[4] Conversely, it is the general rule that the acceptance of such a license implies no covenants by the licensee in respect to the avoidance of activities outside the scope of his license.[5] The few cases which find a contrary result may either be viewed as deviant,[6] or as based on considerations extrinsic to the language of the agreement itself.[7]

5.01 Nonassertion Clauses

In some situations in which licenses are granted under specified patents, the licensee may desire assurance that the licensor has no other patents relevant to the licensed subject matter. If the licensor's portfolio is a limited one, such assurance may most readily be given by a covenant against the existence in that portfolio of additional

---

[4]"Infringement of the patent can no more be a legal injury to a bare licensee than a trespass on Blackacre could be an injury to one having a nonexclusive right of way across Blackacre." Western Elec. Co. v. Pacent Reproducer Corp., 42 F.2d 116 (2d Cir. 1930), *cert. denied*, 282 U.S. 873 (1930). For the incidents of conveyance which *do* give the grantee a voice in the enforcement of his or her grantor's patent, *see* Chapter 6.

[5]"This limited license for 'home' use production contains neither an express nor implied agreement to refrain from production for 'commercial' or any other use as part consideration for the license grant." Automatic Radio Mfg. Co. v. Hazeltine Research, Inc., 339 U.S. 827 (1950).

[6]*E.g.*, Shaw v. E.I. DuPont de Nemours & Co., 226 A.2d 903, 152 USPQ 364 (Vt. 1966).

[7]*E.g.*, Aktiebolaget Bofors v. United States, 153 F. Supp. 397, 114 USPQ 243 (Ct. Cl. 1957); Metro-Goldwyn Mayer Corp. v. Fear, 104 F.2d 892, 42 USPQ 101 (9th Cir. 1939); Ethyl Corp. v. Hercules Powder Co., 232 F. Supp. 453, 139 USPQ 471 (D. Del. 1963).

pertinent values. In other cases, however, particularly where complex patent holdings are involved, the problem may be dealt with in another way by a "nonassertion clause" of the following sort:

> LICENSOR agrees that with respect to any United States patent which, on the date of this Agreement, it owns or under which it has the right to grant licenses of the scope of the licenses granted in this Agreement, or any United States patent which may later issue on a pending application for patent which, on the date of this Agreement, it owns or under which it has the right to grant licenses of the scope of the license granted in this Agreement, it will not assert against LICENSEE, or its vendees, mediate or immediate, any claims for infringement based on the manufacture, use, or sale of any apparatus made or sold by LICENSEE under the license granted in this Agreement and upon which royalty has been paid in accordance with the provisions of Article ___.

In line with the analysis given earlier in this chapter, it should be apparent that a nonassertion agreement of the kind just stated is, in legal effect, the full equivalent of a supplementary nonexclusive license. In some cases, it might well be called by the nonexclusive license name, but in other cases there is an advantage to the drafter in being able to distinguish "licensed patents" from "nonasserted patents" in the royalty-prescribing parts of the agreement and elsewhere. In such cases, the nonassertion language may be useful, but the extreme breadth of the particular language used above should be recognized.

Depending on context and on the subject matter of the primary license, it may be important to the licensor, particularly where he has a complex portfolio, to limit the nonassertion grant by some such added sentence as the following:

> This agreement of nonassertion shall apply, however, only to patents and to claims of patents which are directed specifically to inventions in (here insert the subject matter of the primary license).

In the absence of such a limitation, the nonassertion might be claimed by the licensee to extend not only to inventions comparable to the inventions covered by the primary license, but also to inventions directed to components and materials useful in licensed products.

Of course, the limitation to be applied can be tailored in any way which will appropriately meet the actual intention of the parties.

5.02 Assignments

"Assignments" is a term the normal connotations of which are as well settled in law as are those of the term "license" which were discussed in the opening paragraphs of this chapter. Its law dictionary definition is:

A transfer or making over to another of the *whole* of any property, real or personal, in possession or in action, or of any estate or right therein.[8] (Emphasis added)

In the patent lexicon, however, the meaning of "assignment" has been given a special and lasting gloss by a key passage of an 1891 Supreme Court decision which has done much to shape the vocabulary of future patent conveyances.

The decision is that in *Waterman* v. *MacKenzie*,[9] and the key passage reads as follows:

> The patentee or his assigns may, by instrument in writing, assign, grant, and convey, either (1) the whole patent, comprising the exclusive right to make, use and vend the invention throughout the United States; or (2) an undivided part or share of that exclusive right; or (3) the exclusive right under the patent within and throughout a specified part of the United States. (Revised Statute) Section 4898. A transfer of either of these three kinds of interests is an assignment, properly speaking, and vests in the assignee a title in so much of the patent itself, with a right to sue infringers. In the second case, jointly with the assignor. In the first and third cases, in the name of the assignee alone. Any assignment or transfer, short of one of these, is a mere license, giving the licensee no title in the patent, and no right to sue at law in his own name for an infringement.

5.03 Exclusive Licenses

The Court's nice cleavage, immediately above, between "an assignment, properly speaking" and a "mere license" is often quoted and has had important consequences in many contexts. From the standpoint of the contract drafter, however, the two terms which the Court so flatly distinguished have been supplemented by the insertion between them of the additional concept, "exclusive license."

The classic limitations of meaning of "license," as recited in the opening paragraphs of this chapter, call into question whether any grant beyond a covenant of nonassertion of rights ought to bear the license name. The question is bootless, however, because historical development has firmly established the phrase, "exclusive license," as an accepted description of certain forms of patent conveyance. It means something more than a "mere license" and something less than "an assignment, properly speaking." Its moreness consists in the addition of at least some rights of exclusion to the bare assurance of nonassertion conveyed by a mere license. Its lessness consists in some subtraction from conveyance of the *whole* property right which assignment naturally connotes.

---

[8]BLACK'S LAW DICTIONARY, 4th ed. (St. Paul: West Publishing Co., 1951).
[9]138 U.S. 252 (1891).

In certain cases the subtraction from the whole title may be trivial—as where some minor power is reserved to the grantor—and in such cases the legal consequences of the "exclusive license," so called, will approximate those of assignment. In other cases, however, the right of exclusion added to the licensor's bare assurances against suit will be minimal—as where there is added only a commitment by the licensor that no second license will be granted for 60 days. In such a case, the very use of the term "exclusive license" seems excessive. Nevertheless, it has become an expression of art which finds wide application in the open area between "assignment" and mere "nonexclusive license."

Some circumstances of its use and the consequences attendant upon their existence will be explored in the immediately following chapter. (Chapter 6.)

5.04 Cross-Licenses

A "cross-license" is a transaction in which (1) a license is granted from Party A to Party B and (2) at least part of the consideration provided by Party B is a license to Party A under patents of Party B. Under this definition, the cross-license obviously represents a combination of two grants, one in each direction. The two grants can be viewed separately and, so viewed, can, if desired, be specified in separate instruments. Where this is the treatment selected, the drafting problems involved are basically those of preparing two distinct license agreements, each appropriately defining the rights being extended under it—there being only enough cross-reference to establish the fact of mutual consideration. On the other hand, because the parties are the same and the grants in some measure reciprocal, economy of documentation can often be realized by embodying the entire transaction in a single agreement in which the two grants are appropriately interleaved.

The variety of circumstances which may arise in cross-licensing are so great as to make impossible any general recommendations respecting form. It should be evident, however, that all suggestions concerning agreement structure which are offered in this work in reference to unidirectional licensing will apply with equal force to an agreement or agreements covering a license exchange. Appendix D at the end of this book attempts to illustrate some of the economies of wording which may be realized in the special case in which the cross-grants are symmetrical (i.e., of the same scope in both directions), so that bilaterally worded contract provisions may be employed.

5.05 Grantbacks

"Grantback" is a term generally applied to the requirement by a primary licensor that his licensee include in the consideration to be paid for the rights extended a cross-license (see Section 5.04, above) under related patents (present or future) of the licensee. The reverse rights so stipulated may, for example, be any of the following:

(1) A simple nonexclusive license under future improvement patents (See Chapter 8) of the licensee;
(2) A nonexclusive license under present and future patents of the licensee in the field of the primary license with, in some cases, the right in the primary licensor to grant nonexclusive sublicenses under these patents; or
(3) An exclusive license under (or outright ownership of) licensee's improvement patents.

The fairness and negotiability (from the licensor's standpoint) of requiring any of the rights enumerated in (1), (2), and (3), above, are, of course, matters that can only be determined in light of the circumstances of the particular case. In this connection, the value of the primary licensor's inventive contribution and the magnitude of the competitive concession represented by his adopting a licensing posture in the first instance will obviously have a bearing.

Beyond this, however, any licensor contemplating grantback practices should be keenly aware of the antitrust pitfalls which may attend an unduly overreaching approach. The principal decisional authority in this field[10] is often cited as having endorsed the action of a licensor in granting an exclusive license on the condition that the licensee assign to the licensor improvement patents applicable to the licensed machine for use in connection with it. It is vital to observe, however, that the effect of the subject decision was merely to remand the problem to the circuit court of appeals with the following observation:

> The District Court found no violation of the antitrust laws in the present case. The Circuit Court of Appeals did not reach that question. Hence it, as well as any other questions which may have been preserved, are open on our remand of the cause to the Circuit Court of Appeals.

> We only hold that the inclusion in the license of the condition requiring the licensee to assign improvement patents is not *per se* illegal and unenforceable.

---

[10]Transparent-Wrap Mach. Corp. v. Stokes & Smith Co., 329 U.S. 637 (1947).

While the circuit court did not in this case (on remand) find antitrust violation,[11] the question of the circumstances in which a required grantback will be found illegal is still very much open.

For a time, the Antitrust Division attacked, on the basis of the *per se* theory, license restrictions which required the licensee to assign or grant an exclusive license to the licensor for any patent which issued to the licensee after the licensing arrangement was executed.

In 1981 a Justice Department spokesman indicated that the department's position would be to attack as *per se* illegal exclusive grantback provisions found in licenses to all or most significant actual or potential competitors—or to trivial licensee competitors of an industry-dominating patent owner—where all technology is subject to grantback regardless of whether the practice of the licensed patent is necessary to the improvement. Anything less, according to the Antitrust Division, will be subject to a rule of reason analysis.[12]

Against this background, a decision whether to include grantback requirements in an important licensing program must obviously be made with a careful eye to its possible antitrust implications in the given context. If the decision is affirmative, the drafting problems presented will be no different from those involved in drafting the principal license as discussed in the following chapters. (See particularly Chapter 8 on "improvements.")

---

[11]Stokes & Smith Co. v. Transparent-Wrap Mach. Corp., 161 F.2d 565, 73 USPQ 200 (2d Cir. 1947).

[12]Abbot B. Lipsky, Jr., "Current Antitrust Division Views on Patent Licensing Practices," 50 ANTITRUST 515 (1981).

6

Exclusive Licenses

For purposes of this chapter, every patent grant which conveys any exclusive rights to a transferee but which falls short of assignment of full ownership will be viewed as an "exclusive license."

6.00 Exclusive Licenses; Antitrust Aspects

Almost any conveyance or acceptance of exclusive rights under a patent (except, presumably, those rights received by an employer from inventors employed by him) raises possible issues of antitrust involvement.

Positions taken at various times by representatives of the United States Department of Justice include, for example, the following propositions:

(1) That exclusive rights under patents are "assets" within the meaning of Section 7 of the Clayton Act,[1] and their acquisition in certain circumstances may violate that Section.

(2) That failure of the grantor to include sublicensing rights in the bundle of values received by his licensee may imply or even require illicit interaction between the licensor and the licensee in respect to the granting (or withholding) of further licenses.[2]

---

[1]*See* L. J. Weinstein, "Application of Section 7 of the Clayton Act to Patents, Copyrights, and Trademarks," 5 PTCJ. Res. & Ed. 329 (1962). *See also* Western Geophysical Co. of Am., Inc. v. Bolt Assocs., Inc., 162 USPQ 502 (D. Conn. 1969) and further proceedings in the same case reported at 164 USPQ 277 (1969).

[2]United States v. Krasnov, 143 F. Supp. 184 (E.D. Pa. 1956), *aff'd*, 355 U.S. 5 (1957). *See also* Moraine Products v. ICI America, Inc., 538 F.2d 134, 191 USPQ 65 (7th Cir. 1976) (rule of reason analysis applied to conduct of exclusive licensor and exclusive licensee when one is approached regarding grant of an additional license).

(3) That granting exclusive licenses for particular fields of business may evidence illegal allocation and segregation of those fields.[3]

To the extent that the foregoing propositions are valid, their application to and effect on a particular transaction will obviously depend very largely on the circumstances which surround the transaction. It is impossible here to do more than note the existence of the problem and to counsel reference to latest developments in this field of law whenever the granting or acceptance of exclusive patent rights is contemplated.

6.01 Exclusive Licenses; Sublicensing Rights

Point (2) of Section 6.00, above, suggests a legal reason in connection with each exclusive license grant for dealing definitely with the disposition of the right to grant further licenses. An additional, nonlegal reason for not leaving this question unresolved is found in the likelihood that, if the licensed subject matter is commercially important, inquiries for additional licenses will eventually be received. In such a situation it will be awkward to find that neither the licensor nor the licensee has power to respond to the inquiry.[4]

From the language of *Waterman* v. *MacKenzie*[5] quoted in Section 5.02 of the preceding chapter, it may be argued that any exclusive license so absolute in its terms as to constitute a *pro tanto* "assignment" of the patent necessarily implies a right in the licensee to further assign the license or to subdivide it by granting nonexclusive licenses under it. Even if this argument holds, however, so little in the way of reservation or limitation is required to disqualify an exclusive grant from treatment as an "assignment," and thus to call into question the scope of the collateral powers conveyed with it, that explicit disposition of sublicensing rights is recommended. A great variety of dispositions are possible, and the following paragraphs merely sketch certain matters which may need to be covered where the decision is to let the exclusive license carry with it the exclusive power to extend licenses to others.[6]

---

[3]*See, e.g.*, R. W. McLaren, "Patent Licenses and Antitrust Considerations," 13 IDEA 61 (Conference Number 1969).

[4]*See*, for an example of the dilemma thus created, Old Dominion Box Co., Inc. v. Continental Can Co., Inc., 273 F. Supp. 550, 155 USPQ 70 (S.D.N.Y. 1967).

[5]138 U.S. 252 (1891).

[6]Of all conceivable allocations of the sublicensing power, this one seems to introduce fewest practical and legal complications, and is therefore ordinarily to be recommended.

ARTICLE

1. LICENSEE shall have the exclusive right under the LICENSED PATENTS to grant sublicenses to others at royalty rates not less than those required to be paid in Article ___ of this Agreement.

2. In respect to sublicenses granted by LICENSEE under this Article ___, LICENSEE shall pay over to LICENSOR that proportion of royalties received from its sublicensees necessary to yield LICENSOR returns on LICENSED PRODUCTS, sold by such sublicensees equal[7] to the amounts which it would have received from LICENSEE on equivalent LICENSED PRODUCTS sold by it.

3. Termination under any of the provisions of Article ___ of the license granted to LICENSEE in this Agreement shall terminate all sublicenses which may have been granted by LICENSEE, provided that any sublicensee may elect to continue its sublicense by advising LICENSOR in writing, within (60) sixty days of the sublicensee's receipt of written notice of such termination, of its election, and of its agreement to assume in respect to LICENSOR all the obligations (including obligations for payment) contained in its sublicensing agreement with LICENSEE. Any sublicense granted by LICENSEE shall contain provisions corresponding to those of this paragraph respecting termination and the conditions of continuance of sublicenses.

4. The granting by LICENSEE of sublicenses under the LICENSED PATENTS shall be in the discretion of LICENSEE, and LICENSEE shall have the sole power to determine whether or not to grant sublicenses, the identity of sublicenses, and subject to paragraphs 1 and 3 of this Article ___, the royalty rates and terms and conditions of such sublicenses.

6.02 Exclusive Licenses; Reservations

The subject of reservations from exclusive license grants that may in some circumstances be required by conflicting grants previously made or contingently likely to be made to others has been treated in Chapter 4, Section 4.00. Beyond the matters treated in that section is the ever present question of whether any rights are to be reserved to the licensor. It is quite common, for example, for the licensor to wish to reserve to himself a license to make, use, and sell (or simply to make and use) either the complete invention covered by a licensed patent or some subspecies of it. The drafter must, of course, bear in mind that in the absence of contractual reference to such a reservation, it does not exist, either by implication or otherwise.

---

[7]There is, of course, no obstacle to reducing this requirement to something less than 100 percent parity if it is in licensor's interest to provide incentive for sublicensing in order to maximize overall returns from the licensed patents, and in some circumstances, there may conceivably be antitrust considerations favoring this. (*See, e.g.,* the "competitive advantage" viewpoints discussed in Western Geophysical Co. of Am. v. Bolt Associates, Inc., 162 USPQ 502 (D. Conn. 1969), *modified,* 164 USPQ 277 (1969).)

There is no obstacle to specifying the kind of reservation just referred to provided its existence is acceptable to or negotiable with the licensee. It is desirable, however, in weighing the value of the reservation and in framing its description, to consider its impact upon the tax status of the transaction from the licensor's standpoint, the question being whether its inclusion disables the licensor from claiming capital gains treatment which might otherwise apply to the proceeds from the license. The subtleties of this phase of the tax law are many,[8] and current authorities should be consulted when a specific problem is in hand.

6.03 Exclusive Licenses; Protection of the Licensor

If a patent is assigned or exclusively licensed for a fixed sum to be paid at all events, either at the time of the grant, or at a specified later time, the licensor's interest will probably not require protection beyond an evaluation of the licensee's credit rating. On the other hand, if the licensor's returns from the transaction are to be in the form of royalties or other payments based upon the licensee's use or sales over time, there may be a need for some form of protection against unexpectedly low or inadequate performance by the licensee. The following subsections A, B, and C discuss approaches frequently taken in this connection.

A. Termination by the Licensor

Straightforward relief from a disappointing performance by an exclusive licensee can be provided by giving the licensor the power to terminate the license outright if the yield from it does not reach a given total by a specified date or does not maintain a specified annual rate of return.

The following language exemplifies this approach in terms of a specified annual minimum royalty:

> If royalties paid to LICENSOR under this agreement do not aggregate a minimum of $_____ for the calendar year ending December 31, 19__, and the same amount for each succeeding year during the continuance of the agreement, LICENSOR may at its option terminate the agreement and the licenses granted in it by providing LICENSEE with notice of termination within thirty (30) days after receipt of the last report for any calendar year in repect to which failure to pay the prescribed minimum occurs, unless LICENSEE shall within thirty (30) days

---

[8]*See* Stephen P. Jarchow, "Recent *Hooker Chemicals* Case Examines Patent License/Sale Dichotomy," 57 TAXES 623 (1979).

from the date of such notice pay LICENSOR such additional sum as may be necessary to bring the payment for such calendar year up to the specified minimum.

B. Conversion From an Exclusive to a Nonexclusive License

The right of absolute termination of license is, of course, a severe sanction, and its inclusion in a particular agreement may well be unacceptable to a prospective licensee. On the other hand, it is a reasonable position for the licensor to maintain in most cases that if the licensee does not, within a specified time, achieve a stated minimum of financial performance, the license shall be converted from exclusive to nonexclusive. This permits the licensor to seek additional channels of exploitation for his patent. A common variant of this arrangement is to provide that the license may be maintained as exclusive if the licensee makes specified annual payments, regardless of the magnitude of his own operations under it. The language below may be appropriate for covering these points.

> In the event royalties payable to LICENSOR under this agreement for the calendar year 19__ or for any subsequent year during the life of the agreement do not equal or exceed one thousand dollars ($1,000), LICENSOR shall have the right, upon sixty (60) days' notice, to convert the license granted in Article __ from exclusive to nonexclusive. LICENSEE may, however, maintain the exclusive character of its license, notwithstanding any such notice from LICENSOR, if it shall, prior to expiration of the sixty (60) day notice period, pay to LICENSOR a sum which, when added to the royalties payable for the year in question, totals one thousand dollars ($1,000). Failure of LICENSOR to give the notice provided for in this Article __ in reference to any given year or years shall not constitute a waiver of the right to give such notice in reference to any subsequent year.

Obviously, the objectives of the clause stated immediately above can be achieved more simply from the licensor's standpoint by causing the licensee to agree in all events to pay a stated minimum annual royalty upon pain of suffering an automatic conversion of the license from exclusive to nonexclusive. Because the amount appropriate for this purpose in an exclusive licensing situation is ordinarily substantial, however, the licensee will frequently prefer the greater flexibility of the stated clause.

C. "Best Efforts" and Other Commitments by the Licensee

A number of decisions have said that even in the absence of express commitments to that effect, there is an implied obligation on the part of the exclusive licensee, if he wishes to maintain his license in a situation in which the licensor's returns depend on his action, to exercise reasonable diligence in exploiting the licensed invention.[9] The extent of this obligation is at best nebulous, however, and collateral circumstances may readily erase it, either substantially or completely.[10]

Presumably because of this uncertainty of outcome in the absence of express provisions, many agreements attempt to deal with the problem by inserting a promise of "best (or "reasonable") efforts," or of "all due diligence," or the like among the commitments required of the licensee. But this approach also tends to be illusory in light of the vague and subjective character of the quoted terminology. Thus, in *Western Geophysical Company of America* v. *Bolt Associates, Inc.*,[11] the court was called on to construe a covenant in the following words:

> WESTERN agrees to use its best efforts to promote worldwide licensing and use of the licensed apparatus. . . .

The licensor contended that since the licensee admittedly had not used the licensed apparatus and had not obtained any sublicenses, it must be inferred that it had not exerted its "best efforts." In rejecting this contention in the light of practical difficulties shown to exist in application of the patented invention, the court observed that:

> The phrase "best efforts" emphasizes a theme rather than defines a particular course of conduct to be pursued. While the quality of the efforts expected from the plaintiff is stated there is not a single direct reference in the agreement to the scope or direction in which the efforts should be made.

This excellent characterization of the problem well illustrates why reliance should not be placed by a licensor on "best efforts" or "due diligence" terminology unless objective criteria of compliance can be delineated. This may occasionally be possible, as where the parties agree that "due diligence," for example, shall be satisfied by

---

[9]*See* Waterson, Berlin & Synder Co. v. Irving Trust Co. (*In re* Fain), 48 F.2d 704 (2d Cir. 1931). Summarizing copyright law, Judge A. N. Hand said: ". . . Where there has been a conveyance upon an agreement to pay the grantor sums of money based upon the earnings of property transferred, the courts have implied a covenant to render the subject matter of the contract productive—if the property was a mine, a covenant to mine, quarry or drill; if it consisted of a patent or copyright, a covenant to work the patent or copyright." (Citing decisions.)

[10]*See, e.g.*, Mechanical Ice Tray Corp. v. General Motors Corp., 144 F.2d 720, 62 USPQ 397 (2d Cir. 1944); Eastern Elec. Inc. v. The Seeburg Co., 310 F. Supp. 1126, 164 USPQ 97 (S.D.N.Y. 1969), *aff'd*, 427 F.2d 23, 165 USPQ 747 (2d Cir. 1970). In the first case, inability to meet outside competition with the licensed article was thought to excuse shifting to a royalty-free design. In the second, the licensor's right of termination was said to be an adequate remedy for nonexploitation, and a claim for damages for breach of an alleged covenant was denied for this and other reasons.

[11]285 F. Supp. 815, 157 USPQ 129 (D. Conn. 1968). This is an interlocutory decision, but is still of interest on the point for which it is cited here. *See also* M. Scales, "Implied Obligations in Patent Licenses," 41 MARQ. LAW REV. 385 (1958).

licensee's allocation of stated manpower to production and sales effort, stated dollars to advertising, and so forth.[12]

From the licensee's standpoint also, "best efforts" is dubious language when viewed against the possibility (unlikely though it may be) that a court may in some controversy construe it strongly in the licensor's behalf. In such a case, particularly if the licensee has extensive resources, who could estimate the proportion of those resources which might need to be applied to the task in question in order to meet an unqualified "best efforts" test?

As a generalization, therefore, the minimum royalty and related devices for protecting the licensor in an exclusive licensing situation which are discussed in subsections A and B, above, are to be preferred to unguarded reliance on "best efforts" and "due diligence" terminology.

6.04 Exclusive Licenses; Enforcement of the Patent

Section 281 of the Patent Act of 1952 (35 U.S.C. §281) provides that:

> A patentee shall have remedy by civil action for infringement of his patent.

Section 100 of the same Act states that:

> The word "patentee" includes not only the patentee to whom the patent was issued but also the successors in title to the patentee.

On the authority of *Waterman* v. *MacKenzie*,[13] discussed in the preceding chapter, it may be concluded that a "successor in title," for the purpose of maintaining a civil action for patent infringement, must be the recipient of an assignment, grant, or conveyance in respect to the patent of either—

(1) The whole patent, comprising the exclusive right to make, use, and vend the invention throughout the United States;
(2) An undivided part or share of that exclusive right; or
(3) The exclusive right under the patent within and throughout a specified part of the United States.

The *Waterman* decision states that:

> A transfer of either of these three kinds of interests is an assignment, properly speaking, and vests in the assignee a title in so much of the patent itself, with a right to sue infringers. In the second case, jointly

---

[12]*See also* the language suggested in reference to "an effective program of licensing" in sample Article XIII in Section 21.04 on page 191.

[13]138 U.S. 252 (1891).

with the assignor. In the first and third cases, in the name of the assignee alone. Any assignment or transfer, short of one of these, is a mere license, giving the licensee no title in the patent and no right to sue in his own name for an infringement.

The situation of the exclusive licensee who is a "mere licensee" within the language of the *Waterman* decision was exhaustively explored by the Supreme Court in *Independent Wireless Telegraph Co. v. Radio Corporation of America.*[14] That case involved radio patents of the inventor, Lee De Forest. These patents had been assigned to the De Forest Radio Telephone and Telegraph Company, but through a series of transactions the Radio Corporation had received exclusive rights to use and sell the patented inventions in the United States for transmission of messages. Independent Wireless Telegraph Company bought, from a source other than the Radio Corporation, apparatus covered by the De Forest patents which was licensed and labeled for use in the amateur and experimental field only. Independent used this apparatus, however, for the commercial transmission of messages, and the Radio Corporation brought suit for infringement.

Prior to instituting the action, the Radio Corporation had requested the De Forest Company to consent to being joined as a co-plaintiff, but that company refused. Because the company was outside the jurisdiction of the court in which suit was to be filed, the bill of complaint, after stating the De Forest Company's refusal to join voluntarily, purported to make it a plaintiff *without its consent.* Independent moved to dismiss the complaint on the ground that the Radio Corporation was not such a licensee as to permit it to sue alone in its own name or in joinder with the owner of the patents. Dismissal of this motion by the Second Circuit Court of Appeals was sustained by the Supreme Court. The decision of Mr. Chief Justice Taft is a compendium of the law on the subject and should be reviewed by any lawyer confronted with a related problem.[15]

While denying the right of an exclusive licensee to bring in a federal court in its own name a patent infringement suit seeking equitable remedies (absent jurisdiction based on diversity of citizenship), the decision found full power in such a licensee to compel participation by the patent owner. The following excerpts adequately summarize the Court's position:

> It seems clear, then, on principle and authority, that the owner of a patent, who grants to another the exclusive right to make, use or

---

[14]269 U.S. 459 (1926).

[15]For an example of the continuing vitality of the *Independent Wireless* case, *see* Ferrara v. Rodale Press, 54 F.R.D. 3, 172 USPQ 488 (E.D. Pa. 1972); for a case questioning the continuing vitality of *Independent Wireless, see* Catanzaro v. ITT Corp., 378 F. Supp. 203, 183 USPQ 273 (D. Del. 1974).

vend the invention, which does not constitute a statutory assignment, holds the title to the patent in trust for such a licensee, to the extent that he must allow the use of his name in any action brought at the instance of the licensee in law or in equity to obtain damages for the injury to his exclusive right by an infringer or to enjoin infringement of it. Such exclusive licenses frequently contain express covenants by the patent owner and licensor to sue infringers, that expressly cast upon the former the affirmative duty of initiating and bearing the expense of the litigation. But, without such express covenants, the implied obligation of the licensor to allow the use of his name is indispensable to the enjoyment by the licensee of the monopoly which by personal contract the licensor has given. Inconvenience and possibly embarrassing adjudication in respect to the validity of the licensor's patent rights, as the result of suits begun in aid of the licensee, are only the equitable and inevitable sequence of the licensor's contract, whether express or implied.[16]

The owner beyond the reach of process may be made coplaintiff by the licensee, but not until after he has been requested to become such voluntarily. If he declines to take any part in the case, though he knows of its imminent pendency and of his obligation to join, he will be bound by the decrees which follow.[17]

The presence of the owner of the patent as a party is indispensable, not only to give jurisdiction under the patent laws, but also in most cases to enable the alleged infringer to respond in one action to all claims of infringement for his act, and thus either to defeat all claims in one action, or by satisfying one adverse decree to bar all subsequent actions.[18]

While all of the above was said in reference to a statute which has now been superseded (i.e., by the 1952 Patent Act), it would appear that the superseding statute intended merely to embrace in more general language the substantive content of the existing law on points such as those now under consideration. Accordingly, the several quotations given above from the *Independent Wireless* case may be considered reliable touchstones for framing pleadings in a situation involving protection of the interests of an exclusive licensee who is not clearly a successor in title to ownership of the patent in the sense of being either an "assignee" or a "grantee."

Some qualifications of the rigor of the *Waterman* case in classing exclusive licensees as "mere licensees," unqualified to maintain suit without the joinder of others, have appeared in later cases, particularly in situations where an aggressive licensee has been made defendant in a declaratory judgment action brought by parties whom the licensee has threatened with suit under the patent. For example, in *United Lacquer Mfg. Corp.* v. *Maas & Waldstein Co.*,[19] it was held

---

[16]269 U.S. at 469.

[17]269 U.S. at 473.

[18]269 U.S. at 468.

[19]111 F. Supp. 139 (D. N.J. 1953).

that an exclusive licensee whose license was limited not only in territory but in time had such ownership as to be susceptible to a declaratory judgment action, even though the nominal owner of the patent had not been joined. This result was deemed to hold, moreover, notwithstanding that the patent owner had obligated himself to protect his licensee to the extent of bringing "at least one suit against an infringing manufacturer." Because this obligation was limited, the court concluded that the licensee must be presumed to have retained the "general right to sue, as substantial owner of the patent, according to the *Waterman* case. . . ." Having that right, he must conversely, according to the court, be qualified to respond to a declaratory judgment suit seeking invalidation of the patent.[20]

It is also clear that, in a still more definitive sense than is brought out in the *United Lacquer* case, above, the contractual arrangements of the patent owner and his licensee cannot determine as against third parties the locus of the power to maintain action. Thus, *Agrashell, Inc.* v. *Hammons Products Co.*[21] involved a situation in which Purex Corp., the owner of the patent in controversy, had granted to Agrashell, Inc.:

(1) The sole and exclusive right and license to manufacture, use, and sell the compositions and processes described and claimed in the Licensed Patent . . . "except for the right expressly reserved by Purex to make, use, and sell such compositions and to convey to purchasers thereof the right to use such processes"; and

(2) A right to sue for infringement in its own name, subject to a requirement of 15 days' notice to Purex of any proposed suit and to the right of Purex to elect to participate in the suit and to receive one half of all sums recovered.

The court found that the reservations contained in (1), above, disqualified Agrashell from being an assignee of the first type described in *Waterman* (see Section 6.04, opening part) and left it at most the assignee of "an undivided part or share." Because in such a situation the analysis of *Waterman* requires joinder of the assignor, the court found that the fact that the agreement purported to give Agrashell the right to sue in its own name was without significance. To the same general effect is *Etherington* v. *S. M. Hardee.*[22]

---

[20]Another case which finds the indispensable party rule somewhat more flexible in a declaratory judgment situation than in a situation in which the patent is directly asserted by a licensee is A. L. Smith Iron Co. v. Dickson, 141 F.2d 3, 60 USPQ 475 (2d Cir. 1944).

[21]352 F.2d 443 (8th Cir. 1965).

[22]182 F. Supp. 905 (S.D. Tex. 1960).

The converse of the question discussed above, the right of the exclusive licensee to bring suit in his own name, is that of the right of a patent owner who has granted a license to bring suit without joining his licensee as an indispensable party. The test of indispensability, stated in broad terms, appears to be whether the rights of the licensee will inevitably be affected by a decree likely to eventuate from the suit. If the answer is affirmative, indispensability is established. Under this test a person holding a general exclusive license would have to be joined, while the holder of a license (exclusive or otherwise) in a field disparate from the subject matter in suit probably would not. The finer parameters of this subject are illuminatingly discussed in *Cold Metal Process Co.* v. *Aluminum Company of America.*[23]

The point of the foregoing somewhat elaborate treatment of the "indispensable party" question is, from the standpoint of the contract drafter, to emphasize that the right to bring and maintain suit on a patent cannot, by contract alone, be assigned arbitrarily as between a licensor and his licensee. On the contrary, overriding considerations of law and equity may frustrate an attempted contractual arrangement which overlooks the "indispensable party" viewpoints developed above.

On the other hand, where the rights being extended to a licensee are sufficient presumptively to establish in the licensee the power to maintain suit without joinder of others, it may still prove useful at a time of controversy to have confirmed this in the licensing documents as the intention of the parties. Similarly, where, under established principles, joinder of licensor and licensee would be a normal prerequisite to suit, it may be advantageous, in order to avoid misunderstanding, to indicate which of the parties has the power of initiative and to express agreement that the other party consents to being joined as coplaintiff.[24]

A subject which is ordinarily within the control of the parties is that of financial responsibility for the costs of litigation that may occur. In respect to this subject, there will certainly be some cases in which the benefits of his license to the exclusive licensee are such that he should agree that all costs of litigation undertaken for protection of the licensed patents shall rest on his shoulders. On the other hand, if there have been or are expected to be large payments to the licensor from the licensee, it may be fair that the licensor,

---

[23]200 F. Supp. 407 (E.D. Tenn. 1961).

[24]Naming both parties as coplaintiffs may be desirable. In Sanofi, S.A. v. Med-Tech Veterinarian Products, Inc., 222 USPQ 143 (D. Kan. 1983), a district court held both a patent owner and an exclusive licensee were entitled to an injunction prohibiting patent infringement, while in a prior New Jersey federal district court decision only the exclusive licensee obtained an injunction.

whether or not he is in a position to be the moving party in litigation, shall agree to underwrite all or part of litigation costs. It is obvious that many differing allocations of the burdens of litigation are possible, and the following examples are therefore to be regarded only as suggestive of possible patterns.

Example 1

ARTICLE VIII

While and as long as its license under this agreement remains exclusive, LICENSEE is empowered—
  (a) To bring suit in its own name or, if required by law, jointly with LICENSOR, at its own expense and on its own behalf, for infringement of the LICENSED PATENTS;
  (b) In any such suit to enjoin infringement and to collect for its use, damages, profits, and awards of whatever nature recoverable for such infringement; and
  (c) To settle any claim or suit for infringement of the LICENSED PATENTS by granting the infringing party a sublicense under the provisions of Article __ of this agreement.

In the event LICENSOR shall bring to the attention of LICENSEE any unlicensed infringement of the LICENSED PATENTS, and LICENSEE shall not, within six months,
  (a) Secure cessation of the infringement, or
  (b) Enter suit against the infringer, or
  (c) Provide LICENSOR with evidence of the pendency of a bona fide negotiation for the acceptance by the infringer of a sublicense under the LICENSED PATENTS, the license herein granted to LICENSEE shall forthwith become nonexclusive, and LICENSOR shall thereafter have the right to sue for the infringement at LICENSOR'S own expense, and to collect for its own use all damages, profits, and awards of whatever nature recoverable for such infringement.

Example 2

ARTICLE VIII

1. While and as long as its license under this agreement remains exclusive, LICENSEE is empowered—
  (a) To bring suit in its own name or, if required by law, jointly with LICENSOR, for infringement of the LICENSED PATENTS;
  (b) In any such suit, to enjoin infringement and to collect for its own use, damages, profits, and awards of whatever nature recoverable for such infringement; and
  (c) To settle any claim or suit for infringement of the LICENSED PATENTS by granting the infringing party a sublicense under the provisions of Article __ of this agreement.

2. In any such suit brought by LICENSEE, LICENSOR will reimburse LICENSEE for one-half the attorney's fees and necessary out-of-pocket costs incurred by LICENSEE, provided, however, LICENSOR'S obligation for such reimbursement shall not exceed one-half the total royalties received by LICENSOR from LICENSEE as of the date on which such suit was filed, and provided further that LICENSOR shall be liable for reimbursement in respect to one suit only.

Example 3

ARTICLE VIII

LICENSOR in its own name, or jointly with LICENSEE if required by law, will bring and will diligently prosecute such suits for infringement of the LICENSED PATENTS as may be reasonably necessary to prevent unlicensed infringers from materially injuring the business of LICENSEE under the LICENSED PATENTS, but it shall not be obligated to bring more than one such suit at a time.

Example 4

ARTICLE VIII

LICENSEE, as exclusive licensee, shall have power to institute and prosecute at its own expense suits for infringement of the LICENSED PATENTS, and if, required by law, LICENSOR will join as party plaintiff in such suits. All expenses in such suits will be borne entirely by LICENSEE, and LICENSEE will pay to LICENSOR twenty-five percent (25%) of any excess of recoveries over expenses in such suits.[25]

---

[25]The usefulness in some contexts of an "excess of recoveries over expenses" provision is illustrated by Contour Chair-Lounge Co., Inc. v. Laskowitz, 124 USPQ 52 (Mo. 1959). The exclusive licensee, Contour, had agreed to pay (1) royalties of $1.50 per chair and (2) "all reasonable and necessary expenses of litigation." Contour sued an infringer, expending $30,000 in the action. It obtained a judgment for $14,000, which it settled for $13,000. In follow-up litigation between Contour and its licensor, the licensor recovered $5,339.50, a sum corresponding to $1.50 for each infringing chair involved in the prior suits.

7

The Granting Clause; Elements of the Grant; Definition of Licensed Subject Matter

The terms of the grant which describe the legal character of the license being extended and the provisions which define the subject matter included in the license are clearly the essence of any patent licensing agreement. This chapter contains suggestions for systematic treatment of both these subjects.

7.00 The Granting Clause

The following granting provisions (some offered in the alternative) are listed as a framework for discussing selected available possibilities. These are stated as though intended to be included in a single sentence, but this is for analytical purposes only. In actual presentation, the granting provisions, like all other provisions of the agreement, should be formulated in sentences of comfortably readable length. As here presented, the various clauses will be separately discussed in Section 7.01 of this chapter.

ARTICLE ___

GRANT TO LICENSEE

(a) The LICENSOR grants (or grants and agrees to grant) to the LICENSEE;
(b) And its subsidiaries, affiliates, and controlled companies;
(c) Under the LICENSED PATENTS;
(d) And for the lives of such PATENTS;

(e) A license (state character—see Section 7.01(E));
(f) Use
    (1) to make, use, and sell products embodying the inventions thereof; or
    (2) To practice the methods and to make, use, and sell the products therein described and claimed; or
    (3) To make, use, and sell machines embodying or for operation in accordance with the inventions therefore; or
    (4) To make, have made, use, sell, lease, or otherwise dispose of products embodying the inventions thereof; or
    (5) To make and use but not to sell products embodying the inventions thereof; or
    (6) To make, use, and sell _____ embodying the inventions thereof; or
    (7) To make in its plant at _____ and to use and sell products embodying the inventions thereof:
(g) Throughout the United States, its territories, and possessions.

7.01 Notes on Granting Clauses

A. *"Grants" or "Grants and Agrees to Grant"*

It is quite common to employ the word "grants" where the license is under patents already in being, and to use "grant and agrees to grant" if the license includes patents to be issued later on applications or inventions identified in the agreement. It is doubtful that there is a significant difference in legal effect of the two expressions, and brevity recommends the use of the single word "grant" in most if not in all cases.

B. *"Subsidiaries, Affiliates, and Controlled Companies"*

Each of the terms used in the above heading has its own intuitive connotations, differing from each of the others. It is unlikely that the conjoint use of all three terms will often be found appropriate in a single agreement, and, of course, none of them should be used unless some extension of the license beyond the direct licensee is intended. When any of them are used, the used terms should be defined at an appropriate place in the agreement. A collection of exemplary definitions follows, but none of these should be adopted unless it precisely fits the intention of the parties in the particular situation in hand.

    SUBSIDIARY of a party means any corporation over 50% of the voting stock of which is directly or indirectly owned or controlled by such party.

SUBSIDIARY of a party means a corporation, company, or other entity more than 50% of whose outstanding securities representing the right, other than as affected by events of default, to vote for the election of directors or other governing authorities are now or hereafter owned or controlled, directly or indirectly, by such party, but such corporation, company, or other entity shall be deemed to be a SUBSIDIARY only so long as such ownership or control exists.

CONTROLLED COMPANY of a party means (1) any SUBSIDIARY and (2) any corporation, company, or other entity, not a SUBSIDIARY, at least __% (e.g., 50% or some named figure less than 50%) of the voting stock of which is directly or indirectly owned or controlled by such party, provided such party also has in case (2) either

    (a) The irrevocable right to name a majority of the members of the governing board of such corporation, or

    (b) Effective managerial control by virtue of a management agreement entered into with such corporation.

An AFFILIATE of a party means any person or legal entity which is a general licensee of such party in the field of this agreement and which has a contract with such party entitling it to receive continuing technical services from the party, but any such person shall be deemed to be an AFFILIATE only so long as it has such a contract and continues to be such a licensee.

Whether subsidiaries and controlled companies of either the licensor or the licensee should be included in the agreement in such a way as to be automatically bound by or benefited by it is, in the first instance, a matter of negotiation between the parties. The matter of the subsidiary's (or controlled company's) being obligated automatically and without consent is also, of course, a matter of the relationship between each subsidiary (or controlled company) and its principal, whether the latter is licensor or licensee in the agreement under negotiation. An unintended piercing of the corporate veil can be avoided in one way, as far as the licensee in a unidirectional license agreement is concerned, by including in the license-granting part of the agreement a clause to the following effect:

✳ This license shall extend to SUBSIDIARIES (or CONTROLLED COMPANIES) present and future, of Licensee who notify Licensor in writing that they accept the terms, including the obligations, of this agreement respecting such license.

There is a special subsidiary-affecting point for the licensee to have in mind in negotiating an agreement in which he is to be subject to minimum annual payments or is to receive benefits (such as a reduction in royalty rate) when his payments reach a certain level. This is the desirability of including in the agreement a provision that when and if his subsidiaries, or some of them, come under the agreement (i.e., by election or otherwise), the payments which they make shall be credited against required annual minimums and other fixed financial obligations of the licensee, to the extent there is advantage in doing this.

Consideration should also be given in each case to the desirability of providing for either the continuance or the termination of rights extended to subsidiaries in the event of any subsequent change in the ownership or rights of the parent company in such subsidiaries.

C. *"Under the LICENSED PATENTS"*

Under the convention being generally observed in this work, the capitalization of "LICENSED PATENTS" identifies this as a specially defined term. Meticulous specification of the patents being licensed is, of course, of the essence of any patent licensing agreement. Where only a limited number of completely identified patents are involved, they may be mentioned directly, and no problem of definition arises. On the other hand, where all patents meeting mutually agreed upon descriptive criteria are to be included, much attention must be paid to specifying the criteria accurately.

Some examples of definitions of LICENSED PATENTS are given in Section 3.01(B) of Chapter 3. A further illustration of the possible complexity of this subject is given in the following combination of definitional paragraphs:

(1) FIVE YEAR PERIOD means the period beginning with the date of execution of this Agreement and ending five years after such date.

(2) LICENSED PATENTS means all United States patents of LICENSOR issuing on (i) inventions first conceived and first actually or constructively reduced to practice at any time during the FIVE YEAR PERIOD in the course of their employment by employees of LICENSOR who are employed to do research, development, or other inventive work, (ii) inventions reduced to practice either actually or constructively prior to the termination of the FIVE YEAR PERIOD and owned or controlled by LICENSOR at any time during the FIVE YEAR PERIOD and (iii) inventions reduced to practice either actually or constructively prior to the termination of the FIVE YEAR PERIOD, with respect to which and to the extent to which LICENSOR shall at any time during the FIVE YEAR PERIOD have the right to grant the licenses and rights agreed to be granted by LICENSOR in this Agreement.

It will be found that while there may be partial overlap among the three sets (i), (ii), and (iii) which are specified in paragraph (2), above, each set adds something to the totality of patents included in the term "LICENSED PATENTS." The adoption of a paragraph having this degree of extensiveness obviously assumes prior searching analysis of what it is the parties really wish to accomplish.

D. "And for the Lives of Such PATENTS"

This provision is clearly variable within wide limits, depending on the intention of the parties. It is rarely in the interest of a licensee to acquire a license which can terminate against his volition prior to expiration of the licensed patents. However, where a deviation from this viewpoint (including the possibility of termination under default) is thought appropriate, this can be accommodated by re-wording the subject clause to read—

> and, except as otherwise provided in Articles __ and __ of this Agreement, for the lives of such PATENTS

and by providing in the cross-referenced Articles such provisions for special termination of licenses as are intended. Suggestions on this subject are included in Chapter 17.

In reference to the "life" of a patent, the decisions are not unanimous, but the greater weight of authority is to the effect that a patent expires at midnight on the anniversary of the date of its issuance, the term of the patent having run from the first minute of the day following the day of its issuance.[1]

This matter may be important in an agreement in which large production is involved, so that one day's royalties could be substantial. In any such case, in view of the slight uncertainty of the law on the subject, it may be well to insert at an appropriate place in the agreement a proviso such as the following:

> (i) A patent shall be understood to expire at midnight of the anniversary of the date of its issuance.

E. Character of License

In a complex licensing arrangement, the description of the scope and character of the license to be granted may itself be a matter of considerable difficulty. Some of the possible complications will be discussed under appropriate headings in succeeding chapters of this work. At this point there will be included only a few remarks on certain so-called "words of art" often encountered in the description of simple licenses.

Often a grant is called "an irrevocable, indivisible, nonexclusive (or exclusive) license." The word "irrevocable" is probably superfluous in most cases—although generally harmless. Irrevocability does not ordinarily have to be spelled out, since, in the absence of counter-

---

[1]*See* In re Donaldson, 138 F.2d 419 (C.C. Pa. 1943); Burnet v. Willingham Loan & Trust Co., 282 U.S. 437 (1931); Standard Oil Co. v. Commissioner of Internal Revenue, 43 Board of Tax Appeals 973, 996, 997 (1941).

vailing language, that attribute of a license may normally be implied. It is the conditions (if any) of revocability that must be specifically defined. These can most appropriately be taken up, both in a given agreement and in the arrangement of this book, under the heading "Termination." For treatment of this subject, see Chapter 17.

As to the term "indivisible," its semantic deficiencies have already been discussed in Section 1.01(B)(2) of Chapter 1, under the heading "Vagueness." As that discussion shows, use of "indivisible" without a specially tailored definition of its intended meaning is undesirable. In particular, care should be taken not to make a license indivisible (without definition) if the license is granted to, say, "the Licensee and its controlled companies." Such wording might logically lead to the construction (probably unintended) that the license may be enjoyed by the Licensee *or* any one of the controlled companies, but not by more than one of them at any one time.[2]

The crucial words "nonexclusive" and "exclusive" have already been fully discussed in Chapters 5 and 6.

F. Use

(1), (2), (3) *"To Make, Use, and Sell,"* etc. The variations in terminology which are listed in Section 7.00 under headings F(1), F(2), and F(3) are dictated by the circumstance that in some cases the claims of licensed patents apply to processes or manufacturing apparatus rather than (or in addition to) end-use products, such as (in the words of the patent statutes) "manufactures" or "compositions of matter." For example, clause (2) obviously assumes a combination of product and process claims, and clause (3) assumes both machine and process claims.

(4) *"To Make, Have Made, Use, Sell, Lease, or Otherwise Dispose of Products Embodying the Inventions Thereof."* Under the applicable statute (35 USC 154) the essence of a patent is a "grant to the patentee, his heirs and assigns, for the term of seventeen years . . . of the right to exclude others from *making, using or selling* the invention throughout the United States . . ." (Emphasis added.)

This being so, it is almost certainly the law that the grant of a license to "make, use, and sell" is a complete waiver of the patentee's right to exclude the licensee from enjoyment of the patented invention within the territory to which the patent pertains. No authority at variance with this proposition is known. It is, therefore, questionable

---

[2] In Ozyagcilar v. Davis, 221 USPQ 1064 (D.S.C. 1983), the absence of any express language providing for dividing or sublicensing of the rights under a license was held to prevent licensee from effecting a division. The license under consideration covered two processes.

whether, as a matter of law, anything is gained by including in the granting clause such words as "to . . . have made, . . . lease, or otherwise dispose of . . ."

The use of these more elaborate grants has undoubtedly developed in part through lack of general acquaintance with the point of law noted above and additionally, through the desire of lay clients to be assured that, as licensees, they will have special rights considered important to them in a particular context. There can be in principle no objection to language adopted for the latter purpose. However, if there is any vagueness in the wording chosen, so that its intention is unclear, it could readily be argued that, since there has been departure from language (i.e., "make, use, and sell") which is by premise comprehensive, the new language must be read restrictively insofar as it permits such reading. In particular, this might be thought an ideal setting for application of the interpretive principle, *"inclusio unius est exclusio alterius."*

The specific phraseology offered under F(4), that is, "to make, have made, use, sell, lease, or otherwise dispose of," is, as far as the present author is aware, sufficiently inclusive to cover all applications of a product license likely to be undertaken by any licensee. However, the drafter having as a client a prospective licensee with unusually complex requirements should give careful thought to whether any of these requirements could be asserted to be left undisposed of by the wording in question.

From the standpoint of the licensor, the grant of the right to "have made" (i.e., in addition to the right to "make") may possibly raise questions as to the purposes for which and the conditions under which the have-made right may be exercised.[3] Depending on circumstances, it may be desirable (from the licensor's viewpoint) to require that these words be qualified by some such definition as the following:

> The license "to have made" granted in this Section __ means only that the licensee may contract with a third party or parties to manufacture for the licensee.

The phrase, "otherwise dispose of," is obviously of great breadth and, as a catchall, may be of value to the licensee. The same phrase,

---

[3]In E.I. du Pont de Nemours & Co., Inc. v. Shell Oil Co., 227 USPQ 223 (Del. 1985), du Pont had granted Shell a nonexclusive license, without the right to sublicense, to make, have made, use, and sell for use and resale an insecticide. Union Carbide wanted to obtain a license to manufacture the insecticide for use in one of its own products. Shell, a nonexclusive licensee without sublicensing rights, could not directly sublicense Carbide. Shell suggested that Carbide make the insecticide for Shell (under Shell's "have-made" provisions) with Shell immediately reselling the insecticide back to Carbide (under the "sell for use and resale" provision).

While the court ultimately held that such an arrangement constituted an impermissible sublicense, the litigation could have been avoided by more careful drafting.

used in the royalty-fixing part of the agreement in the context, "products otherwise disposed of," can also be of value to the licensor in making it clear that licensed goods are intended to be subject to royalties even though they are disposed of by the licensor other than by conventional sale. Thus, the following type of definition may often be found useful, if not in connection with the granting clause, then in the part of the agreement which defines royalty obligations:

> The expression "LICENSED APPARATUS—otherwise disposed of" as used in this Agreement means (1) LICENSED APPARATUS not sold but delivered by LICENSEE to others (including deliveries for export), regardless of the basis for compensation, if any; and (2) LICENSED APPARATUS, put into use by LICENSEE for any purpose other than routine testing of such APPARATUS.

(5), (6), and (7) To "Make" (Only), to "Use" (Only), to "Sell" (Only)— *With or Without Limitations.* As a generalization, the rights to "make," "use," and "sell" conveyed by the patent grant are separable rights and may be conveyed independently of one another.[4] Thus, for example, the right to "make and use" might be granted without concurrently extending the right to "sell." But, as a second generalization, there is a "presumption that the grantor intended to make his grant enjoyable."[5] Therefore, a vaguely worded grant which seems restrictive in its terms will not be so construed if such construction would make the grant useless from the licensee's standpoint. Thus, a license to "make," without more, would probably be found to imply the right to use or sell (or, in some circumstances, both) on the theory that without such an implication, the grant would be of no value to the licensee. Accordingly, the sense-making attributes of the granting language employed—if this language covers less than the full right to "make, use, and sell"—need to be thoughtfully evaluated.

The question of what limitations of scope, quantity, geography, or other parameters may legally be incorporated in a license to "make, use, and sell," or to do any one or two of these, leads into a field of law which is beyond the ambit of this work. In broadest possible terms the answer depends upon the competitive context and upon the effect which the desired limitation may have on that context.[6] Foot-

---

[4]"This right to manufacture, the right to sell, and the right to use, are each substantive rights and may be granted or conferred separately by the patentee." Adams v. Burke, 84 U.S. (17 Wall) 453, 456 (1873).

[5]Edison Elec. Co. v. Peninsular Light Co., 101 F. 831, 836 (6th Cir. 1860).

[6]"A restriction is not invalid per se merely because it is part of a patent license agreement. Reasonableness of the provisions, both from the viewpoint of the licensor's business needs and the public interest, is relevant on the question of illegality." American Optical Co. v. New Jersey Optical Co., 58 F. Supp. 601 (D. Mass. 1944).

note 7, below, cites a few relevant decisions selected as of the date of this writing, but other and latest sources should be consulted in reference to the resolution of particular questions which may arise.

G. "Throughout the United States, Its Territories, and Possessions"

Under the Act of 1952 the patent grant runs throughout the "United States, its territories and possessions." If exactly this language is used in the description of the license being conveyed, there should be no question that the licensor intends, as far as territorial extent is concerned, to waive in respect to the licensee whatever rights of exclusion he holds under the patent.[8] Any other language employed at this point may raise questions of construction as to what territorial coverage the parties had in mind.[9]

That a license empowering a licensee to make, use, and sell throughout the United States, its territories, and possessions, automatically includes the right to sell in foreign countries (subject to the existence of adverse foreign patents) seems not to have been ruled upon expressly. It would, however, appear to be inherent in the fact that the postulated language is coextensive with the scope of the patentee's rights that the language implies a territorially unrestricted waiver of these rights. On the other hand, the matter is not free from the possibility of controversy, and in order to avoid either misunderstanding or the implication of unintended restrictions which might be illegal, it may be desirable to append to the license grant a qualifying paragraph such as the following:

> Nothing in this Agreement is intended to preclude the export or the sale for export of products licensed in the Agreement to be made, used,

---

[7]United States v. Glaxo Group Limited, 163 USPQ 668 (D.D.C. 1969)— where griseofulvin in patented form was sold in bulk under an agreement prohibiting resale in bulk, this was held a per se violation of the Sherman Act. *See also* Baldwin-Lima-Hamilton Corp. v. Tatnall Measuring Systems Co., 169 F. Supp. 1 (E.D. Pa. 1958), *aff'd and reh'g denied*, 268 F.2d 395 (3d Cir. 1959), *cert. denied*, 361 U.S. 894 (1959); and United States v. Studiengesellschaft Kohle, 670 F.2d 1122 (DC Cir. 1981).

[8]Although not necessarily under any other patents, including dominant patents. For discussion of possible need to clarify this point, *see* Chapter 14, Section 14.01 on "Negation of Implications."

[9]*See, e.g.*, Superior Testers, Inc. v. Damco Testers, Inc., 309 F. Supp. 661, 164 USPQ 424 (E.D. La. 1970), in which it was held that the grant of "an exclusive license to use the invention in Louisiana and Mississippi" did not intend the term "Louisiana" to be construed in a technical sense but meant the area defined by the parties' prior business dealings in Louisiana. The last-mentioned area was found to include off-shore rights.

and sold (or "made, used and sold or otherwise disposed of," if that phraseology is employed in the basic grant).

If royalties are to be paid under the license, addition of the following words to the clause just suggested may be appropriate:

> and on which royalties shall be paid as provided in Article __ of this Agreement.

The effect of any departure from statutory language in the grant should, of course, be carefully evaluated as to its effect on export rights. For example, in *Elliott Co.* v. *Lagonda Mfg. Co.*,[10] by an agreement made to settle litigation involving several patents relating to boiler-tube cleaners, defendant was licensed to manufacture, use, "and sell to others for use throughout the United States" the combination of a particular patent. The Court concluded that the words "sell to others for use throughout the United States" must have been intentionally selected and must be given their ordinary meaning as words of limitation, especially as no similar words were used in the grant pertaining to another patent recited in the contract. Accordingly, the Court held that the contract language in question limited the defendant to a sale of the relevant devices for use in the United States.

If foreign patents exist corresponding to those under which United States rights are granted, experience demonstrates that their status requires clear definition to avoid future controversy. Ordinarily, the following language (which integrates suggestions made above) will be consistent with the licensor's intent (although not always with the licensee's uninformed understanding):

> Nothing in this Agreement is intended to preclude the export or sale for export of products licensed in the Agreement to be sold or otherwise disposed of and on which royalties shall have been paid as provided in Article __ of the Agreement, subject, however, to the understanding that no rights are granted or implied in respect to such exported products under any patent of Licensor or any other person in any foreign country.

Sale of a product for export in unassembled form is now by statute considered to be infringement[11] and, therefore, would come within the grant clause and royalty requirements of most license agreements.

Of course, the parties to a licensing arrangement may agree for mutual convenience that the royalty base shall include unassembled sets of parts, whether sold for export or otherwise.

---

[10] 205 F.152 (W.D. Pa. 1913).

[11] Title 35 USC §271(f)(1) and (2).

7.02 Definition of Licensed Subject Matter

Given a decision that the license which is to be granted is to be either (1) exclusive or (2) nonexclusive, and having settled the further legal elements of its character (see Section 7.01), an additional issue to be settled is the precise definition of the technical subject matter which is to be licensed. Here, of course, a basic question is whether or not it is intended to license for manufacture, use, and sale everything that is claimed in the LICENSED PATENTS. If the broad grant is intended, it becomes important to use language which clearly exhausts the scope of the licensed monopoly. For this purpose, a definition of LICENSED PRODUCTS such as the following may be appropriate:

ARTICLE I

1.00 LICENSED PATENTS means . . . (See Section 3.01(B) of Chapter 3 and Section 7.01(C) of this Chapter 7).

1.01 LICENSED PRODUCTS means any and all products which employ or are produced by the practice of inventions claimed in the LICENSED PATENTS.

(In this example, as in all other cases in which short and simple definitions are possible, the drafter obviously has the alternative of using and repeating the defining language itself throughout the agreement. In any given instance, this is largely a matter of deciding which practice will produce the more readable agreement.)

Where full scope licensing is desired, failure to use exhaustive wording such as that proposed above may raise unnecessary and undesirable questions as to what limitations, if any, were intended. For example, if a license is granted under a patent entitled "Electromagnetic Machinery," and the license grant reads "to make, use, and sell electric motors," a question immediately arises whether there was an affirmative intention to withhold "electric generators" (which are also of the genus "electromagnetic machinery"). This question exists in theory even though the patent is in its descriptive parts addressed only to electric motors. Moreover, while in the situation of the preceding sentence, the question may seem trivial, its triviality can vanish with some slight shift in the interests of the parties or with new technological insights concerning the applicability of the patented invention.

There may, of course, be strategic advantage from a licensor's standpoint in limiting every license grant to precisely the scope requested by the licensee, whether or not this coincides with the scope of the licensed patents. If this is indeed a planned course of action, however, it should be wittingly undertaken and not inadvertently fallen into through failure to compare the terminology of the license grant with the scope of claim coverage of the licensed patents. After all, the legal uncertainties which attach to "field licensing"[12] are such that they should not be invoked without reason and by accident.

Notwithstanding all the foregoing, there will certainly be cases in which the scope of a license grant cannot be specified merely by reference to the content of the licensed patent. Such a case arises, for example, when a license is desired by a prospective licensee for a particular product line, and the prospective licensor has patents which encompass and/or overlap this product line but are not coextensive in coverage with it. Here, unless more is to be conveyed than the licensee needs or wants, the licensed product scope must be specified either by a term which is completely self-descriptive (as "electric motors" might be, for example) or by a term like "LICENSED PRODUCTS" which is itself tied to a carefully designed definition. The following illustrates the case in which reliance on a stipulatively defined term may be almost imperative.

1.02 LICENSED PRODUCTS means—

(a) Wireless communication systems and apparatus for transmitting, receiving, repeating, modifying, responding to, or utilizing information conveyed by energy propagated through space, including (without limiting the generality of the foregoing) radio broadcast, television broadcast, radio telephone, radio telegraph, and radio facsimile systems and apparatus; and

(b) Parts, components, subassemblies, circuit elements, or materials primarily designed for use in any of the systems and apparatus of (a), above, but excluding parts, components, subassemblies, circuit elements, and materials which are developed or designed primarily either (i) for general use or (ii) for specific use other than for use in such systems and apparatus.

Many variants of the problem of subject matter scope will be encountered in practice, and each must, of course, be dealt with in its own terms. The objective of the preceding commentary is primarily to emphasize the importance and intrinsic difficulty of the subject. On this point, a reconsideration of the materials of Chapter 3 (Definitions) may be helpful.

---

[12]*See, e.g.*, Baxter, "Legal Restrictions on Exploitation of the Patent Monopoly: An Economic Analysis," 76 YALE L.J. 267, 356–367 (1966). Courts, nevertheless, uphold reasonably defined fields. United States v. Studiengesellschaft Kohle, 670 F.2d 1122 (DC Cir. 1981).

8

Licenses Under Improvements; Releases for Past Infringement

8.00 Improvements

The inclusion or noninclusion in a given license of improvements which may be developed by the licensor subsequent to the effective date of the licensing agreement[1] is a matter which obviously depends upon the overall objectives of the contracting parties. If the licensor maintains a substantial program of continuing research and development, the value of future improvements may conceivably outweigh the value of the initially licensed invention, and, in such a case, improvements would ordinarily not be licensed on a catchall basis. On the other hand, if the licensed development is believed to be substantially complete, so that major improvement by the licensor is unlikely, it may be reassuring to the licensee and not seriously prejudicial to the licensor to extend improvement rights. Even here, it will ordinarily be wise from the licensor's standpoint to limit this grant to improvements which the licensor may invent prior to the end of a specified period following the date of the agreement.

Where rights in respect to improvement inventions are to be included in a license agreement, there should be careful definition of the term "improvement." Depending on the wishes of the parties, it may be made to include, for example:

(1) Anything that performs the same function as the specifically licensed invention in a better or more economical way;

---

[1] "Improvements" and other closely related inventions which are in existence prior to the date of the contract will presumably be included (or excluded) by specific reference or will be covered—if the parties so intend—under the terms of a nonassertion clause. (*See* Section 5.01).

(2) Any beneficial modification of a component (or material) useful in the licensed invention; or

(3) Anything that performs functions similar to those of the licensed invention as described in a licensed patent and infringes the claims of the licensed patent (or some one of the licensed patents, if there are several).

Altogether, category (3) of the foregoing is most likely to approximate what the parties have in mind in any undifferentiated reference to "improvements." However, because of uncertainty as to what individual courts might, in their wisdom, do with this term if undefined,[2] it is highly desirable that the parties eliminate potential argument by providing a stipulative definition of their choosing. The following is a possible approach:

> "Improvement," as used in this agreement, means any modification of a licensed device described in a LICENSED PATENT, provided such modification, if unlicensed, would infringe one or more claims of the LICENSED PATENTS.

If the LICENSED PATENTS cover a variety of products, only some of which are actually intended to be licensed, the word "device" should, of course, be replaced by a term which aptly describes the licensed subject matter. Similarly, if the license pertains to a process rather than to a product, a variation such as the following may be called for:

> "Improvement," as used in this agreement, means any modification of a licensed process described in a LICENSED PATENT, provided such modification, if unlicensed, would infringe one or more claims of the LICENSED PATENTS.

---

[2]*See, e.g.,* U.S. Industries, Inc. v. Camco, Inc., 277 F.2d 292, 125 USPQ 216 (5th Cir. 1960). Here, controversy centered in part on the effect of licensing language which specified that "no license is granted for the manufacture, use or sale of any improvement in valves which has been or may be acquired by Olsco or Garrett or either of them." Olsco and Garrett were the licensing parties and the very patent licensed by the agreement in issue (a King patent No. 2,339,487) disclosed and claimed both (1) valves and (2) systems using valves. Licensing of systems was not controverted, but the contention was made that the valve claims (or some of them) were excluded by the force of the language quoted above. Much depended on the meaning of the word "improvement" in the context of the quoted language. As to this, the court said: "We need not seek to determine whether the term 'improvement' had all of the connotations of the patent art and had to have, therefore, the essential characteristics of a patentable novelty over a pre-existing device. Whether so limited or not, it is clear that as used here it referred to changes, betterments, modifications, or adaptations thought to improve which were disclosed outside of King 487. This would comprehend structures or devices covered in other patents or by other practices. As to such non-King 487 "improvements" the prohibition applied without regard to whether the grantors owned or acquired them in the past or future."

Where the nature of the licensed subject matter leaves any room for doubt on the point, it may be prudent from the licensor's viewpoint to add to the affirmative provisions suggested above an exclusionary clause such as the following:

"Improvement does not mean or include developments in respect to components, materials, or processes useful in practicing the inventions of the LICENSED PATENTS, but which do not themselves infringe the licensed claims of the LICENSED PATENTS.

A granting clause pertaining to "improvements," defined as above suggested or otherwise, might, if time limitation is intended, read as follows:

LICENSOR further agrees to grant to LICENSEE licenses of the scope specified in Paragraph 1 of this ARTICLE __ in respect to patents on any improvements (as defined in Paragraph __, above) which are first conceived and actually or constructively reduced to practice prior to the second anniversary of the effective date of this agreement and as to which, prior to that anniversary, LICENSOR has or shall have the right to grant such licenses without payment to others than employees of LICENSOR.

8.01 Releases for Past Infringement

Where an agreement is intended not only to provide for a prospective license but also to dispose of infringement or claimed infringement which has preceded the date of agreement, a release clause is ordinarily called for. In most instances, there will be payment for the past infringement, either at the royalty rates provided for in respect to future operations under the agreement or at a compromise rate (or lump sum) negotiated in order to facilitate settlement.[3] Occasionally, where past infringement has been inconsequential, payment in respect to it will be waived. Regardless of the financial arrangements, however, there is need on the part of the licensee to have some clear disposition of questions of past liability. A release clause of the following kind is common:

LICENSOR releases LICENSEE and all purchasers and users of LICENSED PRODUCTS acquired, mediately or immediately, from LICENSEE from all claims, demands, and rights of action which LICENSOR may have on account of any infringement or alleged infringement of any LICENSED PATENT by the manufacture, use, lease, sale, or other disposition of LICENSED PRODUCTS which, prior to the effective date of this agreement, were manufactured, used, sold, or otherwise disposed of by LICENSEE.

Occasionally, as where a license is being extended to a party whose intentions in respect to good-faith performance of his own

---

[3]*See* Chapter 9, "Reports and Payments," for further discussion of these points.

commitments may be in some doubt, the release given for past infringement may be conditioned upon such good-faith performance being realized. That the accomplishment of this objective is a matter of some difficulty, however, is suggested by the result obtained in *Gallowhur Chemical Corporation* v. *Schwerdle*.[4]

In the *Gallowhur* case, a patent suit had been settled by an agreement containing the following provisions:

> Now, therefore, in consideration of the premises and the faithful performance of the covenants herein contained, the parties hereto do hereby mutually agree as follows:
>
> * * *
>
> 3. Licensor and sublicensee agree that the aforesaid actions shall be dismissed without costs to either party and with prejudice and the execution of this agreement constitutes a release and satisfaction of all antecedent claims between the parties hereto, whether or not contained and/or referred to in the aforesaid action.

A patent license on a royalty basis was also provided. The agreement being subsequently terminated for default of royalty payments and the patents having expired, the licensor brought suit for misuse of trade secrets—an issue not clearly present in the earlier litigation.

The court rejected the plaintiff's contention that the release (held by the court to extend not only to patent rights but also to claims for breach of confidential relationship) had become ineffectual because of failure of consideration. It took the view that the release was conditioned not upon performance of the license terms but merely upon execution of the agreement.

To avoid this kind of result, a clause to the following effect may be considered:

> LICENSOR agrees that, providing LICENSEE fully and faithfully discharges all obligations undertaken by it in this agreement, including but not limited to the obligation to pay royalties, for the full term of this agreement, i.e., until December 31, 1979, LICENSOR will at that time release LICENSEE and all purchasers and users of LICENSED PRODUCTS acquired, mediately or immediately, from LICENSEE from all claims, demands, and rights of action which LICENSOR may now have on account of any infringement of any LICENSED PATENT by the manufacture, use, lease, sale, or other disposition of LICENSED PRODUCTS which, prior to the date of this agreement, were manufactured, used, sold, or otherwise disposed of by LICENSEE. Failure of LICENSEE at any time to so discharge its obligations shall constitute a waiver of the benefits of this paragraph __ and shall forthwith restore to LICENSOR its full rights as they existed on the date of this agreement.

It may be doubted, of course, that a provision of this kind would toll the provision of 35 USC §286 that:

---

[4]117 A.2d 416, 108 USPQ 260 (NJ Super. Ct. Ch. Div. 1955).

no recovery shall be had for any infringement committed more than six years prior to the filing of the complaint or counterclaim for infringement in the action.

Accordingly, a breach or failure of performance occurring more than six years after the date of agreement might find the licensor powerless to sue for infringement in respect to preagreement activities of the licensee. In the negotiating situation which would make the suggested paragraph desirable, however, the matter of real concern is that the licensee, postulated as of doubtful reliability, will immediately or soon commit a breach, thus invoking the waiver of release at a time when some period of preagreement infringement can still be reached under the statute.

Insofar as an agreement of the kind just discussed is entered into as an incident to the settlement of pending litigation, it would obviously be important, in order to preserve the values of the suggested paragraph, to arrange that the litigation be dismissed "without prejudice,"—or, in any event, that the dismissal not be specified as "with prejudice." (See the more complete discussion of these matters in Chapter 19.)

9

Royalties, Reports, and Payments

The consideration paid for licenses granted can, of course, take many forms. It may, for example, be specified as a lump sum to be paid at, or soon after, the date of execution of the agreement or, alternatively, in stated installments over a period of time.[1] Again, it may be a specified amount of money coupled with a reverse license extended under patents of the licensee. In some cases, only a cross-license from the licensee will be called for. Each of the schemes of compensation just referred to has its own problems of definition, some of which will be touched on in other parts of this work. The present chapter is, however, concerned with the case in which consideration is to be paid in whole or in part in the form of "royalties," that is to say, incremental payments proportioned in some way to the extent of use of the licensed inventions.

9.00 Determination of Amount of Royalties

No definitive statement can be made here concerning the "appropriate" amount of royalties, since this is strictly a matter for negotiation between the parties on a "what-the-invention-is-worth" basis.

---

[1]Particularly in a period in which interest rates are high, it needs to be borne in mind that a given sum to be paid over an extended period of time is of much lower effective cost to the paying party than the same total amount paid immediately. For example, in a time of 8 percent interest rates, the "present value" cost to the payor of a consideration of $250,000 paid in 10 annual installments of $25,000 each may be as little as $170,000, depending on which installment payments are to be made. This is a point which may be of considerable utility to a negotiating party who keeps in mind the power of "present value" formulas.

The rationale of royalty determination was stated as well as can be offered in *Georgia-Pacific Corp.* v. *U.S. Plywood-Champion Papers, Inc.*[2] in the following generalization:

> Where a willing licensor and a willing licensee are negotiating for a royalty, the hypothetical negotiations would not occur in a vacuum of pure logic. They would involve a market place confrontation of the parties, the outcome of which would depend upon such factors as their relative bargaining strength; the anticipated amount of profits that the prospective licensor reasonably thinks he would lose as a result of licensing the patent as compared to the anticipated royalty income; the anticipated amount of net profits that the prospective licensee reasonably thinks he will make; the commercial past performance of the invention in terms of public acceptance and profits; the market to be tapped; and any other economic factor that normally prudent businessmen would, under similar circumstances, take into consideration in negotiating the hypothetical license.

Where consumer goods, slated for quantity production for sale in a highly competitive market, are involved, tolerable royalties, measured on selling price, may run from a fraction of a percent to a few percent. Where specialty apparatus of a class normally carrying relatively high profit margins is the subject of the license, higher royalty rates, approaching, say, 5 percent, or even higher values, may be negotiable. In a very few instances, as where the use of the invention (perhaps a new and important catalyst) contributes extremely large added value to the products in which it is used, royalties as high as 50 percent (measured on the selling price of the catalyst or similar value-adding constituent) can be justified and will be found acceptable.

Royalties may, of course, be calculated in such varying ways as (1) a percentage of the selling price of products sold; (2) a percentage of manufacturing cost of licensed products (or products made by use of the licensed invention); or (3) a fixed sum per unit of product manufactured or sold. Reference to these alternatives will be made at subsequent points in this chapter.

Contract drafting in respect to royalty payments divides itself rather naturally into (1) the problem of defining the base on which royalties are to be computed and (2) the procedures under which royalties payable are to be calculated, reported, and accounted for. It ordinarily works well to treat these two matters separately, focusing one part of the agreement on each. Accordingly, the following sections will outline an approach suitable to this course.

Attention must be paid to case law decisions in drafting royalty payment provisions in licenses transferring rights under both patents

---

[2]318 F. Supp. 1116, 166 USPQ 235 (S.D.N.Y. 1970), *modified*, 446 F.2d 295, 170 USPQ 369 (2d Cir. 1971).

and other forms of intellectual property.[3] In general, royalty obligations for use of patent rights will survive patent expiration or patent invalidity, if the royalty payments are allocated between nonpatent and patent rights, while a single royalty payment obligation for a combination of both patent and nonpatent rights will become unenforceable upon either expiration or invalidity of licensed patent rights. Thus, royalty payment obligations allocated between patent rights and nonpatent rights as recited in paragraphs 5.01, 5.02, and 5.03 of the hybrid agreement set forth in Appendix F are recommended.

9.01 General Statement of Royalty Obligation

The statement of royalty obligation, as here visualized, has as its primary objective a clear description of the licensee's activities on which royalties are to be paid. The statement will necessarily take different forms depending on the nature of the licensed invention involved, that is, whether this invention is, in the terms of the patent statutes, a process, a machine, a manufacture, or a composition of matter. It will also vary depending on whether the licensee's objective is use of the licensed invention for manufacturing purposes (as may be the case in respect to a machine or process) or is, on the other hand, sale or other disposition of embodiments of the invention. The following are alternatively usable paragraphs drawn to fit at least several of the possible cases.

   (a) LICENSEE will pay LICENSOR royalties at the rate(s) specified in Article __ of this Agreement on all LICENSED PRODUCTS sold or otherwise disposed of under any subsisting and unexpired claim of any LICENSED PATENT.

   (b) LICENSEE will pay LICENSOR royalties at the rate(s) specified in Article __ of this agreement on all ROYALTY-BASE PRODUCTS sold or otherwise disposed of under any unexpired claim of any LICENSED PATENT.

   (c) LICENSEE will pay LICENSOR royalties at the rate(s) specified in Article __ of this agreement on all ROYALTY-BASE PRODUCTS produced by use of a claimed invention of any of the LICENSED PATENTS which is unexpired at the date of such use.

   (d) LICENSEE will pay LICENSOR royalties at the rate(s) specified in Article __ of this agreement on all ROYALTY-BASE PRODUCTS which are (i) produced by use of a claimed invention of any

---

[3]*See, e.g.,* St. Regis Paper Co. v. Royal Industries, 552 F.2d 309, 194 USPQ 52 (9th Cir. 1977), *cert. denied* 434 U.S. 996 (1977); Pitney Bowes, Inc. v. Mestre, 701 F.2d 1365, 218 USPQ 987 (11th Cir. 1983), *cert. denied*, 464 U.S. 893 (1983).

of the LICENSED PATENTS which is unexpired at the date of such use and (ii) sold or otherwise disposed of by LICENSEE at any time.

In accordance with the convention recommended at the outset of this work, it is assumed that all words in the several paragraphs above which are fully capitalized have been specifically defined at the beginning of the agreement or elsewhere. If the licensing situation is a simple one, involving only one or two patents, for example, specific reference to these patents may obviously be substituted for the generalized term LICENSED PATENTS. Similarly, definition of LICENSEE may be superfluous in many cases. On the other hand, the terms LICENSED PRODUCTS and ROYALTY-BASE PRODUCTS, where they are appropriate at all, are generally so important in their consequences as to merit stipulative definitions which have been thoroughly examined by both parties. Definition of the former term is discussed in Section 7.02 of Chapter 7. Some approaches to defining the royalty base are developed in the following sections.

A. Defining the Royalty Base

This problem has, over the years, engendered much license-involving litigation. In the litigated cases, there appear to be two principal sources of controversy: (1) vagueness as to the general subject matter intended to bear royalties and (2) uncertainty concerning intended peripheral metes and bounds of royalty-bearing subject matter otherwise reasonably identified.

(1) *Vagueness as to Subject Matter.* The vagueness problem is well illustrated by *Heath* v. *A.B. Dick Company*[4] and *Muth* v. *J.W. Speaker Corporation.*[5]

In the *Heath* case, the commitment was to pay royalties of "ten cents (10¢) per pound of the film material used in the stencilization of stencil sheets *under this license.*" This followed an agreement of the licensor to grant "a nonexclusive license under the aforesaid patents relating to the stencilization of stencil sheets."

In a suit for royalties the defense was on the ground that the licensee's products were covered only by claims which had been disclaimed from the licensor's patent. It was shown, however, that this fact had been known to the licensee prior to the execution of the license agreement, and it was held therefore that its commitment was to pay without regard to consideration of valid claim coverage.

The *Muth* case was generally to the same effect, subject to the qualification that in this case there was some doubt as to whether

---

[4]253 F.2d 30, 116 USPQ 358 (7th Cir. 1958).
[5]151 F. Supp. 188, 114 USPQ 327 (D. Wis. 1957).

the covering agreement was a patent license agreement or something broader. Although the existence of a patent was referred to in the recitals of the agreement and seems to have been a principal basis for the agreement, it was held that a commitment to pay "a five percent royalty on each Brake Saver Signal Light sold" implied a commitment to pay without regard to questions of patent coverage.

Avoidance of this kind of litigation-provoking uncertainty should, of course, be the primary concern of every drafter. Limitation of the royalty commitment to goods "sold or otherwise disposed of under any subsisting and unexpired claim of any LICENSED PATENT," as proposed in example (a) of Section 9.01 above, should meet the problem presented in the *Heath* and *Muth* cases—assuming, of course, that the intention of the parties is to protect the licensee to this extent. Other protection normally provided to the licensee against changes in the enforceability of the licensor's patents is suggested in Chapter 13 under the title "Validity and Construction of Patents."

(2) *Uncertainty Concerning Metes and Bounds.* Two cases which well illustrate this aspect of the royalty defining problem are *Pearson, Inc.* v. *Rust*[6] and *Farmland Irrigation Company* v. *Dopplmaier.*[7] Both these cases are discussed in Section 3.01(A) of Chapter 3. It will suffice at this point to remind the reader that in the *Pearson* case royalty base described as comprising "each and every cotton picking machine and all cotton picker parts and equipment embodying the invention or inventions of said Letters Patent" was held to cover all elements of an integrally combined cotton-picker and tractor. This was in spite of the fact that the equipment as initially licensed had been in the form of a trailer adapted to be pulled by a conventional tractor.

A more recent case[8] reaches the same result as *Pearson.* The licensee was to pay royalties on each bow and replacement part sold, but not on accessories. The invention covered a compound bow system originally used only with long bows. The licensee developed a cross-bow using the invention of the licensed patent rights, and argued that the "bow" described in the agreement consisted of the prod of the cross-bow and not the stock. The court held the prod and stock together constitute a complete "bow," because it is almost impossible to use the prod without the stock.

Insofar as avoidance of future controversy in cases of this kind is achievable by the contract drafter, such avoidance must lie in the preparation of "precising definitions" (see Section 3.01) which describe as farsightedly as possible the peripheral elements which are

---

[6]268 S.W. 2d 893, 101 USPQ 424 (Ark. 1954).

[7]308 P.2d 732, 113 USPQ 88 (Cal. 1957).

[8]Allen Archery, Inc. v. Precision Shooting Equipment, Inc., 865 F.2d 896, 9 USPQ2d 1728 (7th Cir. 1989).

and are not to be included in the royalty base. Some examples which undertake this approach follow:

Example 1

1.00 LICENSEE shall pay royalties to LICENSOR at the rate of two percent (2%) of the net selling price of all electrical transformers sold or otherwise disposed of . . .

1.01 An electrical transformer for purposes of Section 1.00, above, shall include the transformer *per se* and all attachments and accessories sold by LICENSEE for close-coupled use with the transformer, including, but not limited to:

(1) Core and coils
(2) Housing
(3) Radiators—fixed or detachable
(4) Forced-air equipment
(5) Electrical bushings
(6) No-load and load tap-changing equipment and control
(7) Insulating fluid
(8) All accessories such as gauges, valves, pumps, relief devices, switches, etc., mounted on the transformer or provided by LICENSEE for the normal operation of the transformer.

Example 2

1.00 LICENSEE shall pay LICENSOR royalties at the rate of __ percent (__%) of the net selling price of Lighting Apparatus sold or otherwise disposed of . . .

1.01 Lighting Apparatus for the purpose of Section 1.00, above, shall include all elevated and/or flush mounted light units complete with light sources (other than spares), ignition or pulsing circuits, master timer assemblies, junction boxes, remote control panels, local control and/or monitor panels, parts associated therewith, and other components forming a part of the installation irrespective of whether supplied for an initial installation or for addition to or modification of an existing installation, but excluding line material, such as poles and cables, which is separate from and external to the Lighting Apparatus components and which serves only to support or electrically connect such components.

Where the initially negotiated choice of a royalty base requires defining language as elaborate as that given in the two examples just stated, one may occasionally find a cleaner solution in agreeing that a *higher royalty rate* shall be applied to a *simpler royalty base*— with the estimated net yield being undiminished. For instance, assuming that in Example 1 the core and coils plus the housing and electrical bushings constitute the essential and universally present elements of every electrical transformer, one might conclude that economy and certainty of accounting could be achieved, with no great change in the final result, by providing something like the following:

> 1.00 LICENSEE shall pay LICENSOR royalties on electrical transformers sold or otherwise disposed of . . . , such royalties to be computed as indicated in Section 1.01, below.
>
> 1.01 Royalties on each electrical transformer sold or otherwise disposed of under the terms of Section 1.00, above, shall be calculated by applying the rate of ten percent (10%) to the sum of the separate manufacturing costs (calculated according to LICENSEE'S customary accounting procedures) or (i) the core and coils in assembled condition, (ii) the housing for the core and coils, and (iii) the electrical bushings to be supplied with the transformer.

The point of all the foregoing is not to recommend any of the specific approaches exemplified but is, rather, to emphasize and illustrate the need for adequate attention to what is potentially one of the most controversial areas of contract wording.

As between stipulating that royalties shall be calculated upon sales (or other commercial disposition) and stipulating that they shall be based upon goods manufactured, the former is generally preferred. One obvious reason for this is that it is easier for the licensee's accounting function to determine when royalties are due and, in general, on what base figures they are to be calculated. Conversely, any auditing of the licensee's figures which may be necessary on the licensor's behalf will ordinarily be simpler if applied to sales proceeds rather than to manufacturing costs. Cases will be encountered, however, in which the manufacturing cost approach has advantages which outweigh the presumptions just referred to. Conversion of any of the exemplary provisions given above to a manufacturing cost basis should be straightforward.

Where the structure of the agreement as a whole is complex, and particularly where there must be a number of references to the base on which royalties shall be paid, it often becomes convenient to adopt a phrase such as "ROYALTY-BASE PRODUCTS," or "CONTRACT PRODUCTS," or the like, as a defined term for this base. The adopted term will, of course, be defined at an appropriate place with whatever particularity is called for by the circumstances.

(3) *Uncertainty as to Licensee's Sales and Distribution System.* It is important for a licensor who is granting a license for running royalty consideration based on a percentage of the licensee's net selling price to ascertain the licensee's capabilities and intentions with respect to the licensee's sales and distribution of licensed products (royalty base products). For example, a licensor who is contemplating direct sales in the United States by a Japanese-based licensee to U.S. customers for the licensed product will probably be disappointed by the amount of royalty income received if the licensee instead sells to an unrelated Japanese trading company at a low price and the trading

company resells in the United States at a price that is 40–50 percent above the price at which it purchased.

Similarly, in the textile field, a licensee that sells licensed product in roll goods form may be selling licensed product at less than 50 percent of the per unit price that sales of the licensed product would achieve if sold as finished product.

In negotiating with a licensee that has the capability of selling licensed product at different levels in a chain of distribution (to one or more of ultimate customers, retailers, wholesalers, or distributors) or in situations as described above in this section (3), it may be desirable for a licensor to specify a fixed per unit royalty indexed for inflation as described in Section 9.06.

B. "Net Selling Price": Deductions and Special Circumstances

In the very common kind of license agreement in which royalties are calculated on the "net selling price" of goods sold, the significance of the quoted term is obviously great. It is important, therefore, to recognize that this term has no fixed meaning, but is, on the contrary, variable in meaning with the usages of particular trades. Thus, in *Friedheim v. Walter H. Hildic Co.*[9] the plaintiff, Friedheim, had been a salesman for the defendant company under a contract which provided for a commission of 10 percent on all net sales over $16,000. Friedheim sold directly to the retail trade, but orders were approved by a jobber who guaranteed the account. Goods were shipped to the retailer direct, freight prepaid, and the jobber was allowed a 15 percent discount. In computing Friedheim's commission, the net sales were figured as gross sales less jobbers' discounts and prepaid freight. Freidheim argued that this was an improper deduction, but at the level of the Supreme Court of South Carolina it was held that such deductions were appropriate to arrive at net sales—*in view of usage in the trade.*

Because of this point, an entirely explicit definition of "net sales" is desirable in any agreement in which this term plays a key role. Wording will, of course, depend on the business context and the intention of the parties, but the following is a form which is frequently appropriate:

> 1.02 "Net selling price" for the purpose of computing royalties under the provisions of Section 1.00, above, means LICENSEE'S invoice price, f.o.b. factory, after deduction of regular trade and quantity discounts, but before deduction of any other items, including but not limited to freight allowances, cash discounts, and agents' commissions.

---

[9] 89 SE 358 (S.C. 1915).

In some cases there is need to provide against the possibility that the licensee may, as a result of favorable organizational arrangement, be able to reduce its effective "net selling price" (to the detriment of the licensor), while still realizing its own full expected income by dealing through specially contrived channels. The following is one type of safeguarding clause designed for use where the main point of concern is the licensee's corporate structure.

> In order to assure to the LICENSOR the full royalty payments contemplated in this agreement, the LICENSEE agrees that in the event any ROYALTY-BASE PRODUCTS shall be sold for purposes of resale either (1) to a corporation, firm, or association which, or individual who, owns a controlling interest in LICENSEE by stock ownership or otherwise, or (2) to a corporation, firm, or association in which the LICENSEE or its stockholders own a controlling interest by stock ownership or otherwise, the royalties to be paid in respect to such ROYALTY-BASE PRODUCTS shall be computed upon the net selling price at which the purchaser for resale sells such PRODUCTS rather than upon the net selling price of the LICENSEE.

Where more subtle devices for minimizing royalty obligations than mere intracorporate arrangements are visualized as possible, wording as elaborate as the following may be called for.

> In order to insure to the LICENSOR the full royalty payments contemplated hereunder, the LICENSEE agrees that, in the event any ROYALTY-BASE PRODUCTS shall be sold (1) to a corporation, firm, or association which, or individual who, shall own a controlling interest in the LICENSEE by stock ownership or otherwise, or (2) to a corporation, firm, or association in which the LICENSEE or stockholders of the LICENSEE, or any subsidiary company of the LICENSEE shall own, directly or indirectly, a controlling interest by stock ownership or otherwise, or (3) to a corporation, firm, or association with which, or individual with whom the LICENSEE or its stockholders or subsidiary companies shall have any agreement, understanding, or arrangement (such as, among other things, an option to purchase stock, or an arrangement involving a division of profits or special rebates or allowances) without which agreement, understanding, or arrangement, prices paid by such corporation, firm, association, or individual for the apparatus licensed hereunder would be higher than the net selling price reported by the LICENSEE, or if such agreement, understanding, or arrangement results in extending to such corporation, firm, association, or individual lower prices for ROYALTY-BASE PRODUCTS than those charged to outside concerns buying similar merchandise in similar amounts and under similar conditions, then, and in any of such events, the royalties to be paid hereunder in respect of such PRODUCTS shall be based upon the net selling price at which the purchaser of PRODUCTS so sold resells such PRODUCTS, rather than upon the net selling price of the LICENSEE; provided, however, that the LICENSEE shall not be obligated under the foregoing to pay royalty based upon selling prices in excess of the standard net selling price at which it or any of the organizations or individuals associated with it as specified in this section shall sell such apparatus to any wholly independent jobber or distributor.

A classical case of contrived royalty minimization is that in which a licensee, in order to reduce his royalty obligations, made an arrangement with his customers under which they bought from him separately, for post-purchase assembly, all but the key invention-embodying element of the product for which he was licensed and on which he was expected to make royalty payments. He thus supplied "under the license" only the skeleton of the licensed product and used this as a basis for calculating the "net selling price" subject to royalties. While, at an appropriate rate, this might have been satisfactory to the licensor, it was not the result contemplated at the royalty rate actually negotiated.

The financial device just described might well be precluded by the second of the safeguarding clauses described above. In the case referred to, however, it was thought prudent in extending a desired license to the same licensee under improvement patents, to specify for the future a fixed-sum payment (rather than a royalty computed as a percentage of the selling price) for each unit of the licensed product thereafter sold.

In a fair number of situations not involving problems of royalty evasion, fixed-sum unit payments may be considered a more reliable basis of compensation than price-variable royalties. The automatic adjustability of the latter form of payment to unpredictable changes in economic conditions will, however, make it the probable choice in the majority of cases. Accordingly, the manipulative tendencies of the licensee may sometimes have to be estimated in deciding how elaborate to make the contractual safeguards against a contrived degradation of the intended royalty base.

In addition to visualizing the complicating circumstances which may arise out of the licensee's "special arrangements," the drafter of a royalty-based license also needs to consider the possibility that the licensee will dispose of substantial quantities of the licensed product other than by sale. Nonselling dispositions might include, for example, leasing or furnishing quantities of samples at no present cost to the recipient. In both these cases, and in imaginable others, the term "net selling price" will have an uncertain application for royalty calculation unless the problem has been dealt with by an appropriate contractual provision.

As a beginning, all nonsales cases can be subsumed under the words "otherwise disposed of,"[10] and these words included in the royalty provisions by reference in those provisions to products "sold or otherwise disposed of." With this antecedent language available it is a straightforward matter, under appropriate accounting guid-

---

[10]For a recommended comprehensive definition of "otherwise disposed of," *see* the last paragraph of subsection F(4) of Chapter 7.

ance, to design a royalty-computing formula which fits the particular case. The following is suggestive of possible approaches.

> Where products are not sold, but are otherwise disposed of, the net selling price of such products for the purposes of computing royalties shall be the selling price at which products of similar kind and quality, sold in similar quantities, are currently being offered for sale by LICENSEE. Where such products are not currently being offered for sale by LICENSEE, the net selling price of products otherwise disposed of, for the purpose of computing royalties, shall be the average selling price at which products of similar kind and quality, sold in similar quantities, are then currently being offered for sale by other manufacturers. Where such products are not currently sold or offered for sale by LICENSEE or others, then the net selling price, for the purpose of computing royalties, shall be LICENSEE'S cost of manufacture, determined by LICENSEE'S customary accounting procedures, plus _____percent (__%).

Of somewhat similar kind is the problem that arises when one must anticipate the possibility that significant quantities of licensed products will be sold, not by themselves, but as components or constituents of more complex products manufactured and sold by the licensee. If this is expected to be a matter of occasional occurrence only, one may perhaps most easily enlarge the definition of "otherwise disposed of" to assure that the definition covers this case. Thus:

> The expression "LICENSED PRODUCTS otherwise disposed of" means (1) LICENSED PRODUCTS not sold but delivered by LICENSEE to others (including deliveries for export), regardless of the basis of compensation, if any; (2) LICENSED PRODUCTS put into use by LICENSEE for any purpose other than routine testing of such PRODUCTS; and, (3) LICENSED PRODUCTS not sold as such but sold by LICENSEE as components or constituents of other products.

In a situation where the above treatment is appropriate and is, therefore, used, the royalty-calculating formula suggested in the next to last preceding paragraph will close the accounting loop. On the other hand, there may also be cases in which it is known or anticipated that the licensee's sales of the licensed products will be almost wholly in combination with other elements so that no directly comparable net selling price can be established. Here, if it is desired to rely on a "net selling price" as distinguished from a "manufacturing cost" approach, the following alternative language may have appeal.

> Where LICENSED PRODUCTS are not sold separately, but are sold in combination with or as parts of other products, the net selling price of the LICENSED PRODUCTS so sold shall be calculated for the purpose of computing royalties due by applying to the total net selling price (as herein defined) of the combined or composite products a fractional multiplier having as its denominator the total manufacturing cost of the combined or composite products (determined in accordance with LICENSEE'S customary accounting procedures) and as its numerator the manufacturing cost of the included LICENSED PRODUCTS (similarly determined).

9.02 Reporting and Accounting Provisions

The royalty base having been firmly defined, there are still details of reporting and accounting procedure which need to be taken care of clearly. The following are convenient reporting provisions where royalties are to be paid under issued patents on the basis of selling prices:

ARTICLE __

LICENSEE agrees to make written reports to LICENSOR quarterly within thirty (30) days after the first days of each January, April, July, and October during the life of the agreement and as of such dates, stating in each such report the number, description, and aggregate net selling prices of _____ sold or otherwise disposed of during the preceding three (3) calendar months and upon which royalty is payable as provided in Article __ hereof. The first such report shall include all such _____ so sold or otherwise disposed of prior to the date of such report [or "between the date of this agreement and the date of such report," if that is the agreed arrangement].

LICENSEE also agrees to make a written report to the LICENSOR within thirty (30) days after the date of any termination of this agreement, stating in such report the number, description, and net selling prices of all __ sold or otherwise disposed of and upon which royalty is payable hereunder but which were not previously reported to LICENSOR.

The obligation to pay royalties shall terminate as to each of the patents under which a license is herein granted on expiration of the patent, except that royalties accrued but not paid prior to such expiration shall be payable with the next report made under the provisions of this Article __. A patent shall be deemed to expire at midnight of the seventeenth anniversary of the date of issuance.

Concurrently with the making of each such report, LICENSEE shall pay to LICENSOR royalties at the rate specified in Article __ of this agreement on the _____ included therein.

Under this agreement _____ shall be considered to be sold when billed out, except that upon expiration of any patent covering such _____, or upon any termination of license, all shipments made on or prior to the day of such expiration or termination which have not been billed out prior thereto shall be considered as sold (and therefore subject to royalty). Royalties paid on __ which are not accepted by the customer shall be credited to the LICENSEE.

In some cases, it will be adequate to limit the reporting obligation in the first paragraph of the provisions recorded above to "the total of the net selling prices" (rather than "the number, description, and aggregate net selling prices"). Particularly where there is a sensitive competitive position between the licensor and licensee, this simplification may also be legally desirable.

While it would seem to be necessarily implied that royalty obligations arising from particular patents will terminate as such patents expire, an express proviso to that effect is desirable in view of the holding in *American Securit Co. v. Shatterproof Glass Corp.*[11] In that case, after finding patent misuse on the ground of coercive package licensing, the court stated that "quite apart from all the foregoing," misuse existed also because royalty was required to be paid on each patent until the expiration of the patent last to expire. Because there was no language in the royalty clause clearly cutting off royalties under older patents as they expired, the court construed a provision that the agreement "shall continue in full force and effect to the expiration of the last to expire of the licensed patents" as "extending" the payment of royalty under the earlier expired patents—with resulting misuse as indicated above.[12] The general theory of the *American Securit* decision was presumably endorsed by the Supreme Court in *Brulotte* v. *Thys Co.*, but the facts of the *Brulotte* case limit its direct authority to a situation in which royalties are levied after all the licensed patents have expired.[13] Accordingly, at least one court has declined to follow the Third Circuit in finding misuse in a requirement that royalty payments be continued undiminished as long as some of the licensed patents remain unexpired.[14] Nevertheless, the existence of the *Securit* and *Deering Milliken* holdings strongly recommends inclusion in a multipatent license agreement of an express cutoff of royalty obligations in respect to individual patents as they expire.

Frequency of reporting on the part of the licensee is a matter to be determined by the mutual convenience of the parties and depends in part on the magnitude of the business expected to be done by the licensee. Quarterly payments and reports are very frequently specified, but semiannual or even annual reports may be preferable if the amounts involved are expected to be small.

9.03 Royalty Payments in Respect to Pending Applications

Licensing negotiations in respect to a given technical development are frequently initiated at a time when patents have not yet

---

[11]268 F.2d 769, 122 USPQ 167 (3d Cir. 1959).

[12]*See also* Duplan Corp. v. Deering Milliken, Inc., 444 F. Supp. 648, 197 USPQ 342 (D.S.C. 1977), *modified,* 594 F.2d 979, 201 USPQ 641 (4th Cir. 1979).

[13]370 U.S. 29, 143 USPQ 265 (1964).

[14]*See* McCullough Tool Co. v. Well Surveys, Inc., 343 F.2d 381, 145 USPQ 6 (10th Cir. 1965).

been issued, but when applications for patent are either on file or in imminent contemplation. In such circumstances, it is common to provide, in effect, that licenses shall be granted "in respect to the applications and patents to issue on them."

There is an anomaly in purporting to grant licenses in respect to applications, because, until these become patents, they create no legal rights of exclusion as to which freedom of action must be purchased. What is really intended, in the ordinary case, is that the licensee shall acquire an assurance (amounting to an exercised option) that he will have rights under the patents when and if they come into existence. To obtain this, the licensee may be willing to pay royalties "under the applications" as if they already existed as patents.[15]

It was thought by some that the decisions of the Supreme Court in *Brulotte* v. *Thys Co.*[16] and in *Lear* v. *Adkins*[17] place obstacles of public interest in the way of this practice. The *Brulotte* case is assumed to be relevant in its holding that payment of license royalties may not be required in respect to a patent beyond its date of expiration. *Lear* is cited largely because of the vague and expansive language of Mr. Justice Black's partially concurring, partially dissenting opinion, which refers to "our patent laws, which tightly regulate the kind of inventions that may be protected and the manner in which they may be protected." (The majority opinion contains nothing directly relevant to the point in issue.)[18]

The Supreme Court in *Aronson* v. *Quick Point Pencil Co.*[19] reviewed a license agreement that called for royalty payments on a pending patent application.

The agreement called for a reduced royalty if a patent did not issue. The Court found no evidence that the patent application was used coercively to extend the royalty payment period.

---

[15]*See* David W. Hill, "The Licensing of Patent Applications: Legal and Competitive Effects," 63 J. PAT. OFF. SOC'Y 483 (1981).

[16]379 U.S. 29, 143 USPQ 264 (1964).

[17]395 U.S. 653, 162 USPQ 1 (1969).

[18]It can be urged that if public policy considerations are to apply, they are most reasonably stated in an address of Mr. Richard W. McLaren, assistant attorney general, given before a "Symposium on Patent Law" in Arlington, Va., on September 25, 1969. Mr. McLaren said:

In addition to staying away from a policy which would prevent the free use of ideas in the public domain, we must also avoid discouraging the exploitation of ideas which have not yet become a part of the public domain. For example, there is a public interest in getting a new invention to the market as soon as possible. Preventing the licensing of patent applications would seem to inhibit this objective.

[19]440 U.S. 257, 201 USPQ 1 (1979).

The terms and circumstances of payment called for under an agreement that licenses pending applications are obviously a matter for negotiation between the parties and the following remarks are addressed to considerations of interest in this connection.

A license may, in one readily imaginable case, be entered into at a time when patent applications have just been filed, or even ahead of that date. If, under these conditions, payments are to be made in respect to activities commencing in the near future, the basis for such payments should be carefully spelled out. Possible alternative bases for royalties are:

(1) All "Contract Products" (defined without specific reference to the content of the applications);

(2) All products utilizing inventions "disclosed" in the applications;

(3) All products utilizing inventions "disclosed and claimed" in the applications;

(4) All products utilizing inventions covered by "allowed claims" of the applications;

(5) Any variation of one of the above.

If alternative (1), (2), or (3) is adopted, it will nevertheless often be reasonable, for the licensee's protection, to make some provision for the contingency that claims will not be allowed in the pending applications or that the allowance of such claims will be excessively delayed. The following are alternative clauses which may be useful to consider in this connection.

Alternative 1

(a) For a period of two years from the date of this agreement, LICENSEE will pay royalties at the rates specified in Section __ on all LICENSED PRODUCTS, as herein defined, which are sold or otherwise disposed of by it within that period.

(b) Payment of royalties shall continue after the end of such two years if at that time LICENSOR shall have obtained the allowance in any of the enumerated applications of a claim or claims readable on LICENSED PRODUCTS sold or otherwise disposed of by LICENSEE, such payment being limited, however, to royalties upon LICENSED PRODUCTS which are covered by such allowed claim or claims.

(c) If at the end of two years from the date of this agreement, no claim applicable to LICENSED PRODUCTS sold or otherwise disposed of by LICENSOR shall have been allowed in any enumerated application, payment of royalties by LICENSEE shall be discontinued by LICENSEE until an applicable claim or claims shall have been allowed. Upon allowance of an applicable claim or claims, payment of royalties shall be resumed and thereafter continued upon LICENSED PRODUCTS covered by such claim or claims.

Alternative 2

The royalties provided for in Section __ shall be paid by LICENSEE in respect to its products utilizing any invention or inventions disclosed and claimed in the enumerated patent applications; provided, however, that if no Letters Patent are granted on any such invention within three (3) years from the date of this agreement, royalty payments shall be discontinued until such date as any such Letters Patent are granted. On any such date, payment of royalties shall be resumed in respect to products of LICENSEE utilizing inventions claimed in such Letters Patent.

Alternative 3

The royalties provided for in Section __ shall be paid by LICENSEE in respect to its products utilizing any invention covered by any pending claim of the enumerated patent applications; provided, however, that if no claim covering an invention utilized in LICENSEE'S products shall be allowed within two (2) years from the date of this agreement, royalties shall, after such two (2) years, be accrued but not paid until such time as Letters Patent containing such a claim shall be issued to LICENSOR. If such Letters Patent are issued within two (2) years from the date when accrual began, the accrued royalties shall be paid over to LICENSOR. If no such Letters Patent shall be issued within the two (2) year period specified in the preceding sentence, the accrued royalties shall be retained by LICENSEE, and royalties shall thereafter be paid only in respect to products of LICENSEE utilizing inventions which, when sold or otherwise disposed of, are covered by claims of issued Letters Patent of LICENSOR that are licensed to LICENSEE under this agreement.

Alternative 4

The royalties provided for in Section __ shall be paid by LICENSEE in respect to its products utilizing any invention covered by any pending claim of the enumerated patent applications; provided, however, that if Letters Patent do not issue within three years from the date of this agreement with a claim or claims covering an invention utilized in

LICENSEE'S products, and none of the enumerated applications (or continuations or divisions of them) pending at the end of the three years contains an allowed claim having such coverage, LICENSEE may thereafter, at its option, terminate this agreement by giving thirty (30) days notice to that effect to LICENSOR.

9.04 Minimum Royalty Requirements

The licensee should, in general, be required to pay a specified minimum for the privilege of keeping the license alive. Particularly where the licensee has the right to terminate the agreement upon due notice, the payment of an annual minimum cannot be considered as imposing an unreasonable burden. At the same time, it assures that the agreement will be a benefit rather than a burden to the licensor.

It should be recognized that the figure should not be less than sufficient to cover the licensor's costs in administering the agreement. Occasionally, it is desirable and fair to the licensee that minimum royalty provisions shall take effect only in the second or third year of the license in order to permit the licensee to get into production before burdening him with substantial costs.

In some cases, as where an important group of patents are being licensed, the minimum annual royalty should be substantial. The mere existence of an unused nonexclusive license detracts from a patent owner's ability to sign up additional prospective licensees. Also, where the licensee is to receive manufacturing information or other benefits which it will realize, if at all, at the outset of the agreement, it is appropriate that a substantial annual minimum be provided and that this continue at all events for a period of several years without the power of termination. The object of such an arrangement would be, of course, to assure that the licensor will receive a payment large enough to be compensatory for the benefits conferred.

For administrative reasons, it is generally desirable, particularly in agreements which give the licensee the right to terminate at any time, to make the minimum royalty payment a definite obligation on the part of the licensee, for example, by the use of the following form:

> In case the royalties paid do not aggregate a minimum of _____ dollars ($_____) for the year ending December 31, 19__, and for each succeeding calendar year during the life of this agreement, the LICENSEE will within thirty (30) days of the end of such year make up the deficiency of the royalties actually paid to such minimum sum.

Under some circumstances, the following form may be useful, but this will have the difficulty of imposing upon the licensor the

administrative burden of reviewing the licensee's operations and deciding whether the licensee's failure to pay the established minimum
justifies termination of the agreement by the licensor:

> In case royalties paid do not aggregate a minimum of _____
> dollars ($_____) for the year ending December 31, 19__, and the same
> amount for each succeeding calendar year during the continuance of
> this agreement, the LICENSOR may at its option terminate this agree-
> ment and the license granted to LICENSEE by thirty (30) days notice in
> writing to the LICENSEE, served on the LICENSEE within thirty (30) days
> after receipt of the last report for such calendar year, unless the LI-
> CENSEE shall within thirty (30) days from receipt of such notice by it
> pay the LICENSOR such additional sum as may be necessary to bring
> the payment for such calendar year up to the specified minimum.

9.05 Keeping and Auditing Records of the Licensee

The following form with reference to the keeping and auditing
of records is suitable for use in the ordinary case:

> LICENSEE agrees to keep records showing the sales or other disposition
> of devices sold or otherwise disposed of under the license herein granted
> in sufficient detail to enable the royalties payable hereunder by LI-
> CENSEE to be determined, and further agrees to permit its books and
> records to be examined from time to time to the extent necessary to
> verify the reports provided for in Article __, such examination to be
> made at the expense of the LICENSOR by any auditor appointed by
> LICENSOR who shall be acceptable to LICENSEE, or, at the option and
> expense of LICENSEE, by a certified public accountant appointed by
> LICENSOR.

In some cases it may be desirable to limit the time within which
an audit may be taken. For this purpose, the following form may be
found appropriate:

> LICENSEE agrees to keep true and accurate records, files, and books of
> account containing all the data reasonably required for the full com-
> putation and verification of the royalties to be paid and the information
> to be given in the reports provided for in Article __ hereof; and LICEN-
> SEE further agrees to permit its books and records to be examined from
> time to time to the extent necessary to verify such reports, such ex-
> amination to be made at the expense of the LICENSOR by an auditor
> appointed by LICENSOR who shall be acceptable to LICENSEE, or by a
> certified public accountant appointed by LICENSOR; provided that only
> those royalties paid by LICENSEE to LICENSOR within the two (2) year
> period immediately preceding the start of the audit, and their sup-
> porting records, files, and books of account shall be subject to audit.

If the licensee is given the right to grant sublicenses to others,
provisions should be included under which the sublicensees will be
required to keep proper records and make them available for appropriate examination.

In some cases, as where the licensor and licensee are competitors with resultant sensitivity about information to be exchanged between them, a foreshortened provision of the following kind may recommend itself:

> LICENSEE agrees to keep records showing the sales of devices sold under the license herein granted in sufficient detail to enable the royalties payable hereunder by LICENSEE to be determined, and further agrees to permit its books and records to be examined from time to time to the extent necessary to verify the reports provided for in Article __, such examination to be made at the expense of the LICENSOR by an independent auditor appointed by the LICENSOR who shall report to the LICENSOR only amount of royalty payable for the period under audit.

9.06 Providing for the Possibility of Inflation or Deflation

If an agreement provides for royalties payable in dollars or cents per unit of goods produced or sold instead of as a percentage of the selling price, it may be advisable to include in the agreement a clause which will recognize the possibility of inflation or deflation. A clause found suitable in certain instances follows, but appropriate financial or accounting advice should be obtained as to the suitability of its wording for a particular purpose:

The royalties payable are to depend upon the purchasing power of the dollar, as reflected by the Monthly All-Commodity Index of Wholesale Prices (hereinafter referred to as the "Index"), issued by the U.S. Government (at present through the U.S. Bureau of Labor Statistics). In order to stabilize the purchasing power of such royalties, they shall be subject to adjustment in each quarterly[20] period covered by this license in the following manner, in accordance with any major fluctuations in the Index:

> If the Index published for the last month preceding any quarterly period shall be more than x or less than y, then the royalties payable for such quarterly period shall be the royalties calculated as provided in Article __, plus the same percent of such royalties as the percent by which the point value of the Index published for the last month of the preceding quarterly period is more than x; or minus the same percent of such royalties as the percent by which the point value of the Index published for the last month of the preceding quarterly period is less than y, as the case may be.

In the preceding clause, the values of *x* or *y* should obviously be chosen in appropriate relation to the actual value of the Index at the

---

[20]This should correspond to the royalty payment and report period in the license agreement, i.e., quarterly, semiannual, or annual.

time the agreement is consummated. The gap between x and y should be large enough that trivial fluctuations of the Index will not require adjustment of the payment rate.

9.07 Nomenclature Information to Be Furnished by the Licensee

The following clause, frequently useful in royalty-requiring agreements, should be considered for the purpose of assisting the auditing function:

> LICENSEE agrees to inform LICENSOR promptly after the execution of this agreement as to the specific nomenclature and type designations under which LICENSEE will render bills covering sales of devices under the license herein granted, and further agrees to inform LICENSOR of any change or new designations which may thereafter be made or adopted for such devices, and LICENSEE in rendering bills for devices sold under the license herein granted, agrees that it will in such bills invariably use the nomenclature and type designation so furnished to LICENSOR.

Again, where the licensor and licensee are in a competitive relationship, the competitive significance of the information to be provided under a clause such as the foregoing should be carefully evaluated, and use of the clause should be avoided if it can be viewed as legally harmful.

10

Special Legal Problems: Misuse Situations and Multipatent Licensing

The doctrine of patent misuse provides an affirmative defense to a suit for patent infringement. A patent owner who is guilty of misuse is not permitted to enforce its patent until the misuse has been purged.

A patent owner misuses its patent by employing the patent to violate antitrust law or by unlawfully attempting to expand the scope of the patent. While a patent licensing practice that violates an antitrust law constitutes patent misuse, a patent owner's conduct may, in certain defined fact patterns, constitute misuse without rising to the level of an antitrust violation. Many changes in misuse law, both statutory and decisional, have recently occurred in a short period of time. Because such changes may continue in the future, it is desirable that persons drafting patent licensing agreements be familiar with current developments in patent-antitrust and patent misuse law.

10.00 Misuse as Defined by the Federal Circuit

The Federal Circuit dealt with patent misuse in a licensing context in *Windsurfing International, Inc. v. AMF, Inc.,*[1] and set forth criteria which must be met in order to successfully invoke the defense of patent misuse. First, the alleged infringer must show that the patentee has unlawfully extended the physical or temporal scope of the patent grant with anticompetitive effect.[2] Second, unless the Su-

[1]782 F.2d 995, 218 USPQ 562 (Fed. Cir. 1986).
[2]782 F.2d at 1001, 228 USPQ at 567.

preme Court has declared the type of licensing agreement at issue to be anticompetitive *per se*, "a factual determination must reveal that the overall effect of the license tends to restrain competition unlawfully in an appropriately defined relevant market."[3] Therefore, absent a Supreme Court pronouncement that a licensing arrangement is *per se* illegal, a rule-of-reason analysis will be used by federal district courts to determine whether the arrangement restrains competition. Because state courts also construe license agreements, and royalty payment obligations, it is still possible that pre-*Windsurfer* case law decisions on patent misuse will be applied in state court proceedings to the extent such decisions do not conflict with 35 U.S.C. §271(d)(4) and (5), discussed below.

Tying, as discussed below in Section 10.2, is the most common basis for a misuse holding. Holdings of misuse by tying have resulted from various types of analysis, usually on a *per se* basis, without inquiring into the effect, if any, on competition. Other licensing arrangements declared *per se* misuse violations by the Supreme Court include conditioning grant of a license on agreement to pay royalties based on total sales regardless of actual use of the patent,[4] projection of royalty payments beyond the expiration of licensed patents,[5] and price fixing of products sold which were manufactured under license.[6]

10.01 Misuse by Tying as Redefined by Statute

In 1988, Congress added subparagraphs (4) and (5) to 35 U.S.C. §271(d).[7] Section 271(d)(4) declares that refusal to license patent rights is not patent misuse. Section 271(d)(5) applies to tying allegations

---

[3]782 F.2d at 1001, 1002, 228 USPQ at 567.

[4]Zenith Radio Corp. v. Hazeltine Research, Inc., 395 U.S. 100, 161 USPQ 577 (1969).

[5]Brulotte v. Thys, 379 U.S. 29 (1964).

[6]United States v. Univis Lens Co., 316 U.S. 241, 53 USPQ 404 (1942).

[7]35 U.S.C. §271(d)(4)(5).

(d) No other owner otherwise entitled to relief for infringement or contributory infringement of a patent shall be denied relief or deemed guilty of misuse or illegal extension of the patent right by reason of his having done one or more of the following:

. . . .

(4) refused to license or use any rights to the patent; or

(5) conditioned the license of any rights to the patent or the sale of the patented product on the acquisition of a license to rights in another patent or purchase of a separate product, unless, in view of the circumstances, the patent owner has market power in the relevant market for the patent or patented product on which the license or sale is conditioned.

and seems to require use of a rule-of-reason analysis of restraint on competition, and definitely requires an analysis for market power. This provision thus appears to legislatively overrule the *per se* misuse rule stated by the Supreme Court in *Morton Salt Co.* v. *G.S. Suppinger Co.*[8] to apply to patent related tie-ins.

10.02 Misuse Based Upon Tying

Tying occurs in a licensing context when a patentee conditions licensing or sale of a patented item (tying item) on the purchase or license of a second item (the tied item). Prior to enactment of 35 U.S.C. §271(d)(5), tying in a patent context had usually been dealt with by the courts on a *per se* basis, without looking at market power or effect on competition.

The Federal Circuit in *Senza-Gel Corp.* v. *Seiffhart*,[9] which was decided before enactment of Section 271(d)(5), approved of a lower court's three-step analysis of patent misuse based upon a tying theory. First the court determined whether the two items alleged to have been tied constitute separable items or actually only one item.[10] Second, is the "thing" tied to the patented item a staple or nonstaple article of commerce? Third, has tying (coercion or conditioning) actually occurred?[11]

After enactment of §271(d)(5), to determine whether an illegal tying arrangement exists, as a first test, the existence or nonexistence of market power in the market for the product or patent on which the license is conditioned must be ascertained, but market power is no longer presumed from the mere ownership of a patent.[12] Apparently, only if market power has been demonstrated, and the three-step test from *Senza-Gel* satisfied, must the rule-of-reason analysis be performed to determine whether competition has been affected. The phrase "under the circumstances" was apparently meant to convey the requirement of a rule-of-reason approach for analysis of tying once market power has been found.[13]

---

[8]314 U.S. 488 (1982).

[9]803 F.2d 661, 231 USPQ 363 (Fed. Cir. 1986).

[10]Jefferson Davis Parish Hospital District 2 v. Hyde, 466 U.S. 2 (1984).

[11]Senza-Gel Corp. v. Seiffhart, 803 F.2d at 664, 231 USPQ at 365 (Fed. Cir. 1986).

[12]35 U.S.C. §271(d)(5). The amended language arguably overrules dicta in case law such as Jefferson Parish Hospital District No. 2 v. Hyde, 466 U.S. at 16, and International Salt Co. v. United States, 332 U.S. 92 (1947), stating that possession of a patent creates a presumption of market power. Note, however, that courts might ignore Section 271(d)(5) in deciding antitrust-based claims of tying.

[13]Cong. Rec. S17,147 (daily ed. October 21, 1988) (remarks of Sens. DeConcini and Leahy).

10.03 The Misuse Problem and "Label Licensing"

The situation occasionally arises that a patent is obtained on an end product, whether chemical, mechanical, or electrical, which is more likely to be produced by a customer of the patent holder than by the patent holder himself. Not infrequently in these situations, the patent holder's interest is in selling materials or parts which are useful in the patented product, although they are not themselves covered by the patent.[14]

It would, of course, be helpful to the patent holder's marketing program if he were able to offer rights under his end-use patent as an inducement to prospective customers to purchase from him the contributive elements or components which he holds out for sale. Unfortunately, however, it became hornbook law[15] that, where the contributive elements are staple articles of commerce, any such strategy misuses the patent and renders it unenforceable.

A. Procedure in Respect to Staple Articles or Commodities

Misuse by tying is still to be avoided by careful drafting, if possible. If an end-use patent is to be licensed by a seller of standard components, it is still desirable to use licensing terms and selling practices which assure that licensing the patent does not significantly distort the competitive market in respect to unpatented supplies or parts. A contractual expedient which the courts have so far recognized as yielding this result is generally referred to as "label licensing," a technique which appears to have been first tested in litigation in *Hall Laboratories, Inc.* v. *Springs Cotton Mills, Inc.*[16]

The *Hall Laboratories* case involved a patent on a process of retarding the corrosion of pipe lines by adding metaphosphates in strategically determined proportions to calcium-containing water. The patent owner did not practice the process directly but sold metaphosphates to those who did. Obviously mindful of the patent "misuse" problem, the court established the following licensing and marketing ground rules:

---

[14]The extent to which the seller's possession of additional patents covering the materials or parts which he sells may affect the legal issues to be discussed in this section is beyond the scope of this book.

[15]*See, e.g.*, §20.03 of Holmes, INTELLECTUAL PROPERTY AND ANTITRUST LAW (New York: Clark Boardman Co., 1983).

[16]112 F. Supp. 29, 97 USPQ 69 (W.D.S.C. 1953), *aff'd*, 208 F.2d 500, 100 USPQ 6 (4th Cir. 1953).

(1) Anyone desiring to use the patented process might do so upon the payment of a royalty at the uniform rate of two cents per pound of metaphosphate employed.
(2) The user might purchase the metaphosphate wherever he chose.
(3) If the user elected to purchase metaphosphate from the patent holder, the two-cent royalty was included in the purchase price and that fact was stated on the package.
(4) If the user desired to purchase metaphosphate from the patent holder for unpatented uses he paid an "ex-royalty" price, which was two cents a pound less than the "royalty-included" price.

It was held that this manner of exploiting the process invention was proper and did not render the patent unenforceable.

A similar result followed in *Calhoun* v. *The State Chemical Manufacturing Company*,[17] involving an unpatented O-ring sold for use in a patented fluid-sealing package construction. The patent owner sold O-rings for use in the patented construction and licensed other O-ring manufacturers to do the same. Purchasers of O-rings were licensed to use them under the patent, but a standard royalty of one-quarter cent was fixed for each packaging construction, and the manufacturing licensees were authorized and required to collect these royalties. Licenses on equivalent terms were also offered directly to end users of the O-rings. This program was found proof against a claimed defense of misuse, the court relying on Section 271 of the Patent Code as well as on the general principles of the *Hall Laboratories* case.

Where the *Hall Laboratories* approach is adopted, it would appear that it must be followed in full detail and with careful attention to the actual effect of its various provisions.[18] Still further it needs to be observed that regardless of the licensing formula used, prophylaxis cannot be assumed if, *in fact*, the total course of conduct adopted seriously alters the competitive flow of unpatented goods. The ske-

---

[17]153 F. Supp. 293, 115 USPQ 120 (N.D. Ohio 157). *See also*, to the same effect, Calhoun v. United States, 339 F.2d 665, 143 USPQ 439 (Ct. Cl. 1964).

[18]Thus, in Barber Asphalt Corp. v. LaFera Grecco Contracting Co., 116 F.2d 211, 47 USPQ 1 (3d Cir. 1940), a licensing program was adopted under which some licensees were charged a royalty of one cent per square yard of concrete treated. This was held discriminatory and a misuse of the patent because of possible inequalities in the competitive burdens to which the second group of licensees were subjected. In contrast, a label licensing procedure avoided a misuse in a complex factual situation in Noll v. O.M. Scott & Sons Co., 467 F.2d 295, 169 USPQ 336 (6th Cir. 1972) (method of crabgrass control).

letonized contractual provisions which follow are offered entirely subject to these caveats.

Example 1

(Notice for use on packages and invoices employed with unpatented constituents sold for use in a patented method and product, the applicable patent being owned by the seller.)

NOTICE TO PURCHASER

The material in this package (or covered by this invoice) comprises constituents understood by ABC Company to be intended for use by the purchaser in producing ceramic bodies which, and the process of making which, are covered by ABC Company's United States Patent No. 4,180,293.

In purchasing this material, you have been charged and invoiced for a royalty at the rate of x percent of the purchase price paid. By this payment, which is ABC Company's standard royalty rate for licensing Patent No. 4,180,293, you have acquired a license under the patent to use the purchased materials to practice the method and to make the ceramic bodies described and claimed in the patent, together with the right to use and sell the bodies so made.

ABC Company will, on request, license any party at its standard royalty rate to practice the patented inventions, using constituents purchased from any source whatever. Persons wishing a copy of ABC's standard license should write to

ABC Company
Box 588
Flint, Michigan

ABC Company will also sell constituents ex-royalty to parties who advise that they are being purchased for use other than in accordance with the inventions of Patent No. 4,180,293.

Example 2

(Provisions for use in an agreement which authorizes a party other than the patent owner to extend licenses under the patent as an incident to the sale of a component useful in the patented invention.)

ARTICLE I

BACKGROUND

1.00 ABC Company is the owner of United States Patent No. 4,180,294 issued September 17, 1977, relating to an irradiating apparatus which utilizes as a key element a specialized electronic tube known in the relevant trade as a "GAMMATRON."

1.01 XYZ Company proposes to engage in the business of manufacturing GAMMATRONS and wishes to be in a position to assure its purchasers of such tubes of a license to use the purchased tubes in apparatus covered by Patent No. 4,180,294.

1.02 ABC Company is willing to grant licenses at a standard royalty rate to any party to practice the invention covered by Patent No. 4,180,294, irrespective of the source of GAMMATRONS used in such practice. It is also willing to authorize any vendor of GAMMATRONS to extend such licenses to purchasers of its GAMMATRONS, subject to the vendor's collection and payment to ABC Company of the standard royalty in respect to practice of the patented invention by use of the purchased GAMMATRONS.

ARTICLE II

DEFINITIONS

2.00 PATENTED EQUIPMENT means irradiating apparatus covered by one or more of the claims of Patent No. 4,180,294 and which, except for the license granted herein would constitute infringement of one or more of said claims. As so defined, PATENTED EQUIPMENT necessarily includes a GAMMATRON.

ARTICLE III

LICENSE GRANT

3.00 ABC Company grants to XYZ Company a nonexclusive license to make, use, and sell or otherwise dispose of PATENTED EQUIPMENT throughout the United States, its territories, and possessions.

3.01 ABC Company also grants to XYZ Company a nonexclusive right to grant to any purchaser or transferee of a GAMMATRON sold or otherwise disposed of by XYZ Company other than as a part of PATENTED EQUIPMENT licensed under Section 3.00 of this ARTICLE III, a nonexclusive license to make, use, and sell or otherwise dispose of PATENTED EQUIPMENT utilizing such GAMMATRON, throughout the United States, its territories, and possessions, provided XYZ Company shall attach to all such GAMMATRONS the following notice:

NOTICE TO PURCHASER

Purchase of this tube includes a license under United States Patent No. 4,180,294 to make, use, and sell or otherwise dispose of one irradiating apparatus covered by the patent and our price includes an allowance for payment to ABC Company of its standard royalty for such license. Our prices ex-royalty will be supplied on request. Licenses at the standard rate and unrestricted as to source of tube are available from

ABC Company
Box 588
Flint, Michigan

ARTICLE IV

PAYMENTS

4.00 XYZ Company agrees to pay royalties at the rate of Fifty Dollars ($50.00) for each PATENTED EQUIPMENT sold or otherwise disposed of by it under the license granted in Section 3.00 of ARTICLE III and at the same rate for each GAMMATRON sold or otherwise disposed of by it subject to the grant of a license to the purchaser or other transferee under the terms of Section 3.01 of ARTICLE III. Reports and remittals of royalty payments due shall be made as provided in ARTICLE V of this agreement.

B. Articles and Commodities Not Suitable for Noninfringing Use

Where the materials or parts sold to an end user are not staple articles or commodities of commerce suitable for noninfringing use, the provisions of 35 U.S.C. 271,[19] as interpreted by the Supreme Court in *Dawson Chemical Company* v. *Rohm & Haas Company*,[20] permit the sale of such materials or parts to carry with it a license for use of the parts or materials in the patented context, without demanding recourse to the complex procedures adopted in the *Hall Laboratories* and *Calhoun* cases. There is, however, uncertainty as to what commodities will be held to be "staple."[21]

Where primary reliance is to be placed on 35 U.S.C. 271, for example in a license grant which authorizes a licensor to extend to his or her licensee royalty-free licenses under an end-use patent as an incident to the sale of constituents or components especially made

---

[19]§271 Infringement of Patent.

. . . .

(c) Whoever sells a component of a patented machine, manufacture, combination or composition or a material or apparatus for use in practicing a patented process, constituting a material part of the invention, knowing the same to be especially made or especially adapted for use in an infringement of such patent, and not a staple article or commodity of commerce suitable for substantial noninfringing use, shall be liable as a contributory infringer.

(d) No patent owner otherwise entitled to relief for infringement or contributory infringement of a patent shall be denied relief or deemed guilty of misuse or illegal extensions of the patent right by reason of his having done one or more of the following: (1) derived revenues from acts which if performed by another without his consent would constitute contributory infringement of the patent; (2) licensed or authorized another to perform acts which if performed without his consent would constitute contributory infringement of the patent; (3) sought to enforce his patent rights against infringement or contributory infringement.

[20]488 U.S. 176, 206 USPQ 385 (1980).

[21]*See, e.g.*, Dr. Salsbury's Laboratories v. I. D. Russell Co. Laboratories, 212 F.2d 414, 101 USPQ 137 (8th Cir. 1954).

or adapted for use in the patented invention, prudence would suggest following the statutory language as closely as practicable. Thus, a grant in the following terms may be visualized:

> LICENSOR grants to LICENSEE a nonexclusive license to make, use, sell, and otherwise dispose of devices covered by any claim of United States Patent No. 4,280,394, including kits of parts which are especially made or especially adapted for the construction of devices that, except for this license, would be an infringement of the patent. LICENSOR also grants to LICENSEE in respect to kits of parts sold or otherwise disposed of as above indicated, and which, as sold, are not staple articles of commerce suitable for substantial noninfringing use, the right to extend to LICENSOR's vendors or transferees assurance of a royalty-free license to use the kits in construction of devices covered by any claim of Patent No. 4,280,394.

Endorsement of the pattern represented by the clause just stated assumes, of course, that the business practices followed will in fact comport with the language of the clause.

10.04 Multipatent Licensing; Suggested Treatment

It is frequently the case that a licensor holds several (a "package" of) patents contingently applicable to the interests of his prospective licensees. Where a given prospective licensee has stated a desire to receive a grant in respect to all applicable patents and a willingness to pay on any reasonably calculated basis for such a grant, no difficulty may be presented in suitably formulating *that license*. However, in view of certain decisions, to be mentioned below, if the patent owner envisions the possibility of granting further and related licenses to other licensees, he needs to anticipate, *in the very first* grant which is consummated, the problems which will arise if the later licensees desire rights under some part only of the entire patent package.

A number of decisions issued prior to enactment of 35 U.S.C. §271(d)(4) and (5), such as *American Securit Co.* v. *Shatterproof Glass Corp.*,[22] *United States* v. *Loew's, Inc.*,[23] and *Hazeltine Research, Inc.* v. *Zenith Radio Corp.*,[24] held that a patent owner may not, as a

---

[22]268 F.2d 769, 122 USPQ 167 (3d Cir. 1959).

[23]371 U.S. 38, 135 USPQ 201 (1962).

[24]239 F. Supp. 51, 144 USPQ 381 (1965). The decision of the district court in this case was reviewed and, in some respects, modified in 1967 by the Seventh Circuit Court of Appeals (388 F.2d 25, 156 USPQ 228) and was additionally reviewed by the Supreme Court in 1969 (395 U.S. 61, 161 USPQ 577) and remanded for further proceedings. However, neither of the reviewing courts found error in the lower court's injunction against (in effect) conditioning the grant of a license under any patent upon the acceptance of a license under any other patent.

condition of extending rights under one or more patents, require that the prospective licensee accept obligations in respect to other patents. There were exceptions to this rule, as where two or more offered patents are crucially related as to subject matter,[25] but these exceptions were not fully articulated by the courts and, therefore, could not be identified with certainty. Accordingly, it used to be that except in extraordinary circumstances (not presently definable), it was recommended that every licensing program involving multiple patents be designed, from the beginning, to anticipate the contingency that some prospective licensee (not necessarily the first) will request or demand a license limited to selected parts of the licensor's patent package. Section 271(d)(5) overrules the *per se* misuse rulings of the above-cited cases in compulsory package licensing situations. However, it does not foreclose rule-of-reason inquiry into whether a particular package licensing procedure constitutes a misuse. Therefore, continued vigilance in negotiating and drafting is required of attorneys advising licensors of more than one patent, or of a patent and any other form of intellectual property, to avoid a misuse holding on a compulsory package licensing theory.

A problem which must be overcome is that of avoiding in a later license any conflict with "more favorable terms" assurances contained in an early one. Obviously, no single pattern can be recommended as fitting all cases likely to arise in this connection, but a program such as the one described below has been found to be useful in a number of contexts.

The procedure is to assign to each patent to be included in the licensing package offered both (1) a primary royalty rate and (2) an incremental royalty rate. The "primary" rate, which may be, for example, from one percent to five percent, will be paid by the licensee if the patent to which it attaches is either (a) the only patent licensed or (b) the most important patent licensed (as indicated by the magnitude of the assigned royalty rate). The "incremental" royalty rate for the same patent may run, say, from a fraction of one percent to one percent or somewhat more, depending on the significance of the invention involved, and will be the rate paid in respect to that patent by the licensee if the invention of the patent in question is utilized *in addition to* the invention of a more important patent on which a "primary" rate is paid. The complete development of such a program can best be visualized by reference to specific contractual provisions, such as the following, which have been drafted to cover a particular case. (The provisions in question have been skeletonized in order to emphasize the matters presently under discussion.)

---

[25]*See, e.g.*, International Mfg. Co., Inc. v. Landon, Inc., 336 F.2d 723, 142 USPQ 421 (9th Cir. 1964). *See also*, for a generalized discussion of this legal area, "Coerced Package Licensing and Royalties—Patent Misuse," 14 IDEA 320 (1970).

ARTICLE I

BACKGROUND

1.01 LICENSOR represents that it is the owner of the patents enumerated in Schedule A, attached to this agreement, and is willing to grant nonexclusive licenses to LICENSEE under any or all of such patents.

1.02 LICENSEE has indicated its wish to acquire licenses under items 1, 2, 5, and 6 of Schedule A, such items being hereafter referred to as LICENSED PATENTS.

ARTICLE II

GRANT BY LICENSOR

2.01 . . . .

2.02 . . . .

2.03 Notwithstanding the grants of Paragraphs 2.01 and 2.02 of this ARTICLE II, no license is granted or implied by this agreement under any patent of LICENSOR other than the LICENSED PATENTS, whether or not the claims of such other patent dominate the claimed invention of any LICENSED PATENT.

ARTICLE III

ROYALTIES

3.01 LICENSEE agrees to pay to LICENSOR a royalty in an amount equal to the "applicable percentage," as defined in Paragraph 3.03 of this Article III, of the net selling price (as defined in Paragraph 4.03 of this agreement) of all CONTRACT PRODUCTS which are sold or otherwise disposed of under the license herein granted.

3.02 LICENSEE also agrees to pay to LICENSOR the "applicable minimum annual royalty," as defined in Paragraph 3.04 of this Article III.

3.03 The "applicable percentage" of the net selling price of each CONTRACT PRODUCT is to be determined from the attached Schedule A by first selecting the relevant group of applicable patents (*i.e.*, the group of unexpired LICENSED PATENTS each of which has one or more claims applicable to such CONTRACT PRODUCT or its manufacture); next selecting from the applicable patents the single patent with an "individual royalty rate" which is the highest individual royalty rate of the applicable patents; and then adding to this highest individual royalty rate the "incremental royalty rate" of each of the remaining applicable patents. The sum resulting from this addition of rates is the "applicable percentage."

3.04 The "applicable minimum annual royalty" is to be determined from the attached Schedule B by first identifying all applicable patents (as selected in Paragraph 3.03 of this Article III) applicable to any CONTRACT PRODUCTS or their manufacturer; next selecting from these applicable patents the single patent with an "individual minimum annual royalty" which is the highest individual minimum annual royalty of the applicable patents; and then adding to this highest minimum individual annual royalty the "incremental minimum annual royalty" of each of the remaining applicable patents. The sum resulting from the addition of minimum annual royalties is the "applicable minimum annual royalty."

3.05 The obligation to pay royalties shall terminate as to each of the LICENSED PATENTS upon its expiration, except that royalties accrued but not paid prior to such expiration shall be payable with the next report submitted by LICENSEE under the provisions of Article IV hereof. Upon expiration of a LICENSED PATENT both the "applicable percentage" and the "applicable minimum annual royalty" payable under the remaining LICENSED PATENTS shall be redetermined in accordance with the procedures specified in Paragraphs 3.03 and 3.04 of this Article III. Where two or more "applicable minimum annual royalties" are in effect during successive periods of any calendar year because of the expiration during that year of one or more LICENSED PATENTS, each of such "applicable minimum annual royalties" shall be prorated to cover only the period during which such applicable minimum annual royalty was in effect.

ARTICLE IV

REPORTS AND PAYMENTS

4.01 LICENSEE will make written reports to LICENSOR semiannually within sixty (60) days after the first days of January and July of each year during the term of this agreement and as of such dates stating in each such report the net selling prices of all CONTRACT PRODUCTS sold or otherwise disposed of under each group of applicable patents (as selected in Paragraph 3.03 of Article III hereof) during the preceding six (6) months, together with a listing of the patents in each such group.

4.02 Simultaneously with each report provided for in Paragraph 4.01 of this Article IV, LICENSEE will pay to LICENSOR the royalties shown by such report to be due and payable.

4.03 (Includes conventional definition of "net selling price").

ARTICLE VII

TERMINATION

7.01 . . . .

7.02 At any time after three (3) years from the effective date of this agreement, LICENSEE shall have the right to terminate this agreement in its entirety or its license under any, some, or all of the LICENSED PATENTS at the end of any calendar year, provided there is no default hereunder, by written notice given to LICENSOR at least ninety (90) days prior to the end of such year.

Schedule A

Licensed Patent	Individual Royalty Rate, percent	Incremental Royalty Rate, percent
(1) —,888	7.50	
(2) —,412	4.00	0.50
(3) —,366	4.00	0.50
(4) —,330	3.50	0.45
(5) —,247	3.50	0.45
(6) —,506	3.50	0.45
(7) —,754	3.50	0.45
(8) —,124	3.25	0.40
(9) —,557	3.00	0.35
(10) —,272	3.00	0.35

Schedule B

Licensed Patent	Individual Minimum Annual Royalty	Incremental Minimum Annual Royalty
(1) —,888	$56,000.00	
(2) —,412	14,000.00	$2,800.00
(3) —,366	14,000.00	2,800.00
(4) —,330	10,000.00	2,000.00
(5) —,247	10,000.00	2,000.00
(6) —,506	10,000.00	2,000.00
(7) —,754	10,000.00	2,000.00
(8) —,124	8,000.00	1,600.00
(9) —,557	6,000.00	1,200.00
(10) —,272	6,000.00	1,200.00

A program developed as indicated by the preceding exemplary provisions is obviously extremely flexible in its application. Any requested selection of patents can be accommodated without doing violence to the structure of preexisting agreements (provided only they are in the same format). There is, of course, a possible dilemma to be confronted in a situation in which a particular prospective licensee wishes to receive licenses under "secondary" patents without concurrently becoming licensed under more important patents by which they may be dominated. That is, however, a dilemma which is inherent in the policy of the law against coercive coupling of patent licenses. Whether it could be surmounted by refusal of unreasonably selected licenses in a particular case is a matter which would depend crucially upon the special facts of the case and is beyond the scope of this work to explore. The possibility of this contingency, however, presumably makes highly desirable the inclusion in the "standard agreement" of a paragraph corresponding to Paragraph 2.03 of the above.

A question which will very probably present itself in the development of a licensing program patterned as above proposed is whether a maximum royalty percentage can be set, upon payment of which the licensee may practice concurrently any number of the licensed patents without further detailed accounting. On the theory that this is a field in which the antitrust rule of reason should apply, it seems plausible to argue that if the maximum royalty set does not differ widely from the "applicable percentage" calculated under the agreement formula for the greatest number of patents believed in good faith to be *likely to be used concurrently at any one time*, then minor discrepancies which may actually arise in practice should not invalidate the program as a whole.

11

More Favorable Terms Provisions

There is no general rule of law which requires the patent owner to extend identical licensing terms to all licensees,[1] or to refrain from granting to a subsequent licensee terms which are more generous in some respect than those contractually assured to a prior licensee. It is therefore quite natural for the prospective acceptor of a license to request that the agreement contain provisions assuring him of protection against the subsequent extension of more favorable terms to others. On the other hand, an overly generalized "no more favorable terms" clause can prove extremely troublesome to the licensor if he is later confronted with a licensing occasion which differs radically in its context from the license which contains such a clause.

The potential for controversy of this subject is well illustrated by the decision of the Fourth Circuit Court of Appeals in *St. Joseph Iron Works* v. *Farmers Mfg. Co.*[2] In this case, Farmers had been granted a license by St. Joseph to make baskets covered by certain patents and pending applications. The covering agreement contained the following clause:

> 9. If First Party grants to any other party license on one or more of the patents or applications for patent, which are the subject matter of this agreement, upon more favorable terms and/or royalty rates than those specified herein, First Party shall give immediate written notice thereof to Second Party. If Second Party so elects, it shall automatically become entitled to such more favorable terms and/or royalty rates.

Subsequently, St. Joseph, which functioned primarily as a manufacturer of basket-making machinery, modified machines that it

---

[1]For a discussion of the legal issues relating to this chapter, *see* K. E. Payne and B. G. Brunsvold, "Five Important Clauses: A Practical Guide," LICENSING LAW AND BUSINESS REPORT 6, no. 1 (1983), pp. 74–77.

[2]106 F.2d 294, 42 USPQ 558 (4th Cir. 1939).

had earlier sold to a certain customer so that these machines would produce baskets which, while unlike those made by Farmers, were nevertheless (as the court found) within the scope of the licensed patents. No royalties were required of the customer, and no notice of the transaction was given to Farmers. Upon later learning of this situation, Farmers declined to pay further royalties and, being sued, counterclaimed for recovery of all royalties paid subsequent to the date of the customer arrangement referred to above. Its argument was that the failure of St. Joseph to charge royalties on the modified machines amounted to granting the customer a license which, being free, was necessarily "more favorable" than that extended by the agreement with Farmers. It won on both its defense and its counterclaim, the court declining to examine closely the question of whether baskets manufactured by the modified machines were precluded by prior art from being viewed as an infringement of the licensed patents. As to this, the court said:

> This rule of construction, which is availed of to save a meritorious patent which would otherwise be held void on account of the breadth of the claims (cases cited) cannot avail plaintiff for the reason that plaintiff cannot be heard to question the validity of the claims of its patent, and the ordinary rule applies that courts will interpret an expression positively recited in the claims as satisfied by any suitable instrumentality capable of performing the stated function successfully. (Case cited.)
>
> Instead of a strict construction, we think the patent, as between the plaintiff and defendants, should be liberally construed to the end that defendant may be protected in the license granted by it by plaintiff, for which royalty is reserved by the contract.

This sort of costly result (probably totally unexpected by the licensor in the St. Joseph case) can only be avoided by thoughtful anticipation during the contract-drafting period of contingencies apt to arise during the further administration of the licensed patents. This kind of anticipation may be assumed to account for the licensor-favoring result which obtained in *Plastic Contact Lens Company* v. *Guaranteed Contact Lens, Inc.*[3]

Litigation arose as the result of discontinuance by two licensees (Guaranteed Contact Lens Company and Quality Optical Company) of royalty payments nominally due under license agreements in respect to contact lens patents owned by Plastic Contact Lens Company (successor of Solex Laboratories). While these agreements had been executed some months after January 1, 1961, each was by its terms made effective on the latter date. Moreover, each agreement contained a "most favorable licensee" clause in the following terms:

> Solex agrees that in the event it should *hereafter* grant a license to another person, firm or corporation under said Patent No. 2,510,438,

---

[3]283 F. Supp. 850, 158 USPQ 544 (S.D.N.Y. 1968).

or under any other United States patent or application licensed hereunder upon terms and conditions more favorable than those herein accorded, *except for the manner of settlement for past infringement,* Solex shall promptly offer Licensee the benefit of such more favorable terms and conditions, which upon acceptance shall be retroactive to the date that such more favorable terms and conditions were accepted by said other person, firm or corporation. (Emphasis added.)

After a brief period during which Guaranteed and Quality paid royalties as prescribed by their agreements, they discontinued such payments. When sued, they defended on the general ground that plaintiff had breached the "most favored licensee" provisions of their agreements through the extension of two other licenses under the circumstances noted below.

The first basis of defendants' complaint was Plastic's granting to Security Contact Lens Corporation a license arguably more favorable in some respects than defendants' licenses. This agreement had been executed December 22, 1960, and became effective January 1, 1961. The second basis of complaint was that in settling a patent suit brought against by George H. Butterfield and Son under patents of that company, Plastic Contact Lens Company had settled on terms which included the granting of a free license to Butterfield under the patents involved in the present suit, together with the right in Butterfield to extend a similar license to four of its own licensees. This agreement was entered into in 1962.

As to the Security license, the court found no conflict with enforceable interests of the licensees because the Security license had been *executed* before the agreements relied upon by Guaranteed and Quality Optical. The court leaned on the word "hereafter" found in the "more favorable terms" clause of the agreement and on a general argument that such clauses are normally intended to have only prospective application.

As to the Butterfield agreement, where the "hereafter" phraseology was clearly inapplicable, the court found an escape for the plaintiff licensor in the agreement's reference to "except for the manner of settlement for past infringement." It apparently concluded that the "manner of settlement for past infringement" could include favorable treatment in respect to *future* infringement, a result which some counsel might think unpredictable. On this front, however, the plaintiff's case was buttressed by the fact that following the Butterfield settlement, plaintiff had informed all its licensees of the terms of settlement and offered revised terms to any licensee who considered the Butterfield settlement "more favorable" and who *was in a position to grant the plaintiff consideration equivalent to that received from the Butterfield interests.* Neither defendant replied to this offer.

On the analysis given above, the court ordered payment by defendants of royalties due under the appropriate terms of their agreements.

Sometimes the needs of the licensee can be met without obliging the licensor to face the uncertain perils of a "most favorable terms" clause by giving the licensee a right to terminate his license at any time—thus providing him with an opportunity to negotiate new terms if he feels that a later licensed competitor has been excessively favored. Where this is not possible, very careful attention should be given by the licensor (and his license draftsman) to the design of provisions which reasonably protect the licensee without excessively tying the hands of the licensor.

The following form may solve the problem of both parties in agreements which exact no consideration from the licensee other than the payment of royalties calculated at a percentage or per-unit rate:

11.00 (a) If the LICENSOR shall grant to any manufacturer or seller of LICENSED PRODUCTS other than a company in which the LICENSOR has a substantial interest, direct or indirect, a license which is under any United States Letters Patent licensed in this agreement and which will permit such manufacturer or seller to manufacture or sell for any use within the scope of the license granted in this agreement and at rates of royalty which, calculated on an equivalent basis in respect to the Letters Patent in question, are lower than those provided in this agreement, then LICENSOR will
  (i) Promptly notify LICENSEE of such license, and
  (ii) Extend to LICENSEE the lower royalty rates of the noticed license, effective as of the date on which they became effective in respect to the noticed license.
11.00 (b) The provisions of Section 11.00 (a), above, shall not apply in respect to any license granted by LICENSOR the consideration for which consists in whole or in part of patent rights or other rights of such substantial value as, in the judgment of LICENSOR, to warrant a reduction in royalty rates below the rates provided in this agreement, or the acceptance of such rights in lieu of royalties.

Where there are financial terms, such as minimum or maximum required annual payments, which, in addition to royalty rates, might conceivably be reduced in subsequent grants by the licensor, the licensee may wish some account to be taken of these in the "more favorable terms" provisions of his agreement.[4] It is probably better from the licensor's standpoint that the various contingencies of this kind be dealt with as explicitly as possible, rather than being lumped in a vague reference to "other terms and conditions." For example, to cover such matters as those just referred to, Section 11.00 (a), above, might be restyled as follows:

11.00 (a) If LICENSOR shall grant to any manufacturer or seller of LICENSED PRODUCTS other than a company in which LICENSOR has a sub-

---

[4]*See* Studiengesellschaft Kohle m.b.H. v. Novamont Corp., 518 F. Supp. 557, 207 USPQ 999 (S.D.N.Y.), *amended*, 532 F. Supp. 234, 209 USPQ 175 (1981), *reversed in part*, 704 F.2d 48, 219 USPQ 289 (2d Cir. 1983).

stantial interest, direct or indirect, a license which is under any United States Letters Patent licensed in this agreement and which will permit such manufacturer or seller to manufacture or sell for any use within the scope of the license granted in this agreement

(i) At rates of royalty which, calculated on an equivalent basis in respect to the Letters Patent in question, are lower than those provided in this agreement, or (ii) on prospectively operative financial terms, other than royalty rates, corresponding to prospectively operative financial terms established in this agreement and more favorable to the licensee than those provided in this agreement,

then LICENSOR will

(i) Promptly notify LICENSEE of such license, and

(ii) Extend to LICENSEE the lower royalty rates or other more favorable financial terms of the noticed license, effective as of the date (or dates) on which they became effective in respect to the noticed license.

Such extension of lower royalty rates or other more favorable financial terms shall only be effective, however, if LICENSEE shall, within sixty (60) days of receipt of the notice referred to in (i), above, advise LICENSOR that it accepts all terms of the noticed license which are more favorable to LICENSOR than corresponding terms of this agreement and which are brought to the attention of LICENSEE in the notice referred to.

On the licensee's side, there is need to recognize that equitable considerations are involved in the enforcement of these clauses and that diligent pursuit of the remedies which they provide may be essential to realization of their benefits. This point is at least partially illustrated in *Harley C. Loney Co.* v. *Mills*,[5] in which the agreement sued upon contained the following provision:

In the event Loney shall hereafter grant a license under the patent aforesaid at a royalty rate or rates lower than the corresponding rate or rates provided for in paragraph 6 hereof, or on any more favorable terms and conditions, Mills shall be entitled to the benefit of such lower royalty rate or rates or such more favorable terms or conditions for its manufacture, use and sale hereunder subsequent to the date of such grant.

Subsequent to execution of this agreement, and following litigation with another party, Loney Company (the licensor) negotiated with the other party an agreement with respect to the same patents as those licensed to Mills which granted a paid-up license for the remainder of the term of the patents for a flat consideration of $13,500. Loney promptly notified Mills (its original licensee) of the granting of this license, but Mills made no response and continued to account for about a year on the established royalty basis. Eventually, however, it notified Loney that it elected to accept the fully paid license, calling attention to the fact that since notice of the availability of such a license, it had paid approximately $10,000 in royalties and

---

[5]205 F.2d 219, 98 USPQ 58 (7th Cir. 1953).

offered to pay a balance sufficient to make a total of $13,500. Loney denied that Mills was entitled to a paid-up license on the terms thus stated, and Mills refused to pay further royalties. The matter being brought to suit, the court held for the licensor and took the view that the licensor's offer to grant Mills a paid-up license on terms as favorable as those accorded to the third party was in the nature of an option which, to be exercised, required specific action. Mills could, in the court's view, exercise the option only by payment of a lump sum of $13,500 in consideration of a license paid up *prospectively from the date of the payment*.

As the cases cited above indicate, adequate contractual treatment of the "most favored terms" problem is a matter of great difficulty. Agreement provisions concerning this subject should be meticulously tailored to the circumstances of the particular situation in hand, and no one of the forms cited in the preceding text should be adopted without the most diligent scrutiny of its *ad hoc* suitability. In many cases, concessions by the licensor (e.g., in the area of terminability of licenses) offered in lieu of "more favorable terms" protection will provide more certainty of result and serve the mutual interests of the parties better than an intricately contrived "favorable terms" clause.[6] However, this is a problem of negotiation, and in those instances in which the licensee considers protection indispensable, the observations of this chapter should be applied.

---

[6]As to the effectiveness of limiting the "more favorable terms" clause to royalties, *see* Prestole Corp. v. Tinnerman Prods., Inc., 271 F.2d 146, 123 USPQ 242 (6th Cir. 1959). "More favorable royalty terms" held to extend to an ancillary grant to a later licensee of free technical assistance. The contract was held breached where Tinnerman failed to disclose the later contract to Prestole to permit Prestole to determine its acceptance of the later contract's terms.

In Shatterproof Glass Corp. v. Libbey-Owens-Ford Co., 482 F.2d 317, 179 USPQ 3 (6th Cir. 1973), a retroactive "release" was held to be, in effect, a "license" for purposes of a more favored licensee clause. On the other hand, in determining whether a particular "release" or "license" grant invokes a favored licensee clause, the court held that all elements of consideration given by the licensee must be evaluated.

12

Transferability of Rights and Obligations Pertaining to Licenses

Provisions reading generally as follows are often encountered in license agreements:

> This license and agreement shall inure to the benefit of and be binding upon the successors, assigns, or other legal representatives of the parties hereto.

Unfortunately, such language is of extremely uncertain effect and may well be in conflict with other provisions of the agreement which purport to specify the assignability or lack of assignability of the license granted and of rights pertaining to it. Its casual use is not recommended.

In determining how, in a particular license agreement, to cover the points toward which the above provisions are presumably directed, focus on the fact that every agreement involves both rights and duties of each of the parties. It is the item-by-item alienability of these rights and the item-by-item delegability of these duties which need to be contractually defined. Having determined the various issues of alienability and delegability as matters of principle, the contract drafter will then be in a position to recommend appropriate contractual language.

12.00 Licensor's Rights and Duties

In the case of the licensor, the duty of continuing the license subject to compliance by the licensee with the conditions of the agreement is, in effect, a servitude running with ownership in the patent and will be binding upon an assignee of the patent even without reference to this subject in the agreement. Similarly, the licensor's

109

right to receive royalties and reports is probably sufficiently non-personal to be assignable whether or not the agreement mentions the point. Accordingly, in a simple patent license agreement, the chief reason for including provisions touching on these issues may well be to avoid any possible misreading of the situation by either the licensor or licensee in case one of them attempts to construe the agreement without adequate legal advice. Where specific language is thought desirable for this reason, the following may serve:

> 12.00 The license granted in this agreement shall be binding upon any successor of LICENSOR in ownership or control of the LICENSED PATENTS, and the obligations of LICENSEE, including but not limited to the obligation to make reports and pay royalties, shall run in favor of any such successor and of any assignee of LICENSOR's benefits under this agreement.

Where the agreement involves more than a simple license grant, as where it includes, for example, an obligation of the licensor to furnish technical information or services, the simple treatment offered above will very possibly not serve. The same basic principle will apply, however; namely, that the several obligations and benefits of the licensor must be sorted out and each appropriately treated as to its qualities of survival under various conditions of transfer.

12.01 Licensee's Rights and Duties

On the authority of *Hapgood* v. *Hewitt*,[1] it has long been held that a nonexclusive license may be assigned by the licensee only when the covering agreement specifically so states, this being on the theory that the privileges and obligations pertaining to the nonexclusive licensee are personal. However, this rule does not hold when the transferee succeeds to the entire business of the licensee and assumes all its assets and liabilities.[2] Moreover, the matter is open to be decided as a matter of state law[3] and, in view of a growing public policy preferring freedom of alienation, may well be determined in favor of assignability in the absence of strong contextual arguments to the contrary.[4] Accordingly, it behooves a licensor who

---

[1]119 U.S. 226 (1886).

[2]Lane & Bodley Co. v. Locke, 150 U.S. 193 (1893); *see also* Syenergy Methods, Inc. v. Kelly Energy Systems, Inc., 695 F. Supp. 1362, 1366 (D.R.I. 1988) (holding that the right not to be sued for patent infringement was transferred to a new corporation that bought only a division of the original corporation).

[3]*But see* Unarco Indus., Inc. v. Kelley Co., 465 F.2d 1303, 175 USPQ 199 (7th Cir. 1972) (licensing of patents is so intertwined with the sweep of federal statutes that federal law must be applied).

[4]Farmland Irrigation Co., Inc. v. Dopplmaier, 308 P.2d 732, 113 USPQ 88 (Cal. 1957).

desires to limit absolutely the assignability of a given license to include appropriate limitations in the covering agreement. The following language may be suitable for this purpose.

> 12.01 The rights and licenses granted by LICENSOR in this agreement are personal to LICENSEE and may not be assigned or otherwise transferred without the written consent of LICENSOR. Any attempted assignment or transfer without such consent shall be void and shall automatically terminate all rights of the LICENSEE under this agreement.

[handwritten margin note: non-assiability clause]

The last sentence of clause 12.01, above, may be essential if the licensor's remedy for an assignment made in spite of the terms of the first sentence is to be anything other than a suit against the licensee-assignor for breach of contract.[5] However, it may no longer be useful as a barrier against assignment in bankruptcy.[6]

In some instances in dealing with a solvent licensee, the licensor will have no real objection to assignment of a nonexclusive license by the licensee provided reasonable assurance of compliance with the terms of the covering agreement is obtained from the assignee. In a case in which a relatively high degree of assignability of the rights and duties of the parties is favored, the following provision may be useful:

> 12.02 LICENSEE's rights under this agreement and the license herein granted shall pass to any assigns for the benefit of the creditors of LICENSEE and to any receiver of its assets, or to any person or corporation succeeding to its business in LICENSED PRODUCTS as a result of sale, consolidation, reorganization, or otherwise, provided such assignee, receiver, person, or corporation shall, without delay, accept in writing the provisions of this agreement and agree to become in all respects bound thereby in the place and stead of LICENSEE, but may not be otherwise transferred without the written consent of LICENSOR.

Clause 12.02, above, provides reasonable safeguards to the licensor, and may be useful to the licensee in that it permits a general assignee of the licensed party to elect whether it will continue the license. Where it is desired by the licensor to make the language of 12.02 somewhat more limiting in respect to the conditions of transferability, the phrase "entire business and good will" may be substituted for the words "business in LICENSED PRODUCTS."

It occasionally occurs that a licensor will have no objection to licensing a new entrant into a field in which he is himself operating,

---

[5]*See* Allhusen v. Caristo Construction Corp., 303 N.Y. 446, 103 N.E.2d 891 (1952).

[6]The Bankruptcy Act of 1978 (Title 11, United States Code) has raised questions concerning the effect of such automatic termination provisions. The Act provides for an automatic stay of all acts to dispose of property (11 U.S.C. §362), which may negate drafting procedures that attempt to provide for automatic termination of a license. *See* §12.02, *infra*.

but would seriously object if the license were to fall (e.g., by assignment) into the hands of a preexisting competitor in that field. Because clause 12.02, as worded above, provides no barrier to the occurrence of such an event, for example through acquisition of the ownership of the favored licensee by the feared competitor, a proviso of the following sort may in some instances be useful as an addition to the suggested clause:

> In no event, however, shall the granted license be assigned to or run in favor of a person who or corporation which, prior to the date of this agreement, was engaged in substantial production or sale of devices competitive with the LICENSED PRODUCTS.

12.02 Bankruptcy Law Considerations

It is not uncommon for an established company to desire to enter into a license agreement with a small start-up firm having a low level of financial resources. A high percentage of such companies become insolvent, which raises the prospect of a trustee in bankruptcy (or the debtor in a Chapter 11 reorganization) becoming capable of assuming or rejecting continued performance under a license agreement. This section explores negotiating and drafting techniques to minimize the undesirable consequences of bankruptcy on the licensing partner of a company that is a prospect for bankruptcy.

A. Legal Effects of the Bankruptcy Code

A license contract typically has continuing performance obligations on both parties that will cause it to be considered an "executory contract" and subject to assumption or rejection by a trustee under the Bankruptcy Code.[7]

As originally enacted, the broad statutory power under 11 U.S.C. §365, of the trustee (or the debtor, in a Chapter 11 reorganization) to assume or reject a license agreement, placed a licensee at risk where the trustee (or debtor) no longer believed the license agreement was advantageous to the licensor. This risk was recognized to have

---

[7]Intellectual property license agreements are generally recognized to be executory contracts, and thus may be assumed or rejected by the trustee/debtor. *See In re* Petur U.S.A. Instrument Co., Inc., 35 B.R. 561 (Bkrtcy. N.D. Wash. 1983) (patent license found executory); *In re* Alltech Plastics, Inc., 3 USPQ2d 1024 (Bkrtcy. W.D. Tenn. 1987) (listing provisions rendering license executory). One technique, however, for avoiding the effect of the Bankruptcy Act is to draft a license agreement so that one party, usually the licensor, has no continuing obligation of performance.

a chilling effect on the licensing of intellectual property,[8] and the Bankruptcy Code was amended to add subsection (n) to §365 of Title 11 U.S. Code. Under the new subsection, intellectual property licensees will have the assurance of being able to continue to use the licensed intellectual property after rejection by a trustee (or debtor).

Under §365(n) any right of exclusivity in the license agreement will still be enforceable by the licensee, but other rights of the licensee cannot be specifically enforced. Section 365(n)(1)(B). In this manner, rejection will not deprive the licensee of the use of the intellectual property, but the licensor/debtor will, consistent with the general goal of §365, be relieved of any other burdens of complying with the rejected agreement such as a promise to sue third party infringers or the obligations of a most favored licensee provision.

Another problem under the federal bankruptcy law is the automatic stay of all acts to dispose of property (11 U.S.C. §362) that voids a clause calling for automatic termination of a license agreement upon the licensee filing for bankruptcy, unless certain exceptions are applicable.

B. Negotiating and Drafting Issues

1. Protection for the Licensee of a Bankrupt Licensor

A licensee of a potential bankrupt licensor usually will want to ensure that the license continues after bankruptcy. This desire for continuity of the license is now protected by statute to the extent of the basic grant clause, but other parts of the license agreement are probably not specifically enforceable against the bankrupt. Subsection (n) of §365 of the Bankruptcy Code now provides statutory protection for a licensee to continue its license under a complicated series of provisions. Analysis of this subsection is suggested before negotiating and drafting agreements with a potentially insolvent licensor.

2. Protection for the Licensor of a Bankrupt Licensee

A licensor of a potentially bankrupt licensee will frequently want to be able to terminate the license agreement if the licensee becomes insolvent. Where personal obligations of a licensee are called for

---

[8]The chilling effect became apparent from Lubrizol Enterprises, Inc. v. Richmond Metal Finishers, Inc., 756 F.2d 1043 (4th Cir. 1985), *cert. denied*, 475 U.S. 1057 (1986). Richmond Metal Finishers ("Richmond") owned metal coating process technology, and granted Lubrizol Enterprises ("Lubrizol") a nonexclusive license to use the technology. A year after granting the license, Richmond filed for Chapter 11 reorganization. Under §365, Richmond successfully rejected its contract with Lubrizol to facilitate the sale or licensing of the technology unhindered by restrictive provisions in the agreement with Lubrizol.

under an agreement, the Bankruptcy Code provides exceptions that after reference to state law will usually prevent a trustee from assuming or assigning the licensee's rights. 11 U.S.C. §365(c) and (e)(2). Thus, it is in the licensor's interest to draft the agreement to emphasize the personal obligations of the licensee and to avoid permitting the free assignability of the agreement by the licensee. A license that runs to "licensee and its assigns" raises an inference that consent of the licensor to assignment has been granted and thus the statutory exceptions in Section 365(c) and (e)(2) may not apply.

Numerous other drafting and negotiating techniques to avoid adverse impacts of the bankruptcy laws are available for various specific license agreement fact patterns. Discussion of such techniques in the content of specific applicable fact patterns is beyond the intended scope of this book.[9]

12.03 Exclusive Licenses

The circumstances associated with the granting of an exclusive license which falls short of a general assignment of the patent involved are usually so special that no general treatment of the problems of transferability is possible.

---

[9]For a discussion of some of the consequences of bankruptcy on the nonbankrupt other party to a patent license agreement, *see* G.A. Frank, "Roll of the Dice—Is One of the Parties to a Patent License Agreement Facing Chapter 7 or Chapter 11 Bankruptcy?" 70 J. Pat. and Trademark Off. Soc'y 728 (November 1988).

13

Validity and Construction of Patents

The decision of the Supreme Court in *Lear* v. *Adkins*[1] abnegates, on grounds of public policy, any power of a licensor to withhold from his licensee freedom at any time to contest the validity of the licensed patent on the basis of facts which justify such action. It is ineffectual and inadvisable for the licensor to require any commitment on the part of the licensee to acknowledge or to forswear attack upon the validity of a licensed patent.[2]

The conclusion just stated does not, however, preclude the use of reasonable guidelines concerning the position and conduct of the parties if new circumstances change the presumptions of patent validity and scope upon which a given agreement was entered into. The following type of clause may still serve for this purpose.

> If, in any proceeding in which the validity, infringement, or priority of invention of any claim of any LICENSED PATENT is in issue, a judgment or decree is entered which becomes not further reviewable through the exhaustion of all permissible applications for rehearing or review by a superior tribunal, or through the expiration of the time permitted for such applications (hereinafter referred to as an "irrevocable judgment"), the construction placed upon any such claim by such irrevocable judgment shall thereafter be followed, not only as to such claim but as to all claims to which such construction applies, with respect to acts occurring thereafter; and, if such irrevocable judgment holds any claim invalid or is adverse to the patent as to inventorship, LICENSEE shall be relieved thereafter from including in its reports apparatus sold thereafter covered only by such claim or by any broader claim to which such irrevocable judgment is applicable, and from the performance of those other acts which may be required by this agreement only because of any such claim; provided, however, that if there are two or more con-

---

[1]395 U.S. 653, 162 USPQ 1 (1969).

[2]But mere inclusion of a "no contest" clause is not a *per se* misuse (only a nullity under *Lear*). Panther Pumps & Equipment Co. v. Hydrocraft, Inc., 468 F.2d 225, 175 USPQ 577 (7th Cir. 1972), *cert. denied*, 411 U.S. 965 (1973).

flicting irrevocable judgments with respect to the same claim, the decision of the higher tribunal shall be followed thereafter, but if the tribunals be of equal dignity, then the decision more favorable to the claim shall be followed until the less favorable decision has been followed by the irrevocable judgment of another tribunal of at least equal dignity. In the event of conflicting irrevocable judgments of the Supreme Court of the United States, the latest shall control.

Beyond the foregoing, it may also be useful, in the light of uncertainties left by *Lear* v. *Adkins* as to where license agreement parties are expected to stand if a post-execution controversy arises between the parties concerning the validity of a licensed patent, to provide procedural ground rules such as the following:

> (a) Nothing in this agreement precludes LICENSEE from contesting validity of any LICENSED PATENT. In the event evidentiary material comes to the attention of LICENSEE subsequent to LICENSEE's execution of this agreement which, in the judgment of LICENSEE, bears upon the validity or scope of any LICENSED PATENT, LICENSOR will in good faith discuss with LICENSEE whether such evidentiary material so affects the validity or scope of the LICENSED PATENT to which it is asserted to apply that the terms of the license in respect to such LICENSED PATENT should be modified.
>
> (b) LICENSEE may prospectively terminate this agreement as a whole or its license and concomitant future obligations in respect to any LICENSED PATENT upon thirty (30) days written notice to LICENSOR. Assertion by LICENSEE, subsequent to the date of its execution of this agreement, of the invalidity of any claim of any LICENSED PATENT, if coupled with or followed by—
>
>> (i) Withholding, or notice of intention to withhold, or denial of obligation to pay, royalties otherwise payable under this agreement in respect to LICENSEE's operations under such claim, or
>>
>> (ii) Initiation or participation in a suit challenging or denying the validity of such claim in reference to LICENSEE's operations under this agreement
>
> may, at the option of LICENSOR, be conclusively presumed to constitute LICENSEE's termination, as of the earliest provable date of such withholding, notice, denial, initiation, or participation, of its license in respect to such claim and of its obligation under this agreement for payment of royalties in respect to LICENSEE's future operations under the claim (but not under any other claim).

The language of the immediately preceding paragraph (b) is predicated upon the assumption that the license under consideration is a royalty-bearing one. Agreements involving other forms of compensation for licenses granted will, of course, require different treatment. It is believed, however, that the sense of what has been proposed can be readily transformed to fit other settings. The language actually adopted in any agreement must, of course, reflect the joint views of the licensor and licensee as to what is reasonable in the circumstances. On the other hand, the arrangement suggested has the virtue from the licensor's standpoint of fixing his rights of recourse with some certainty in the event of an unexpected challenge to validity, while, from the licensee's standpoint, it leaves him with the complete freedom to mount such a challenge, which *Lear* v. *Adkins* makes mandatory.

Inclusion of provisions such as those stated in paragraph (b), above, is, of course, without prejudice to the further inclusion in the agreement of a right on the part of the licensor to cancel the agreement in its entirety in event of the licensee's unjustified default in payments or in any other substantial element of performance required by the agreement. (See Chapter 17, Section 17.01.)

For evidence of the possible value (and arguable dangers) of the provisions suggested above, from the standpoint of clarifying the licensor's right of termination, see *Crane Co.* v. *Aeroquip Corp.*[3] This case should be reviewed for its demonstration of the complex issues which *Lear* introduces into the subject of license termination.

As to the binding effect of a prior consent decree, see *Schlegel Mfg. Co.* v. *King Aluminum Corp.*[4] and *KSM Fastening Sup., Inc.* v. *H.A. Jones Co.*[5]

A patent licensor who is interested in avoiding a validity contest with its licensee in a federal district court may want to consider use of a clause requiring the licensee to initiate reexamination proceedings in the United States Patent and Trademark office,[6] or a clause requiring that all validity disputes be submitted to binding arbitration.[7]

---

[3]356 F. Supp. 733, 177 USPQ 666 (N.D. Ill. 1973), *rev'd on other grounds*, 504 F.2d 1086, 183 USPQ 577 (7th Cir. 1974).

[4]369 F. Supp. 650, 181 USPQ 619 (S.D. Ohio 1973), *aff'd sub nom.*, Schlegel Mfg. Co. v. USM Corp., 525 F.2d 775, 187 USPQ (6th Cir. 1975), *cert. denied*, 425 U.S. 912 (1976).

[5]776 F.2d 1522, 227 USPQ 676 (Fed. Cir. 1985).

[6]For a discussion of the reexamination statute (35 U.S.C. §132) and the advantages and disadvantages of reexamination to a licensor and a licensee, *see* Arthur S. Garrett and E. Robert Yoches, "Licensing and Reexamination," LICENSING LAW AND BUSINESS REPORT 4, no. 6 (1981), pp. 169–175.

[7]Under 35 U.S.C. §294 arbitration awards on the issues of patent validity and infringement are final and binding on the parties to the arbitration proceeding.

14

Representations and Warranties; Negation of Implications; Indemnification

Certain representations may *ordinarily* be considered as implicit in any license agreement. These include, for example, representations that the licensor has the power to extend the license rights which the agreement purports to extend and that he has not taken and will not take any action derogatory to those grants. In some situations, however, as where there has been controversy or expressed uncertainty about these matters, it may be important to the licensee that representations of this kind be expressly confirmed by the agreement itself.

In distinction from the foregoing, there are certain rights and obligations, that may or may not be implied, depending entirely on context. These include, for instance, an intention to confer, as an incident to a license grant under a subordinate patent, a coextensive license under an earlier and dominant patent of the licensee, or in another case, an intention to extend sales-permitting licenses under foreign patents which correspond to a licensed United States patent. Where extension of these rights is *not* intended by the licensor, it will be prudent for him to make this clear in appropriate provisions of the agreement. Conversely, where the licensee expects such rights, he should contend for their express recitation.

Again, in connection with the sale of assets which include patent rights or know-how, there are certain warranties which may or may not be implicit in the general terms of the transaction, which may or may not be important to the interests of the transferee, and which may or may not be within the power of the transferor to give. In such circumstances, each party needs counsel as to the best way of treating these matters within the structure of the agreement.

119

This chapter will attempt to highlight some items in the field of warranty and representation which deserve to be examined carefully while the agreement is in the drafting phase.

14.00 Representations and Warranties

A. In Connection With a Simple License Grant

It can hardly be harmful to the licensor and may in some circumstances be useful to the licensee to have in the agreement a representation and warranty of the following scope with respect to patent rights being extended:

> LICENSOR represents and warrants in respect to the LICENSED PATENTS that it has legal power to extend the rights granted to LICENSEE in this agreement and that it has not made and will not make any commitments to others inconsistent with or in derogation of such rights.
>
> (But see in this connection Chapter 4 on "Reservations and Exceptions.")

B. In Connection With a Grant of Future Rights

Where rights are promised to a licensee in respect to future inventions of the employees of a corporation or other business entity and where access to those inventions is a major consideration from the licensee's standpoint, it may be prudent for the licensee, unless the relevant business practices of the licensor are well known and entirely reassuring, to press for the following kind of express commitment:

> LICENSOR will throughout the term of this agreement, as far as it is reasonably practicable for it to do so, cause its employees who are employed to do research, development, or other inventive work to disclose to it inventions within the scope of this agreement and to assign to it rights in such inventions such that LICENSEE shall receive, by virtue of this agreement, the licenses agreed to be granted to it, it being understood that if due care and diligence are used, any inadvertent failure to comply with this section of the agreement shall not constitute a breach of the agreement.

The following is a somewhat more stringent provision on the same point:

> LICENSOR will acquire from its employees who are employed to do research, development, or other inventive work, and from corresponding employees of its subsidiaries, rights to inventions made during the term of this agreement which relate to the subject matter of licenses agreed to be granted to LICENSEE, such that LICENSEE shall, by virtue of this

agreement, receive from LICENSOR, without payments beyond those provided in Article ___, the licenses so agreed to be granted.

If any qualification of this type of commitment is made necessary by the business practices of the licensor, such as its practices in contracting with government agencies, the qualification should, of course, be expressly stated in a further clause supplementary to that just set forth. The following is suggestive of what may be required:

> It is recognized that LICENSOR may have contracted or may hereafter contract, directly or indirectly, with governmental agencies to do development work financed by such agencies on terms which require LICENSOR to assign to the agencies its right to grant licenses in respect to inventions arising out of such work or which otherwise restrain LICENSOR from granting licenses to others under such inventions. Inability of LICENSOR in respect to such inventions to grant the licenses purportedly agreed to be granted in this agreement shall not be considered a breach of the agreement.

A clause of the kind just offered can obviously be expanded to cover other business arrangements which the licensor must anticipate and except from the sweep of the agreement. It is quite common also for the licensor of future rights to require a protective stipulation such as the following in respect to patents or licensing rights which may at some time be acquired by the licensor for a price so high as to make it uneconomic to include them in the agreement without assurance of additional consideration:

> If LICENSOR acquires from others than employees of LICENSEE patents or licensing rights in patents on terms which require monetary payment by LICENSOR, such patents shall not be subject to this agreement except as the parties may subsequent to the date of the agreement expressly agree.

Alternatively, if the licensee wishes greater assurance of access to after-purchased patents of the licensor than is provided by the clause just presented, the following somewhat more expansive language may be considered:

> If LICENSOR, subsequent to the date of this agreement, acquires from others than employees of LICENSOR patents or licensing rights in patents on terms which require payment of monetary or other consideration by LICENSOR, such patents shall become subject to this agreement only if LICENSEE agrees to pay LICENSOR a proportionately reasonable share of such consideration.

C. In Connection With the Outright Sale of Patents or of a Business to Which Patent Rights May Be Relevant

Where patents or related values are sold, either as such, or with other assets, the purchaser may either demand a warranty of title, or in the absence of question-raising facts, rely upon the implied warranties which would normally attach to such a transaction. If the transaction involves the acquisition of a business of some technical content, then, regardless of whether patents as such are part of the assets being sold, the buyer may desire patent-related assurances of the following kind:

(1) Except as detailed in Appendix A, attached to this agreement, there are no patent infringement suits or asserted patent infringement claims pertaining to (the transferred business) pending against SELLER on the date of this agreement.

(2) Except as stated in Appendix B attached to this Agreement, SELLER is not, at the date of this agreement, operating under or paying royalties under any patent license or technical information agreement applicable to (the transferred business), nor is it committed in any way to enter into such an agreement.

14.01 Negation of Implications by Licensor

While some of the suggestions which follow may be excessive in connection with the grant of a simple nonexclusive license under United States patents, it will ordinarily be prudent for the licensor at least to consider whether his interests require adoption of any or all of them. Such consideration should take into account not only the possibility that some of the propositions which are negated by the suggested language might, in the absence of negation, be implied in law, but also the very real chance that some of them (if not expressly disclaimed) may be believed by the licensee to apply, whether such belief is in accordance with or contrary to law. Experience shows that the latter possibility contains seeds of controversy costly enough, regardless of outcome, to justify fully the negotiating and drafting time required to resolve doubts in advance.

SUGGESTED NEGATIONS

(a) Nothing in this agreement shall be construed as

(i) A warranty or representation by LICENSOR as to the validity or scope of any LICENSED PATENT; or

(ii) A warranty or representation that anything made, used, sold, or otherwise disposed of under any license granted in this agreement is or will be free from infringement of patents of third parties; or

(iii)   A requirement that LICENSOR shall file any patent application, secure any patent, or maintain any patent in force; or

(iv)   An obligation to bring or prosecute actions or suits against third parties for infringement (except to the extent and in the circumstances stated in Article __); or

(v)   An obligation to furnish any manufacturing or technical information; or

(vi)   Conferring a right to use in advertising, publicity, or otherwise any trademark or tradename of LICENSOR; or

(vii)[1]   Precluding the export or sale for export from the United States of LICENSED PRODUCTS on which royalties shall have been paid as provided in Article __ (subject, however, to the understanding that no rights are granted or implied in respect to such exported products under any patent of LICENSEE or any other person in any foreign country); or

(viii)   Granting by implication, estoppel, or otherwise, any licenses or rights under patents of LICENSOR other than LICENSED PATENTS, regardless of whether such other patents are dominant of or subordinate to any LICENSED PATENT.[2]

(b) LICENSOR makes no representations, extends no warranties of any kind, either express or implied, and assumes no responsibilities whatever with respect to use, sale, or other disposition by LICENSEE or its vendees or other transferees of products incorporating or made by use of (i) inventions licensed under this agreement or (ii) information, if any, furnished under the agreement.

14.02 Indemnification

A. By the Licensor

In only special situations should a licensor of only patent rights undertake to indemnify his licensee against the possibility that ac-

---

[1]The objectives of this paragraph are fully discussed in subdivision (G) of Section 7.00 of Chapter 7. The paragraph is repeated here as a contribution to the completeness of this section of the work.

[2]With respect to implication of a license in connection with the sale of goods for particular uses, *see* Bandag, Inc. v. Al Bolser's Tire Stores, Inc., 750 F.2d 903, 223 USPQ 982 (Fed Cir. 1984); Oster v. Grant-Southern Iron & Metal Co., 381 F. Supp. 290, 182 USPQ 124 (E.D. Mich. 1974).

tivities conducted under the license might infringe patents or other rights of third parties. This is because the licensor would rarely be in a position to foresee the nature of his licensee's future activities and thus to evaluate the magnitude of the risks in extending indemnity.

Indemnification by a licensor is much more common in agreements that transfer the right to use trade secrets and know-how. For example, when circumstances known in advance tend to fix the licensee's design and when the payments likely to be made by the licensee are large, the risks of indemnification may seem reasonable. In such a case (and only in such a case or one comparable to it) provisions of the following kind might be found applicable:

ARTICLE ___

INDEMNIFICATION

.00 LICENSOR will assume the defense of any suit brought against LICENSEE or its vendees, mediate or immediate, for infringement of any United States patent or for wrongful use of proprietary information of any third party insofar as such suit is based upon a claim that the infringement or wrongful use is attributable to LICENSEE's application without substantial modification of TECHNICAL INFORMATION supplied under this agreement. In any such suit, LICENSOR will indemnify LICENSEE against any money damages or costs awarded in such suit in respect to such a claim.

.01 The obligations of LICENSOR stated in Section   .00, above, apply only if (a) LICENSEE shall promptly inform LICENSOR in writing of any claim within the scope of Section   .00, (b) LICENSOR is given exclusive control of the defense of such claim and all negotiations relating to its settlement and (c) LICENSEE shall assist LICENSOR in all necessary respects in conduct of the suit.

.02 LICENSOR's total liability to incur out-of-pocket costs in the defense of any suit or suits and to pay damages awarded in any suit or suits shall be limited to the amount theretofore paid to LICENSOR by LICENSEE under this agreement, and LICENSEE will advance to LICENSOR any amounts required to be expended by LICENSOR in excess of that limit. Amounts so advanced shall be credited to future payments due from LICENSEE to LICENSOR as a result of LICENSEE's operations under this agreement.

.03 The foregoing paragraphs of this ARTICLE ___ state the entire liability of LICENSOR to LICENSEE in respect to LICENSEE's use of TECHNICAL INFORMATION, and, except as specifically provided in those paragraphs, LICENSOR shall not be liable either directly or as an indemnitor of LICENSEE because of any claim arising in any way from LICENSEE's use of TECHNICAL INFORMATION.

B. By the Licensee

There are imaginable cases in which the licensee or some customer of the licensee, being dissatisfied with or assertedly injured by a product manufactured under the license, might seek remedy against the licensor. This could arise, for example, in a case in which a device or commodity manufactured under a process license operated unsatisfactorily or injuriously, with this result being ascribed by the complainant to fault in the licensed process.

Whether licensor liability could actually attach under these circumstances may be questioned, but arguments have been put forward for finding liability in at least some such situations.[3]

While these arguments have most cogency in those cases which involve the furnishing of technical information and/or technical assistance (as distinguished from mere patent licenses), they are not entirely without application to the case of aggressively marketed patent licenses. For this reason, any party engaged in a systematic licensing program (whether or not know-how is provided) may prudently consider whether his program involves undesirable risk of warranty-type liability. If it does, he may seek protection against claims of the licensee by including in the contract papers a denial of implied warranties along the lines of clause (b) suggested at the end of Section 14.01 of this chapter. Beyond this, as protection against still further extension of evolving doctrines of "strict liability" toward persons with whom the seller is not in direct privity,[4] the licensor may elect to require assurance of indemnification by his licensees in some such terms as the following:

> LICENSEE will hold LICENSOR harmless against all liabilities, demands, damages, expenses, or losses arising (i) out of use by LICENSEE or its transferees of inventions licensed or information furnished under this agreement or (ii) out of any use, sale, or other disposition by LICENSEE or its transferees of products made by use of such inventions or information.

---

[3]Norris, "Tort Liability That May Attach to Intellectual Property Licensing," 61 J. PAT. OFF. SOC'Y 607 (1979).

[4]*See* Restatement (2d) Torts (1965), Section 402A.

15

Assumption by Licensee of Responsibility for Prosecution of Patent Applications of the Licensor

In some instances, particularly where the licensor is an individual inventor anxious to minimize his responsibility for the further development and protection of his invention, there is attraction in the idea that the licensee shall take over direct prosecution of pending applications of the licensing inventor and/or of applications still to be filed on his behalf.

If payment to the licensor is to be in the form of a lump sum, to be paid at all events, there may well be no objection to such an arrangement. On the other hand, if the financial returns to the licensor (either from the immediate licensee or from future licensees) are to be in any way dependent on the quality of the patent protection obtained (as where royalties are to be paid on products manufactured "under the patents"), assumption of prosecution responsibility is laden with danger to the licensee. At the very least, dissatisfaction by the licensor with the returns realized, insofar as these depend on the scope of patent claims obtained from the Patent Office, may lead to controversy and recrimination. At the worst, it may lead to litigation charging negligence or bad faith in the handling of the applications, and in any such litigation, the licensee will have difficult burdens of proof.[1]

There is probably no completely effective safeguard against these results if an arrangement is made for prosecution of applications by in-house counsel of the licensee. In any such arrangement there is a

---

[1]*See* Beattie v. Prod. Design & Engineering, Inc., 198 N.W.2d 139, 173 USPQ 757 (Minn. 1972).

prima facie conflict of interest which it would be extremely difficult to negate or insulate against by attempted contractual limitations of responsibility or liability. The situation is one which strongly recommends isolation devices such as those now to be described.

In one approach, the licensee may (by agreement with the licensor) simply agree to underwrite, on a progressive payments basis, the patent prosecution expenses of the licensor up to a stated maximum of payment, this maximum to be exceeded only if, in the sole judgment of the licensee, further payments are in its interest. (There is, of course, nothing in this plan which precludes the licensor from underwriting expenses above the limit of payments established by the license agreement.)

In a second approach, likely to be preferred by the licensor if he wishes to minimize his personal responsibility, provisions such as the following may be offered:

ARTICLE ___

FILING AND PROSECUTION OF APPLICATIONS

1. LICENSOR will, within thirty (30) days after execution of this agreement, disclose to LICENSEE all information in its possession pertaining to the LICENSED INVENTIONS which may be necessary or useful for the preparation and filing of patent applications for the protection of such LICENSED INVENTIONS. LICENSOR will, thereafter, from time to time, on request, supply such additional information as may be necessary or desirable to facilitate prosecution of such applications.

2. LICENSEE will, upon receipt of the information referred to in Paragraph 1, above, accept liaison and financial responsibility for
   (a) Preparation, by a patent lawyer in independent practice who shall be nominated by LICENSEE and approved by LICENSOR, of a patent application or applications on patentable aspects of the LICENSED INVENTIONS,
   (b) Filing, upon execution by the inventor, of such application or applications in the United States Patent Office, and
   (c) Prosecution by such lawyer of the application or applications to allowance or to the point of necessary appeal from a final rejection by an Examiner of the United States Patent Office.

3. Except as may be later separately agreed in writing, LICENSEE does not assume financial or other responsibility for
   (a) The filing or prosecution of any appeal from a final rejection by an Examiner of the Patent Office of any patent application on a LICENSED INVENTION, or
   (b) The conduct of any interference in which the application or applications may become involved.

4. LICENSEE will arrange for the prompt furnishing to LICENSOR of copies of
   (a) Any applications filed in the United States Patent Office as provided in Paragraph 2, above,
   (b) Any papers received from the Patent Office pertaining to such applications, and

(c) Any papers filed in the Patent Office pertaining to such applications.

5. LICENSOR shall have the right at any time, by notice to LICENSEE given as provided in Article __ of this agreement, to assume and continue at his own expense direction of the prosecution of any application filed as provided in Paragraph 2, above. Upon receipt by LICENSEE of any such notice from LICENSOR, LICENSEE shall forthwith be relieved of all further financial and other responsibility in respect to the application affected by the notice. Failure of the LICENSOR to give notice as provided in this Paragraph 4 shall be taken as conclusive evidence of the satisfactory discharge by LICENSEE of its responsibilities under this Article __, and LICENSOR's sole remedy for dissatisfaction with LICENSEE's discharge of responsibilities shall be by the timely giving of such notice.

The pattern established by the several paragraphs set forth immediately above may, of course, by varied within wide limits, depending on the situation of the parties. The essential features of the pattern, however, are that the scope of the licensee's responsibilities shall be clearly defined and that the licensor's remedies for dissatisfaction with the discharge of those responsibilities shall be explicitly delimited. The device of assigning the prosecution of applications to independent (rather than inhouse) counsel is at least a partial barrier against later claims of bad faith in the preparation or handling of patent applications because of the licensee's self-interest.

16

Notices Under the Agreement; Patent Marking; Applicable Law; Arbitration

16.00 Notices Under the Agreement

Many licensing agreements provide for "notice" to be given in respect to various matters, such as termination of licenses, claims of default, or exercise of an option. To avoid uncertainty and possible controversy as to the legal effectiveness of notices purportedly given, it is desirable to specify in reasonable detail the mechanism of notice which the parties regard as acceptable and the persons to whom or the offices to which notices shall be sent.

Notice clauses such as the following are customary:

Alternative 1

Any notice, report, request, or statement provided for in this agreement shall be deemed sufficiently given when sent by certified or registered mail addressed to the party for whom intended at the address given at the outset of this agreement or at such changed address as the party shall have specified by written notice.

Alternative 2

(a) Except as otherwise provided in paragraph (b) of this Section ___, notices under this agreement, including correspondence items concerning the agreement, shall be served upon the party to whom directed by depositing them postage prepaid in the U.S. mails, registered or certified, and addressed to the served party as follows (or to other addresses established as provided in paragraph (b) of this Section ___):

131

Vice President, Research Division
ABC Corporation
190 DeMont Street
New York, New York 10020

General Manager, Power Tools Dept.
XYZ Corporation
180 Water Street
Flint, Michigan 48502

(b) Notice served as provided in (a), above, shall be deemed given three (3) days following the date of deposit in the U.S. mails. If notice is given other than as provided in (a), then the burden of proving service and receipt by the addressee shall be upon the party alleging service of notice. Either Party may change its effective address by giving thirty (30) days notice of the new address in the manner provided in (a), above.

In some cases, as where the parties are located in different countries, there may be reason to specify that notice may be given by telegram, cablegram, or radiogram. In any such case, however, thought should be given to specifying a mutually agreeable mode of fixing the effective date of the notice. (Compare the first sentence of paragraph (b) of Alternative 2, above, with Alternative 1.)

16.01 Patent Markings

Failure of a licensee to mark on licensed goods the numbers of applicable patents under which it is licensed may, under the patent statutes,[1] prevent the licensor from collecting damages for past infringement (i.e., infringement occurring prior to actual notice to the infringer of his infringement) in a suit brought against a third party on such patents.

Also, if the licensee marks a manufactured product with the number of a licensed patent, the licensee will be estopped to argue that the product does not infringe the licensed patent.[2] A licensee that refrains from marking a manufactured item, which is identical to an item previously manufactured and properly marked, cannot relieve itself from royalty payments.[3]

---

[1] U.S.C. §287.

[2] Crane Co. v. Aeroquip Corp., 364 F. Supp. 547, 179 USPQ 596 (N.D. Ill. 1973), *rev'd on other grounds*, 504 F.2d 1086, 183 USPQ 577 (7th Cir. 1974). (The Seventh Circuit found that defendant's devices infringed and did not reach the marking issues.) *But see* SmithKline Diagnostics, Inc. v. Helene Laboratories Corp., 859 F.2d 878, 890 (Fed. Cir. 1988) (dicta questioning the validity of the "marking estoppel" doctrine).

[3] Gridiron Steel Co. v. Jones & Laughlin Steel Corp., 361 F.2d 791, 149 USPQ 877 (6th Cir. 1966).

Accordingly, if the licensor visualizes the possibility of litigating his patents, he should consider the need for a commitment from the licensee such as the following:

> LICENSEE agrees to mark all LICENSED PRODUCTS sold or otherwise disposed of by it under the license granted in this agreement with the word "Patent" and the number of the licensed patent.

Where more than one patent is involved, the following form may serve:

> LICENSEE agrees to mark all LICENSED PRODUCTS sold by it under the license granted with the word "Patent" or "Patents" and the number or numbers of the LICENSED PATENT or LICENSED PATENTS applicable thereto.

Compliance with provisions such as those just offered is at least a formal burden to the licensee and may reasonably be resisted if there is basis for believing that the licensed patents are not likely to come into litigation or that the licensor's needs in litigation will be served by prospective relief (e.g., an injunction) without serious concern about recovery of past damages. Where the licensor does not feel a present need for insisting on marking by his licensee, but wishes to preserve the option of doing so at a future date, a temporizing clause such as the following may serve both parties' interests:

> LICENSEE agrees to observe the reasonable requirements of LICENSOR with respect to the marking of articles sold under the license herein granted with the word "Patent," followed by the number or numbers of the patent or patents applicable thereto under which a license is granted hereunder.

This kind of provision leaves it to the licensor's post-execution initiative to determine whether and to what extent marking of licensed patents shall be insisted upon.

A patent licensee who is transferring rights under process patents likely to be litigated should review 35 U.S.C. §287(b)(1)–(6), enacted in 1988. 35 U.S.C. §287(b)(4)(B), which applies to process patent marking and notice issues, provides an option to a licensee, who receives a request for disclosure for the identity of any process patent being used. The option is the choice of (1) identifying the patent to the requester or (2) notifying the licensor of the request for disclosure. Section 287(b)(4)(C) eliminates any requirement on the part of the licensee to respond to a request for a disclosure if the licensee is marking in the manner prescribed by §287(a) the patent number of the process patent on all products made by a patented process which have been sold by the licensee in the United States.

The above-described additions to Section 287 under the Process Patents Improvement Act of 1988 suggest that the licensor may desire the following language to be included in the marking provision of any license transferring rights under process patents that have a likelihood of being litigated:

LICENSEE agrees to mark any products made using a process covered by any LICENSED PATENT with the number of each such patent and, with respect to LICENSED PATENTS, to respond to any request for disclosure under 35 U.S.C. §287(b)(4)(B) by notifying LICENSOR of the request for disclosure.

16.02 Applicable Law

Questions of applicable law are more apt to arise in connection with agreements between citizens of different countries than where all parties are citizens of a single country.[4] Even in the latter case, however, and even where the country is the United States, differences in commercial law and interpretive viewpoints exist from state to state. Therefore, in some situations, as where many licenses, geographically distributed, are to be issued by a single licensor, it may be desirable to the issuing party that the law of a single preselected state shall apply to all similarly patterned contracts. This section discusses the possibility of achieving such a result.

As a classic work in the field[5] shows, the determination of applicable or governing law in reference to a contract can be a matter of considerable complexity. For example, the rule to be applied may differ in dependence on whether one is concerned with the validity of the contract, or with its performance or discharge.[6] The conventional as well as the evolving wisdom of the subject was well summarized by the Court of Appeals of New York in *Auten* v. *Auten*,[7] a case which has landmark qualities because of its determination of the applicability in the state of New York of the relatively novel "center of gravity" rule.

The *Auten* case involved a separation agreement negotiated in New York between a husband and wife, both of English origin, which provided for support payments to be made to the wife in England. Payments being in default, the wife filed a petition for separation in England, which, however, was not pressed. She later sued in New York on the support agreement and was met with the defense that the English separation suit constituted a repudiation and rescission of the agreement. The lower courts, applying New York law, found the defense good. The Court of Appeals reversed and remanded on the ground that the applicable law was that of England (which pointed

---

[4]*See, e.g.,* Warner & Swasey Co. v. Salvaghin Transferica, S.p.A., 633 F. Supp. 1209, *aff'd,* 806 F.2d 1045 (Fed. Cir. 1986).

[5]J.H. Beale, THE CONFLICT OF LAWS (Mt. Kisco, N.Y.: Baker, Voorhis & Co., 1935).

[6]*Id.* at 1077 and 1100.

[7]308 NY 155, 124 N.E.2d 99 (1954).

toward a different result). It reached this conclusion by rejecting the customarily applicable rules of conflict of law, which it summarized as follows:

> Most of the cases rely upon the generally accepted rules that "All matters bearing upon the execution, the interpretation and the validity of contracts . . . are determined by the law of the place where the contract is made," while "all matters connected with its performance . . . are regulated by the law of the place where the contract, by its terms, is to be performed."
>
> Many cases appear to treat these rules as conclusive. Others consider controlling the intention of the parties and treat the general rules merely as presumptions or guideposts to be considered along with all the other circumstances.

Laying aside all these various "rules of thumb," the New York Court found the law of England to be appropriate to the case in hand under the "center of gravity" approach. Within this approach, it said, "the courts, instead of regarding as conclusive the parties' intention or the place of making or performance, lay emphasis rather upon the law of the place which 'has the most significant contacts with the matter in dispute.'" Because the main purpose of the contract in issue was to provide support to the wife in England through payments made in that country, its "center of gravity" was found to lie within English law.

The *Auten* case was decided without the benefit of an indication in the contract of the intention of the parties concerning applicable law. It is a rule frequently stated, but qualified by so many exceptions as to provide a dubious basis for reliance, that the parties may determine applicable law by a clear manifestation of intention. According to Beale,[8] this rule is limited, among other ways, by the necessity that the choice shall be *bona fide* (i.e., not for the purpose of avoiding unfavorable law of the place of making or the place of performance). Also, the choice must not be exotic, that is, totally unrelated to the context of the agreement. Therefore (again according to Beale), "the courts have generally confined the parties in their choice of law to the place of making or the place of performance." The Uniform Commercial Code, while governing only in respect to the specific transactions within its ambit (which presumably does not include license agreements as such), may nevertheless suggest an important policy trend in its provision that "when a transaction bears a reasonable relation to this state and also to another state or nation the parties may agree that the law either of this state or of such other state or nation shall govern their rights and duties."[9] How far New York State would, in view of the *Auten* decision, honor an

---

[8]Beale, CONFLICT OF LAWS, at 1081.

[9]*See, e.g.*, Conn. Gen. Stat. §42a–1–105(1) (1959 Conn. Pub. Act. 133, §1–106).

elective departure from the "center of gravity" of a licensing transaction is presumably not yet determined.

In the face of these at least partially conflicting trends and viewpoints, the parties to a license agreement may well have maximum likelihood of seeing their selection respected if the home location of the licensor is designated as the situs of applicable law. Even if this location is not the place of final execution of the contract, it will ordinarily be closely connected with important aspects of its performance (e.g., the filing of reports and the making of payments). Accordingly, its selection might well qualify as reasonably meeting the requirements of the traditional rules (as summarized in the *Auten* case, above) as well as those of the Uniform Commercial Code and of New York law. For these reasons, unless the parties wish to influence the choice of law in some other direction (at risk of seeing their attempted selection ignored), the resolution of the matters as just stated is recommended.

If it is the decision of the parties that they will undertake to stipulate applicable law, there still remains a word to be said about the form of the stipulation.

An issue of local law or local viewpoint may arise as to (1) the interpretation, (2) the construction, or (3) the application of particular provisions of a given contract. While the enumerated terms tend to overlap in common usage, various writers have emphasized differences in their possible semantic and legal significance.

Taking the distinction part way, A. L. Corbin has suggested:[10]

> By interpretation of language we determine what ideas that language induces in other persons. By "construction of the contract," as that term will be used here, we determine its legal operation upon the action of courts and administrative officials. If we make this distinction, then the construction of a contract starts with the interpretation of its language but does not end with it; while the process of interpretation stops wholly short of a determination of the legal relations of the parties.

It would appear, however, that "construction" itself may involve two concepts, namely, (1) the legal effect intended by the parties, and (2) the legal effect permitted by the law and policy of the forum. The term "application" may usefully describe the second of these.

In view of the distinctions just noted, parties purporting to stipulate "applicable law" should presumably avoid such narrow language as

> The law applicable to this contract shall be that of the State of New York

and should prefer wording such as:

---

[10]CORBIN ON CONTRACTS (St. Paul: West Publishing Co., 1960). Sec. 534, at 9 (reproduced with the permission of the copyright owner, West Publishing Co.).

    This agreement shall be construed, interpreted, and applied in accordance with the laws of the State of New York

or:

    This agreement shall be governed in all respects by the laws of the State of New York, except that its conflict of law rules shall not apply.

16.03 Arbitration

Contemplation of the possibility that controversy may arise under even the most artfully drawn contract may lead the parties to consider providing in advance for arbitration of disputes.[11]

Arbitration as a means for resolving conflict has much to recommend it in situations in which the issues are reasonably clear-cut and capable of compact presentation to an arbitrator (or arbitrators). However, it is difficult to know in advance whether every controversy which might arise under a particular license agreement will be of this character. Moreover, any controversies which are appropriate for arbitration can be arbitrated (if the parties so choose) by an *ad hoc* agreement made at the time conflict appears. Therefore, careful consideration should be made of the advantages and disadvantages in a particular licensing situation of a commitment for submission to arbitration of *all* disputes arising under the agreement.

Some licensing situations exist in which the parties must anticipate the likely occurrence of a series of conflict-inviting circumstances of a particular kind which will need to be settled as they arise. An example of this might be presented by the foreseeable prospect that the licensee will produce a succession of slightly different products, some of which will be and some of which will not be clearly within the scope of the licensed patents and hence subject to royalties.[12] In such a case, the parties, recognizing the problem in advance, might wish to establish a procedure for arbitrating infringement questions as they present themselves. An arbitration clause directed specifically to this issue might be in such terms as the following:

    Any controversy or claim arising under or related to this contract which involves a question of infringement or any of the LICENSED PATENTS shall be settled by arbitration in accordance with the Patent Rules of the American Arbitration Association, and judgment upon the award

---

[11]For relevant commentary, *see* Davis, "Resolving Patent Disputes by Arbitration and Minitrial," 65 J. PAT. OFF. SOC'Y 275 (1983).

[12]A broad provision, by which the parties to a licensing agreement agreed to submit any controversy arising under the agreement to arbitration, has been held to include arguments over the scope and infringement of the patent. Rhone-Poulenc Specialites Chimiques v. SCM Corp., 769 F.2d 1569 (Fed. Cir. 1985).

rendered by the Arbitrator(s) may be entered in any Court having jurisdiction thereof.

The American Arbitration Association is a nationally recognized body of high standing, the services of which are extensively used in commercial and labor disputes. It has regional offices in many parts of the country. Execution of an arbitration clause in the form suggested above is in effect a commitment that any resulting arbitration shall be conducted under the administration of the Association using an arbitrator or arbitrators selected from a panel of experts in patent law. Copies of the Association's rules may be obtained from its headquarters in New York or in other major cities. Many states (and the United States) have statutes respecting the enforceability of arbitration awards properly arrived at, and the "entry of judgment" clause which concludes the arbitration provision stated above is recommended by the American Arbitration Association to invoke the applicability of these statutes.

Where the agreement in question deals with foreign licensing or is between nationals of different countries, there may be a preference by one or both parties for reference of any arbitrable matters to the International Chamber of Commerce. The following is a very generalized clause for carrying out such a preference.

> Any controversy or dispute arising out of or in connection with this Agreement, its interpretation, performance, or termination, which the parties are unable to resolve within a reasonable time after written notice by one party to the other of the existence of such controversy or dispute, may be submitted to arbitration by either party and if so submitted by either party, shall be finally settled by arbitration conducted in accordance with the rules of conciliation and arbitration of the International Chamber of Commerce in effect on the date hereof. Any such arbitration shall take place in the City of New York, New York, United States of America. Such arbitration shall be conducted in the English language and the arbitrators shall apply the laws of the State of New York.
>
> The institution of any arbitration proceeding hereunder shall not relieve Licensee of its obligation to make payments accrued hereunder pursuant to Paragraph 6 hereof to Licensor during the continuance of such proceeding. The decision by the arbitrators shall be binding and conclusive upon the parties, their successors, and assigns and they shall comply with such decision in good faith, and each party hereby submits itself to the jurisdiction of the courts of the place where the arbitration is held, but only for the entry of judgment with respect to the decision of the arbitrators hereunder. Notwithstanding the foregoing, judgment upon the award may be entered in any court where the arbitration takes place, or any court having jurisdiction.

It is, of course, entirely within the power of licensing parties to specify that arbitration shall be conducted before a preselected arbitrator of their choice, with or without reference to selected applicable rules of the American Arbitration Association or other established body. Many state arbitration statutes and the national statute[13] are aimed at assisting the implementation of such agreements.

For years, patent validity issues were judicially considered inappropriate for arbitration.[14] However, Congress by enacting 35 U.S.C. §294 decided that arbitration of patent validity and infringement issues was in the public interest.[15]

---

[13]9 U.S.C.A. §§2-207 (West 1970 and Supp. 1989).

[14]*See* Beckman Instruments, Inc. v. Technical Dev. Corp., 433 F.2d 55, 167 USPQ 10 (7th Cir. 1970) *cert. denied*, 401 U.S. 976 (1971).

[15]It is now possible, though not necessarily desirable, to draft a patent license agreement to effectively subject to arbitration all disputes that might arise thereunder, except disputes concerning the antitrust effects of performance under the agreement. *See* Vol. 11, no. 4 of the APLA Quarterly Journal (1983), which contains a collection of articles on arbitration of patent license and related contractual disputes.

17

Term and Termination of the Agreement

17.00 The Significance of "Termination"

It is quite common in agreements of all kinds to encounter reference to the "life" or "term" of the agreement or to be told that the agreement shall "terminate" under such and such conditions. There is anomaly in these modes of expression, because, in a very real sense, it can be argued that an agreement never wholly "terminates," although its legal force may in due course tend to approach zero for all practical purposes. What really happens to an expiring agreement is that the various rights and obligations attaching to it come to an end sequentially (rarely all at one time), until at some moment no significant right or obligation can be found to remain. This moment, if it could be identified with certainty, might reasonably be spoken of as the "termination" of the agreement, but, as experience shows, this conservative usage is not the common one.

For example, patent license agreements often contain a provision such as the following:

> This agreement shall run to the end of the life of the last to expire of the LICENSED PATENTS and shall thereupon terminate.

But one then finds that, in spite of the purported "termination," the licensee is still committed to pay accrued royalties and to make reports, while the licensor has rights of audit and recovery and/or certain other rights. But how do these obligations and rights, invocable after the date of ostensible "termination," subsist, if not under the agreement itself? Lazarus, though in his shroud, still lives.

The point is not merely a philosophical one; large stakes and costly litigation sometimes turn on it. Thus, in a certain agreement

141

entered into in 1932 between RCA, on the one hand, and Westinghouse and General Electric Company, on the other hand, rights, including sublicensing rights, were exchanged between the parties. One of the provisions of the agreement was: "The termination date shall be December 31, 1954." Another provision expressly continued beyond the 1954 date *licenses* under patents based on pretermination inventions, but there was no provision expressly extending RCA's right to grant sublicenses under Westinghouse or General Electric patents beyond that date. This right was valuable, and General Electric brought suit, joined in by Westinghouse and supported by the U.S. government, to establish that the sublicensing right had ended on the "termination date" of the agreement. The court found to the contrary.[1] In light of the total context, and in spite of the seemingly unqualified definition of "termination date," standing alone, Judge Maris concluded that the sole purpose of that definition was to establish a cutoff of the period during which new inventions would become subject to the agreement. Sublicensing rights were held to be part and parcel of the "licenses" granted and to be coextensive with them in duration.

Review of the *RCA* decision and of the contract provisions to which it refers shows what ambiguities may arise if the drafter fails to recognize "termination" as a multipronged concept. It demonstrates also the importance of defining each prong separately if every contractual right and obligation is to end on a certain date or upon the occurrence of unmistakably identifiable events. Because certainty in respect to these matters may be of crucial significance to the parties (as the *RCA* case demonstrates), the termination article of the agreement deserves and demands the drafter's most assiduous attention.

17.01 Formal Treatment of the Termination Problem

One must conclude that traditional usage probably rules out the possibility of wholly dispensing with the word "termination" and its semantic equivalents, such as "expiration." Accordingly, the practical approach is probably to define whichever of these terms is used in such a way as to preserve those incidents of the agreement which the parties really intend to survive the so-called "termination" or "expiration." The preparation of such a definition imposes on the drafter the salutary burden of seeking out and listing all aspects of the negotiated transaction which are actually intended to outlast the "agreement's" ostensible demise. In pursuance of this theory, the

---

[1]United States v. Radio Corp. of Am., 117 F. Supp. 449, 100 USPQ 157 (D. Del. 1954).

"Term and Termination" article of the agreement may be formulated generally as follows:

ARTICLE XVII

TERM AND TERMINATION

17.00 The word "termination" and cognate words, such as "term" and "terminate," used in this ARTICLE XVII and elsewhere in this agreement are to be read, except where the contrary is specifically indicated, as omitting from their effect the following rights and obligations, all of which survive any termination to the degree necessary to permit their complete fulfillment or discharge:

 (a) LICENSEE's obligation to supply a terminal report as specified in Section __ of ARTICLE IX of this agreement.

 (b) LICENSOR's right to receive or recover and LICENSEE's obligation to pay royalties (including minimum royalties) accrued or accruable for payment at the time of any termination.

 (c) LICENSEE's obligation to maintain records and LICENSOR's right to conduct a final audit as provided in ARTICLE IX of this agreement.

 (d) Licenses, releases, and agreements of nonassertion running in favor of customers or transferees of LICENSEE in respect to products sold or transferred by LICENSEE prior to any termination and on which royalties shall have been paid as provided in ARTICLE IX of this agreement.

 (e) Any cause of action or claim of LICENSOR accrued or to accrue, because of any breach or default by LICENSEE.

17.01 (a) If LICENSEE shall at any time default in the payment of any royalty or the making of any report hereunder, or shall commit any breach of any covenant herein contained, or shall make any false report and shall fail to remedy any such default, breach, or report within thirty (30) days after written notice thereof by LICENSOR, LICENSOR may, at its option, terminate this agreement and the license herein granted by notice in writing to such effect.

 (b) Unless previously terminated in accordance with other provisions of this agreement, this agreement and the licenses granted hereunder to LICENSEE shall run until expiration of the last to expire of the LICENSED PATENTS and shall thereupon terminate.

Suggestions concerning rights of the licensee to "terminate" the agreement or any of the licenses granted to it under the agreement appear in Section 10.01 of Chapter 10 and in Chapter 13, which should now be reexamined. It is believed that the wording of Paragraph 17.00, above, is broad enough to qualify in the intended way any relevant termination provisions which may be adopted in accordance with the proposals made in either of the chapters referred to.

17.02 Some Tax Considerations in Reference to Termination Provisions

As stated in Chapter 1, the rapidly changing character of tax law, both statutory and interpretive, makes it inexpedient in the present work to attempt generalized advice on this subject. It is not amiss to note, however, that in connection with assignments and exclusive licenses respecting patents, the reservation by the grantor of a power of termination of the rights granted may, if excessive, deprive him of a right to capital gains treatment otherwise contingently available in respect to his proceeds under the covering agreement. In some instances, this may be a matter of substantial financial consequence.

The principal distinction to be drawn is between (1) a power of the grantor to terminate at will, which will almost certainly preclude a capital gains claim, and (2) a power to terminate only upon the occurrence of a condition subsequent which arises independently of the action of the grantor. A condition of the latter kind, which may be, for example, a material default of the grantee, will not, it appears, defeat capital gains even though termination is accomplished by independent action of the grantor taken after occurrence of the condition subsequent.[2] Thus, the language of clause 17.01(a), offered in Section 17.01 of this chapter, should, because it is of condition subsequent character, have no unfavorable tax consequences, even if used in connection with the grant of an exclusive license. A similar conclusion would seem to apply to the termination and conversion provisions suggested in subsections (a) and (b) of Section 6.03 of Chapter 6 (Exclusive Licenses).

Termination rights of the *licensee* in an exclusive license and termination rights of either party in a *nonexclusive license* are usually devoid of tax consequences.

---

[2]For more extended discussion of this subject *see, e.g.*, M. F. Beausang, Jr., "Tax Consequences of Termination Provisions of Exclusive License Agreements," 50 J. PAT. OFF. SOC'Y 717 (1968).

18

Interpretation of the Contract; Preclusion of Prior Understandings; Restriction of the Mode of Amendment

Most persons engaged in commercial enterprise have encountered a situation in which a contract seemingly clear on its face has been asserted by the other party to be interpretable in an unexpected way or to be qualified by prior or subsequent understandings collateral to the contract itself. Patent license agreements are by no means sheltered from such contentions, and it is the program of this chapter to consider how far drafting can guard against their success.

18.00 Interpretation

Vagueness attaches to all use of language (Chapter 1) and, therefore, all language must be "interpreted." The canons of interpretation by reference to extrinsic data vary from the "traditional" rule that "parol evidence"[1] may not be introduced unless there has been a prior judicial discovery of ambiguity in the instrument, to the suggestion of the Restatement of Contracts Section 230 (1932) that the meaning of an integrated contract[2] should be that which "would be attached to the integration by a reasonably intelligent person acquainted *with*

---

[1]"PAROL EVIDENCE . . . with reference to contracts . . . is the same as extraneous evidence or evidence *aliunde*." BLACK'S LAW DICTIONARY (4th ed. rev., St. Paul: West Publishing Co., 1976).

[2]*See* Section 18.01, this chapter.

*all the circumstances prior to and contemporaneous with the making
of the integration.*" (Emphasis added.)

The continuing struggle between these generally opposed viewpoints is well illustrated in a patent context by the decision of the
Seventh Circuit Court of Appeals in *Ortman* v. *Stanray Corporation.*[3]
In this case the contract provided that plaintiff (Ortman) would assign
all its patent rights in a certain invention to defendant (Stanray) in
return for payments based on defendant's "quarterly cost for milling
head inserts of the type disclosed and claimed in the said patent
application." Payments were to be made for 10 years or "for the life
of any patent issued on the said patent application . . . whichever
period is longer."

The part of the agreement over which controversy arose read as
follows:

> (4) Assignor, on thirty (30) days advance written notice to or from
> Standard, shall be revested with the entire right, title and interest in
> and to the said patent rights if Standard fails or refuses to make the
> payments to Assignor provided for in paragraph (2) hereof or if Standard
> discontinues manufacturing or acquiring milling head inserts of the
> type disclosed and claimed in the said patent application serial No.
> 812,320 for more than one (1) year.

After paying royalties for five years, defendant, apparently on
advice of counsel that its cutting device was not covered by the patent,
notified plaintiff of termination of the contract pursuant to paragraph
(4) and discontinued all payments. Plaintiff sued for infringement
and for *breach of contract.*

In respect to the breach of contract claim, defendant argued that
it had acted within the clear intendment of paragraph (4). It objected
to admission of collateral evidence offered by plaintiff to show that
this paragraph was primarily a security device for plaintiff and was
not intended to create a termination power in defendant. The lower
court decided this issue in favor of defendant on the ground that a
condition precedent to the admission of any evidence relating to the
meaning of a contract is an initial determination by the court that
the contract is ambiguous. The subject contract was found susceptible
of a clear and reasonable interpretation on its face, that interpretation being favorable to defendant's position.

The court of appeals reversed and remanded, concluding that the
"terms of this contract are not so plain and clear that there can be
no question as to the meaning." Admission of "relevant" collateral
evidence on meaning was directed.

So far, the court was operating within the "traditional" rule
which predicates the admissibility of parol evidence on a prior finding

---

[3]437 F.2d 231, 168 USPQ 617 (7th Cir. 1971).

of ambiguity. The principal opinion went on, however, to analyze the law of the forum (Illinois) in terms which included the following:

> Thus, relevant parol evidence is always admissible to assist in the determination of what the words used in an integrated writing mean; and the parol evidence rule is placed in its proper role of focusing interpretation on the meaning of the terms embodied in the writing and of rendering all evidence inoperative to vary those terms once their meaning has been discovered. Admitting evidence of prior negotiations and agreements for the purpose of discovering the meaning of the terms used in the integration does not violate the parol evidence rule.

This statement was supported by the following reference to a portion of a tentative draft that became RESTATEMENT (SECOND) OF CONTRACTS §214, comment *b* (1981):

> The expressions and general tenor of speech used in negotiations are admissible to show the conditions existing when the writing was made, the application of the words, and the meaning or meanings of the parties. Even though words seem on their face to have only a single meaning, other meanings often appear when the circumstances are disclosed.

This view of the law certainly does not represent the present position of all jurisdictions.[4] Nevertheless, it is consistent with the general trend[5] toward increased availability of extrinsic evidence to illuminate contract terms which, although not patently ambiguous, are made contingently unclear by arguments of one party or the other.[6]

An important distinction must be drawn, however, between (1) clarification of meaning by extrinsic evidence and (2) substitution of extrinsically evidenced understandings for substantive agreements clearly recorded in a final and integrated contract. The first may be permissible, at least within the limits of the legal principles developed above. The second is impermissible, and its impermissibility leads to recommendations concerning contract form set forth in Section 18.01, below.

As to the first point, clarification of meaning by extrinsic materials, drafting foresight can accomplish little in the face of the increasingly exploratory attitude of the courts, if there is a provable

---

[4]Indeed, the principal opinion in the subject case is, in the concurring opinion which accompanies it, criticized as excessive even in its interpretation of Illinois law.

[5]*See* J. H. Wigmore and A. Kocourek, WIGMORE: EVOLUTION OF THE LAW, on evidence, 2470 (3d ed., New York: Burt Franklin, 1940). For further illustration of the trend in action, *see* Autogiro Co. of Am. v. United States, 384 F.2d 391 (Ct. Cl. 1967).

[6]For California rule that parol evidence may not apply in contest between party to the contract and a nonparty, *see* Von Brimer v. Whirlpool Corp., 362 F. Supp. 1182, 1189–90, 180 USPQ 182, 185 (N.D. Cal. 1973).

negotiating record which arguably qualifies the terms of the written contract. That is to say, reliance on the hopefully favorable aura of an artfully selected word will prove illusory if the record suggests that the parties may have intended the word's less usual rather than its more usual application. One can finally erase the potential upsetting power of a prior recorded negotiating position of the other party only if the ultimate contract wording, read against the negotiating record, leaves no doubt that the position was abandoned in the final agreement between the parties.

18.01 Preclusion—by Integration—of Asserted Prior Understandings

It is ordinarily the intention of the parties involved that a formal written contract, duly executed, shall supersede and exclude from consideration prior collateral negotiations and near agreements of the parties insofar as they relate to matters expressly dealt with in the contract itself. Absent strengthening factors, however, this presumption of intention (if, indeed, it is one) is weak and may be overthrown by evidence that the parties did not regard the written instrument as an integration of their mutual commitments.[7]

Inclusion in the instrument of an express indication of intention to integrate should obviously be a favorable factor if the integrity of the agreement is put in question. At the least, it will increase the burden of plausibility of the party who claims prior collateral understandings additive to or subtractive from the written instrument. As one source puts it, the rule "which forbids proof of an oral agreement to add to or vary a valid written agreement is particularly applicable where the writing contains a recital that it contains the entire agreement between the parties."[8]

At the time an agreement is entered into, all parties will ordinarily concur that leaving the integrity of the written document open to collateral attack is undesirable. The drafter will, therefore, rarely

---

[7]*See, e.g.*, Royal Industries v. St. Regis Paper Co., 420 F.2d 449, 164 USPQ 236 (9th Cir. 1969). In this case Royal claimed the power to terminate a license granted to St. Regis because of the failure of St. Regis to adhere to a commitment, not recorded in the license agreement but alleged to have been made orally in the course of its negotiation, that it would maintain its prices at levels established by Royal. The case was decided favorably to St. Regis on other grounds, on the basis that under California law, the rule cannot be applied to exclude evidence tending to prove that the rule itself is inapplicable because the parties did not intend the writings to be an integration of their total understanding. *See also* cases discussed in American Indus. Fastener v. Flushing Enters., 362 F. Supp. 32, 179 USPQ 722 (N.D. Ohio 1973).

[8]30 Am. Jur. 2d 154, Sec. 1018.

be opposed in including, to buttress this sentiment, an integration clause such as the following:

> This instrument contains the entire and only agreement between the parties and supersedes all preexisting agreements between them respecting its subject matter. Any representation, promise, or condition in connection with such subject matter which is not incorporated in this agreement shall not be binding upon either party. No modification, renewal, extension, waiver, and (except as provided in Articles _____ and _____ hereof) no termination of this agreement or any of its provisions shall be binding upon the party against whom enforcement of such modification, renewal, extension, waiver, or termination is sought, unless made in writing and signed on behalf of such party by one of its executive officers. As used herein, the word "termination" includes any and all means of bringing to an end prior to its expiration by its own terms this agreement, or any provision thereof, whether by release, discharge, abandonment, or otherwise.

(Where both parties are not corporations this form will obviously require appropriate modification.)

A clause of the type offered above should have considerable force as a defense against free-swinging interpretation or qualification of the integrated agreement by reference to other sources of the parties' intention than the agreement itself. Use of the clause (or of a similarly directed alternative) is, therefore, recommended, particularly in any agreement which represents the culmination of a long negotiation. It should be recognized, however, that even such a clause will not insulate the agreement against attack on grounds of fraud or mistake, nor will it preclude a court from recourse to evidence of prior negotiating exchanges bearing on the completeness of the instrument where a strong equitable argument can be made for such action.[9]

For the application of the clause in the face of a claim of modification by subsequent agreement, see Section 18.02, below.

18.02 Amendment by Subsequent Agreement

A further principle which militates against the guaranteed success of any attempt to make a written agreement wholly self-sufficient and self-limiting is that stated by Corbin as follows:

---

[9]*See* International Milling Co. v. Hachmeister, 380 Pa. 407, 110 A.2d 186 (1955). Here, in a transaction for purchase and sale of flour, the agreement form employed specified that: "This Contract constitutes the complete agreement between the parties hereto; and cannot be changed in any manner except in writing subscribed to by Buyer and Seller or their duly authorized officers."

Nevertheless, the buyer was permitted to show that this particular contract form had been adopted at the insistence of the seller, and was understood by both parties to be subject to specifications not stated in the contract itself.

Any written contract, other than specialties not now being considered, can be rescinded or varied at will by the oral agreement of the parties and this is held to be true, except as otherwise provided by statute, even of a written agreement that the contract shall not be orally varied or rescinded.[10]

The rationale of this rule is the very simple one that those who have power to make a contract must obviously have equal power to change it by mutual consent—including a change which abrogates a no-oral-modification provision.

The principle just stated has such persuasive force that few states have attempted to override it by statutes of general application.[11] New York State, however, has in its Personal Property Law a Section 33-c (Consol. Laws c. 41) which reads as follows:

An executory agreement hereafter made shall be ineffective to change or modify, or to discharge in part, a written instrument hereafter executed which contains a provision to the effect that it cannot be changed orally, unless such executory agreement is in writing and signed by the party against whom enforcement of the change, modification or discharge is sought or by his agent.

This statute was construed in *Green* v. *Doniger*[12] in a case having an integration clause reading as follows:

This constitutes the entire agreement and understanding between us and it may be terminated by either of us at any time upon thirty (30) days notice to the other; and it shall not be considered modified, altered, changed or amended in any respect unless in writing and signed by both of us.

In the litigation one party alleged a change in compensation arrangements accomplished by oral discharge (abandonment) of the written agreement. It was held that because of the separate reference to termination in the opening part of the clause quoted above, the remainder of the clause would not, even in the light of the language

---

[10]A. L. Corbin, CORBIN ON CONTRACTS (St. Paul: West Publishing Co., 1960), Sec. 1295, at 206. *See also, e.g.*, Wymard v. McCloskey & Co., 217 F. Supp. 143 (E.D. Pa. 1963): "The law is crystal clear that a written contract may be modified orally. Consolidated Tile and Slate Co. v. Fox, 410 Pa. 336, 341, 189 A.2d 228 (1963). Even where the contract provides that any non-written modification will not be recognized. Wagner v. Graziano Construction Co., 390 Pa. 445, 448, 136 A.2d 82 (1957)."

[11]While the Uniform Commercial Code is not directly applicable to license agreements, its widespread adoption and its treatment of the oral-modification problem may portend a change in this policy. Section 2-209 of the Code (Connecticut version) provides in its most relevant parts as follows:

(2) A signed agreement which excludes modification or rescission except by a signed writing cannot be otherwise modified or rescinded. . . .

(4) Although an attempt at modification or rescission does not satisfy the requirements of subsection (2) . . . , it can operate as a waiver.

[12]300 N.Y. 238, 90 N.E.2d 56 (1949).

of Sec. 33-c of the Personal Property Law, be construed to preclude the kind of change asserted by the claiming party.

It is to be hoped that the somewhat different clause suggested in Section 18.01 of this chapter would, if construed under the New York statute, lead to a different result from that realized in the *Doniger* case. Moreover, the suggested clause, because of its requirement that any amendatory *or* terminating agreement be signed by an "executive officer," should discourage the kind of claim which is occasionally made that modification has been affected by an agent who, although far down the line of executive command of the party denying the modification, acted with apparent or purported authority to bind his company.

19

Settlement of Patent Litigation

Much patent litigation is settled by negotiated agreement prior to final adjudication of the legal issues involved. Because settlement patterns can vary so widely, no general treatment of the contracting problems involved is possible or desirable. It may, however, be useful to discuss certain points which recurrently arise in situations proposed to be settled by the acceptance by one party of a license under patents of the other party and/or by appropriate release of various claims asserted in the litigation.

19.00 Releases

It is, of course, important to any party who, by payment of money or other valuable consideration, is attempting to buy freedom from claims asserted in litigation to assure that the freedom purchased is as absolute as the circumstances permit. But where the litigation concerns patents, and especially where the parties have or may expect later to have mutual patent or other relationships in addition to those directly affected by the litigation, the omnibus kind of release found useful in some other situations (e.g., accident claims) will hardly serve.

If, as an incident of the settlement, a license under patents is taken in respect to the future activities of the accused infringer, the problem becomes one of appropriately combining the future license with a suitably worded release for the past. In this case, the general licensing and release considerations reviewed in Chapters 7 and 8 will have direct application.

On the other hand, it is not uncommon for the party accused of infringement to wish to avoid the apparent concessions involved in acceptance of a license (by that name) and to insist that in consideration for any amounts to be paid, the grant by the other party be in exculpatory terms (i.e., releases and assurances against further assertions of past or future infringement). A formula which may serve both parties in this kind of situation is suggested by the following provisions:

> (1) ABC, for itself, its successors, and assigns, releases and forever discharges XYZ, its past and present directors, officers, employees, successors, assigns, customers, and other transferees from any and all promises, causes of action, claims, and demands whatsoever in law or in equity, arising or claimed to arise out of any infringement or asserted infringement of any patent, issued or issuing at any time, by any spring valves manufactured, used, sold, or otherwise transferred by XYZ at any time prior to the effective date of this agreement.

> (2) ABC covenants that at no time will it, its successors, or its assigns make any claim or commence or prosecute against XYZ, its directors, officers, successors, assigns, customers, or other transferees any suit, action, or proceeding of any kind based upon assertion of infringement of any patent, issued or issuing at any time, by any spring valve which is the same or substantially the same in design as a spring valve manufactured, used, sold, or otherwise transferred by XYZ prior to the date of this agreement.

The sense of the two preceding paragraphs is, of course, that the accused infringer is released from any and all claims of patent infringement with respect to past manufacture and sales of all equipment of the designated class, and is further assured of freedom from infringement claims in respect to all future equipment of the same class which follows generally the existing designs of the settling defendant. In this form of settlement the situation is necessarily left open in respect to new equipment designs which may be created.

A settlement of this type is probably most appropriate where the principal issue in litigation has been one of infringement. If, on the other hand, the controversy has centered mainly on the validity of the asserted patents, the settling defendant (assumed to be the accused infringer) will probably prefer in lieu of paragraph 2, above, assurance of a fully paid license (or covenant of nonassertion) in respect to the patents in suit—such license (or nonassertion) to be unlimited as to types of equipment covered. Whether this should also include assurance of nonassertion of other presettlement patents and patent applications of the complainant will depend on the circumstances. (See Chapter 5, Section 5.01.)

It may or may not be consistent with the objectives of the parties to include in the agreed settlement releases or other rights in respect to foreign patents. If disposition of foreign claims is not intended, the reference to "patents" in paragraphs 1 and 2, above, may be limited to "United States patents," and a "foreign patents" paragraph such as the following may usefully be added:

(3) Nothing in this agreement shall be construed as granting to either of the parties rights under any patents of any foreign country, or as limiting the right of either party to assert in foreign countries against the other party or those in privity with it claims based on patents of those countries. Conversely, nothing in this agreement shall limit or bar assertion of any defense available to either party in respect to any claim of patent infringement asserted against it or those in privity with it by the other party in any foreign country.

Intended exclusions from a release drawn in seemingly comprehensive terms should be identified specifically in the excluding provisions and may not safely be assumed to be implicit in vague or generalized language used in such provisions. This is well illustrated by the decision of the Court of Appeals of the Seventh Circuit in *Green* v. *Valve Corporation of America*,[1] in which the court examined the effect on the broad release clause contained in a settlement agreement of a qualifying paragraph quite similar to paragraph 3, above. In this case, it was the contention of one of the parties that the qualifying paragraph (and particularly that part of it preserving the right to assert defenses against foreign patents) left it free in the United States to initiate a suit against the other party to the settlement agreement for antitrust violation arising from the latter's fraudulent procurement of palpably invalid foreign patents. Against the history of the earlier (settled) controversy and the indications seen in the settlement agreement that it was intended to be comprehensive except as to expressly reserved subject matter, the court found no basis in the foreign patents paragraph for permitting attack on (as distinguished from defense against) a foreign patent position of the other party. While this decision necessarily depends closely on the specific facts of the case before the court, it nevertheless demonstrates adequately that one who would withhold rights or remedies from an agreement ostensibly designed to settle pending controversy would be well advised to negotiate for unequivocal withholding language.

If, as frequently occurs in patent litigation, the patent claim is joined with a claim for misappropriation of proprietary information or breach of confidential relationship, the release clauses adopted will, of course, have to recognize this fact also. The following clause suggests a linguistic approach (additive to those materials offered above) which may be considered in this connection.

(4) ABC, for itself, its successors, and its assigns, releases and forever discharges XYZ, its past and present directors, officers, employees, successors, assigns, customers, and other transferees from all promises, causes of action, claims, and demands whatsoever in law or in equity which, as against XYZ, its past or present directors, officers, employees, successors, customers, or other transferees, ABC, severally or jointly with others, ever has had, now has or may at any time have or claim

---

[1] 428 F.2d 342, 166 USPQ 161 (7th Cir. 1970).

to have and which arise or are claimed to arise out of any disclosure or acquisition by or from any person prior to the date of this Agreement, of any information of any kind, allegedly confidential or otherwise, and relating to the field, art, technology, design, development, manufacture, lease, sale, or business of spring valves.

Where, as will probably be the case, the effectiveness of the releases proposed to be given is contingent upon delivery of payment or action dispositive of litigation by the party to be released, the terms of agreement should obviously recognize this fact. A clause such as the following may serve this purpose.

(5) The releases and covenants not to sue set forth in this Agreement are conditioned upon compliance by XYZ with all the provisions of Article II of this agreement and shall be effective only upon such compliance and upon entry of an order of dismissal of Civil Action No. _____, as provided in Article X of this agreement.

19.01 Discontinuance of Suit

Settlement arrangements ordinarily make explicit provision for formal discontinuance of the pending litigation. The terms of discontinuance are obviously consequential, and some consideration of available alternatives is, therefore, worthwhile.

In the circumstances under contemplation (i.e., the active pendancy of suit), discontinuance requires initiative by the party plaintiff. Voluntary dismissal by a plaintiff in a federal court is governed generally by Subdivision (a) of Rule 41 of the Federal Rules of Civil Procedure, as follows:[2]

Rule 41. Dismissal of Actions.

(a) VOLUNTARY DISMISSAL: EFFECT THEREOF.

(1) *By Plaintiff; By Stipulation.* Subject to the provisions of Rule 23 (e), of Rule 66, and of any statute of the United States, an action may be dismissed by the plaintiff without order of court (i) by filing a notice of dismissal at any time before service by the adverse party of an answer or of a motion for summary judgment, whichever first occurs, or (ii) by filing a stipulation of dismissal signed by all parties who have appeared in the action. Unless otherwise stated in the notice of dismissal or stipulation, the dismissal is without prejudice, except that a notice of dismissal operates as an adjudication upon the merits when filed by a plaintiff who has once dismissed in any court of the United States or of any state an action based on or including the same claim.

---

[2]Fed. R. Civ. P. 41(a), as amended 1946 and 1948. The reference to Rule 23(e) relates to class actions, and the reference to Rule 66 relates to an action wherein a receiver has been appointed.

(2) *By Order of Court.* Except as provided in paragraph (1) of this subdivision of this rule, an action shall not be dismissed at the plaintiff's instance save upon order of the court and upon such terms and conditions as the court deems proper. If a counterclaim has been pleaded by a defendant prior to the service upon him of the plaintiff's motion to dismiss, the action shall not be dismissed against the defendant's objection unless the counterclaim can remain pending for independent adjudication by the court. Unless otherwise specified in the order, a dismissal under this paragraph is without prejudice.

There could readily be cases in which, the necessary statutory conditions being met, the parties would see advantage in recourse either to subdivision (i) of paragraph (1) or to paragraph (2) of 41(a) — or to some other procedure recommended by litigation counsel in the particular case in question. More frequently, however, subdivision (ii) of paragraph (1), providing for dismissal by stipulation, will provide an appropriate guide, and further comment will be with reference to this procedure — although the caveats expressed below apply more generally.

A significant point to be observed is that "unless otherwise stated," dismissal by stipulation is "*without prejudice.*" A generally applicable viewpoint is that when an action is dismissed "without prejudice," it is as if the action had never been brought, and, accordingly, such a dismissal will not bar a later suit on the same claim. Conversely, a dismissal "with prejudice," although not a judgment on the merits in the true sense, nevertheless operates as such with respect to the identical parties and their privies, and is *res judicata* as to a later suit on the same claim. The distinction between "with" and "without" is obviously crucial and should be kept well in mind by both parties to a projected disposition of litigation by dismissal under a settlement agreement. It will ordinarily be of interest to the defendant in an infringement suit that dismissal of the suit shall be "with prejudice," and, depending on the terms of settlement, this result may be perfectly acceptable to the plaintiff. Where this is the situation, the agreement covering settlement will presumably provide for the execution on behalf of the parties (e.g., by their respective counsel) and for the entry before the court of a stipulation generally in the following form:

STIPULATION OF DISMISSAL

It is hereby stipulated between counsel for the respective parties that the above action be, and the same hereby is, dismissed with prejudice, without costs or disbursements, and that an order to that effect may be entered without further notice.

_____

Attorneys for Plaintiff

_____

Attorneys for Defendant

Cases can be imagined in which a stipulation of dismissal such as that suggested above would still be effective to end litigation forever, even though the words "with prejudice" were omitted or even if the words "without prejudice" were substituted for them. This could be so, for example, if the covering agreement provided for acquisition by the defendant of an unqualified license under the controverted patent upon payment of consideration actually delivered at the time of execution of the agreement. In contemplation of different kinds of situations, however, it is instructive to consider briefly the history (so far as publicly recorded) of certain litigation between Technograph Printed Circuits, Ltd. and Radio Corporation of America (RCA) over alleged infringement by RCA of three patents of Technograph. This litigation was begun by Technograph in 1962 by suit against RCA in the district of Delaware, a court of the Fourth Circuit. In 1963, the principal patents in question were held invalid by the District Court of Maryland in litigation reported as *Technograph Printed Circuits, Ltd.* v. *Bendix Aviation Corporation.*[3] This decision was affirmed *per curiam* by the Fourth Circuit Court of Appeals.[4] The Supreme Court denied certiorari.

Presumably in the light of these developments, Technograph and RCA, in 1966, stipulated to a dismissal of the Delaware case. The stipulation was "with prejudice" as to one patent and "without prejudice" as to the other two. As to the latter two, the parties stipulated that the action could be reinstated at any time by motion of either party.

Later, Technograph sued other parties in an Illinois District Court, and that case was converted to a class action into which the court proposed to sweep all but certain carefully defined accused infringers. Presumably in resistance to the threat of involvement in this new action, RCA moved to reinstate the Delaware case as to the two patents to which the "without prejudice" stipulation applied. This motion was granted by the Delaware court, subject, however, to specification by the court that "nothing . . . done . . . shall have any bearing upon whether or not RCA is included" in the Illinois class action. On this record, the Illinois court denied RCA's motion for its exclusion from the prospective class action.[5] The terms of the court's inclusion order had expressly excepted parties as to which prior litigation had been dismissed "with prejudice." Obviously, in the subject case, these words made a difference.

There may also be cases in which the plaintiff insists that the litigation be subject to conditions precedent or be defeasible upon

---

[3]218 F. Supp. 1, 137 USPQ 725 (D. Md. 1963).
[4]327 F.2d 497, 140 USPQ 285 (4th Cir. 1964).
[5]285 F. Supp. 714, 157 USPQ 313 (N.D. Ill. 1968).

specified conditions subsequent. Where defeasance upon conditions subsequent (e.g., failure of the defendant to adhere to promises made) is the objective, dismissal "with prejudice" would obviously be inappropriate, and a dismissal without qualification (and accordingly "without prejudice" under Rule 41(a)(1)) may be indicated.

Alternatively, if, in order to give finality to the settlement, a dismissal "with prejudice" is to be entered as soon as certain conditions have been met, a stipulation specifying such dismissal might be signed by the parties in duplicate and held in abeyance by counsel subject to a provision in the settlement agreement such as the following:

ARTICLE VII

DISCONTINUANCE OF SUIT

Unless prior to January 1, 1982, ABC shall have asserted a breach by XYZ of its commitments under ARTICLE V of this agreement, then, on that date, the attached stipulation of dismissal of suit shall become effective and may then or thereafter be entered by either party without notice to the other party.

To be in accord with a contractual provision such as that just stated, the stipulation as executed would presumably bear the record date of January 1, 1982. The period of suspension of effectiveness of the stipulation would obviously have to be limited to a term known to be acceptable to the court before which the case is pending.

19.02 Avoidance of Publicity

The typical settlement of litigation represents a deeper compromise of opposing viewpoints than occurs in less controversial negotiations. Not uncommonly, the patent rights granted in such a settlement are acquired on financial terms calculated more with an eye to the probable costs of completing the litigation than upon the conventional economic criteria for determining the value of a license or release. In such circumstances, one or both of the parties may be interested in avoiding any announcement of the settlement which might suggest to the public that there has been a capitulation (one way or the other). To serve this interest, it may be appropriate to include in the settlement contract language such as the following:

ARTICLE X

PUBLICITY

1. No public statement respecting the terms or circumstances of the settlement represented by this agreement shall be made by either party except in the following form:

ABC Company and XYZ Company have announced that their litigation respecting patents on _____ has been settled upon a mutually acceptable basis. The suit pending between them in the Federal District Court for the Southern District of New York is being dismissed.

Neither party shall authorize, nor, so far as within its power, permit, publicity concerning the settlement except as provided in this Article X.

If the avoidance of publicity is considered a matter of extreme consequence by one party, that party may wish to press for the addition to the paragraph immediately above of a requirement for preventive action in some such language as the following:

2. Promptly upon the entry by the court of an Order of Dismissal of the litigation being settled by this agreement, each party shall distribute to its officers, employees, and sales representatives, a notice as follows, the notice to be signed by an officer of the distributing company:

The patent litigation between ABC Company and XYZ Company which has been pending for several years in the United States District Court for the Western District of _____, in reference to _____ has been settled upon terms satisfactory to each of the parties.

Neither party desires to attempt to take commercial advantage of the settlement through public or private comment, and you are therefore instructed that no director, officer, employee, sales representative, or other person acting on behalf of this company is to make any statement about the litigation or its settlement which departs from or goes beyond the express terms of the information contained in the first paragraph of this instruction.

There are, of course, situations in which the possibility of announcing the acceptance of a license by the other party is one of the considerations affecting the licensor's decision to discontinue litigation. In such a case, the highly conservative practices suggested above will not apply, although the parties may still want some understanding as to the terms in which announcement of settlement shall be made.

20

Execution of Agreements: Problems of Authority and Proof

When all aspects of the proposed transaction have been agreed upon and reduced to writing, some question may still remain on one side or the other as to the authority of the person acting in behalf of the other side to enter into such a transaction and/or to execute the confirming agreement papers. In a very high proportion of licensing situations, this question will be trivial in that either the authority of those purporting to represent the respective parties is self-evident or the risk of loss through lack of authority on either side is minimal. There are certain cases, however, in which the careful counsel (drafter or otherwise) will want specific assurances. There are, moreover, still other cases, particularly where the possibility of litigious controversy over the agreement is imaginable, in which forethought concerning the provability of the contract itself will be worthwhile.

This chapter touches on certain aspects of the preceding matters.

20.00 Authority to Contract

A. The New Enterprise Situation

One situation which may raise an issue of the basic authority of an acting party is that in which the party represents, or purports to represent, a newly organized corporation, partnership, or other business entity. In this kind of situation, there will occasionally be uncertainty as to which individuals among the recently associated interests have power to make commitments binding upon the entire enterprise. In such a case, it will certainly be appropriate to request access to the background documents (e.g., corporate charter and by-

161

laws, partnership agreement, or joint-venture contracts) which deal with this point. Moreover, if the documents produced are unclear as to the locus of authority, it may be prudent to require, and to arrange the papers to accommodate, signature[1] by all contingently interested persons and legal entities.

A related situation in which multiple signatures may be desirable is that in which the technical values being bargained for have arisen outside the structure of the business entity presently claiming power to deliver them. A case of this kind would be one in which there is known to be in the background an inventor or entrepreneur with imaginable personal claims on part of the proceeds of the values being dealt with. Here again, inquiry concerning the chain of title may be a desirable first step, followed, if indicated, by a requirement that all claiming parties join in the grant which is in issue.

A suitable formalistic device for dealing with the background inventor or entrepreneur situation just suggested is represented by the following "Assent," which is intended to become an integral part of the principal agreement papers and to be located immediately following the signatures of the primary negotiating parties:

ASSENT

John P. Jones, whose address is _____, warrants that he is the owner of the entire right, title, and interest in and to the LICENSED PATENT, identified as such in the agreement to which this Assent is appended, including the right to recover for and to grant releases for past infringement, and that he has granted to the LICENSOR named in the agreement an exclusive license under the LICENSED PATENT with the right to grant sublicenses and to recover for and to release past infringement, which license continues in force on the date when he executes this Assent. The said John P. Jones hereby acknowledges that the LICENSOR has the right and license to grant the rights, releases, and sublicenses granted to LICENSEE in the agreement, and to the extent that any of his rights are or may be affected, agrees to be bound by the terms and conditions of the said agreement, and further agrees that he will look to LICENSOR and not to LICENSEE, for any and all royalty payments and other remunerations, if any, due or which might become due him by virtue of the licenses, rights, and releases granted to LICENSEE under the agreement. He further agrees that if the exclusive license which he has granted to LICENSOR and which is now in effect and under the authority of which the present agreement has been entered into between LICENSOR and LICENSEE is cancelled or terminated for whatever reason, the rights, licenses, and releases granted under the agreement shall continue in full force and effect, the same as if he, John P. Jones, had been the original LICENSOR. He further agrees that the terms, conditions, and obligations of this Assent shall be binding upon himself, his heirs, assigns, and legal representatives.

---

[1]*See* discussion of forms of signature under 20.01, below.

ASSENT DATED:

JOHN P. JONES

Witness

An alternative mode of dealing with the uncertainties of a situation such as that exemplified immediately above would be to receive covenants of quiet enjoyment and assurance of indemnification from the principal negotiating party whose contracting powers are in question. It must be recognized, however, that the value of such commitments depends entirely upon the degree of financial responsibility of the party giving them.

B. The Problem of Intracorporation Authority

Where one is dealing with an established corporation, the problem of intracorporate authority is seldom worrisome. Perhaps the one case which suggests proceeding with caution, or at least with extra careful formality, is that in which the magnitude of the commitments by the parties is so great as to raise the possibility of a later claim of lack of authority (i.e., in reference to the individual purporting to represent one party) if the transaction eventually turns out badly from the standpoint of that party. Consideration of this possibility may justify some reminiscence concerning the nature of authority in corporate organizations.

It is useful to recall that "authority to contract" as seen from the corporation viewpoint is or may be separate from "authority to sign."[2] Thus, in *Catholic Foreign Mission Society of America* v. *Oussani*,[3] it was held that a resolution of a religious corporation that "the president has authority to sign and execute all documents" did not give the incumbent of the position *power to contract* independently of the directors with respect to real estate. Conversely, as one author has

---

[2] "The power to contract and the power to execute a contract by signing it in behalf of the corporation are separate and distinct. Ordinarily, however, it would seem that where there is no charter provision, statute, bylaws, or usage to the contrary, that an officer of a corporation who has power to enter into a contract, i.e., to agree upon the terms so as to bind the company, has power to bind the company in the formal act of executing the contract by signing the name of the corporation thereto. But it is sometimes provided . . . that a certain officer, or officers, shall sign specified contracts, or all contracts on behalf of the corporation. In the latter case, power to sign does not, of course, necessarily include power to enter and to negotiate and enter into the contract." W. M. Fletcher, CYCLOPEDIA OF THE LAW OF PRIVATE CORPORATIONS (rev. ed., Chicago: Callaghan & Co., 1964).

[3] 215 N.Y. 1, 109 N.E. 80 (N.Y. 1915).

said, "The authority to execute a written memorandum may be proved by implication from authority to make the contract, but it is not a necessary implication." [4] The power to contract and the power to sign documents, except as they clearly inhere (i.e., as a matter of usage or conventional implication) in particular offices or titles,[5] necessarily derive from paths of delegation and redelegation established by express action of the board of directors or equivalent primary authority.

The parallel but noncoincident lines of authority for "acting" and for "signing," especially in respect to distinctive activities, such as patent licensing, are often expressed within a given corporation by separate authorizing documents. Thus, there may be, on the one hand, a resolution of the Board conferring on various officers and managers authority on behalf of the corporation to *execute* documents of specified kinds, including, for example, agreements of a class which would include patent license agreements. On the other hand, there may be a quite separate resolution which delegates authority to named levels of management for decision making in respect to the purchase or sale of such commodities as patent rights, authority being sometimes reserved to the Board itself for purchases above a certain level of cost.

C. A Married Individual In a Community Property State

In dealing with a married individual who is acting as an assignor or licensor and resides in a community property state, a prospective patent licensee or assignee may want to check on the application of the state's community property laws to the transfer of personal property and rights thereunder.[6] Generally, a husband has the power to transfer community personal property provided he does not defraud his wife.

20.01 Execution

Contracts are, of course, traditionally entered into by subscription of appropriate signatures, followed by actual or symbolic delivery

---

[4]A. L. Corbin, Corbin on Contracts (St. Paul: West Publishing Co., 1962), Sec. 525, at 781.

[5]Titles such as "President," "Chief Executive Officer," and "General Manager" have plenipotentiary implications, and except in such matters as sales of real estate or other fixed assets and in respect to expenditures large in relation to the size of the enterprise, may generally be relied upon as conveying authority to act. Other titles, such as "vice president," must be examined in context to determine their probable scope of authority. Thus the title "Vice President, Engineering," might imply relatively little authority in financial or patent matters.

[6]Patents have the attributes of personal property. 35 U.S.C. §261.

of the document by the party last to sign. The conventions of simple signature are so generally understood as not to justify extended discussion. It is perhaps worth noting, however, that in arranging the contract papers for subscription there may be important differences in legal consequences between a signature such as

John B. Jones
President,
XYZ Corporation

and a signature such as

XYZ Corporation
by—John B. Jones
President

While context might preclude such a result, the first form above is capable of the construction that it is the act of the signing individual only, and that the title and corporation reference are appended merely for identification and without implication that the corporation itself is committed. The second form, therefore, is the correct one if the corporation rather than the individual is intended to be bound. Bear in mind, however, that there may be cases in which both the corporate signature and the individual signature should be obtained—as where the corporation and the signing officer claim to share rights in the subject matter of the contract.

Where the parties are both corporations, it is useful in focusing attention on the question of authorization to precede the signatures by a terminal agreement paragraph resembling one of the following:

Example 1

IN WITNESS WHEREOF, each of the parties hereto has caused this agreement to be executed in duplicate originals by its duly authorized officers or representatives.

Example 2

IN WITNESS WHEREOF, each of the parties hereto has caused its corporate seal to be affixed and duly attested and this agreement to be signed by its authorized representative.

If one party is an individual, Example 2 (for instance) may be modified as follows:

IN WITNESS WHEREOF, XYZ Corporation has caused its corporate seal to be affixed and duly attested and this agreement to be signed by its authorized representative, and John B. Smith has signed the agreement in his own behalf.

Where one of the parties is a partnership, it is sufficient (at least in the absence of local law to the contrary) for only one general partner to sign the agreement. The preceding form may be used in such a case, substituting for the last clause the following:

> and (name of partnership) has caused this agreement to be signed by _____, a general partner.

20.02 Authentication

Assuming that authority to act and to sign in a particular capacity has been plausibly demonstrated by the individual who is to function in that capacity, there may still be a need to consider the problems of proof of due execution which may arise if the contract ever must be litigated. At the time an agreement is entered into, the possibility of denial of either signature or authority to sign by either party will always seem remote. Nevertheless, in a situation of very substantial importance, with large financial issues at stake, even this remote possibility justifies at least minimal precautionary arrangements.

The traditional device for assuring provability of a vital signature is, of course, the use of subscribing or attesting witnesses who either witness the signing or receive acknowledgment of signature from the signing party. While "unofficial" and casually summoned subscribing witnesses may serve and be effective, provided they can be found and produced when need arises, more formalistic devices are to be preferred in cases of great importance. Some of these are noted below.

A. Execution by an Individual Acting in His Own Behalf

The device most readily applicable in reference to an individual contracting party is that of "acknowledgment" before a public officer (e.g., judge, clerk, notary public, or commissioner) authorized to receive and certify such acknowledgments. The statutes of most states now specify the form of acknowledgment and certification which will be recognized within the state in question as a basis for "recording" a document (e.g., a deed or will) that has been executed with recording in mind.

However, even for purposes of recording, the statutory form of acknowledgment must only be followed "substantially." Accordingly, where later proof of execution rather than recording is the principal object of certification, the wording may presumably be whatever is preferred by the parties. Nevertheless, in the absence of reasons to the contrary, adoption of the statutory form of the state of execution is probably indicated—among other things to avoid resistance to certification by a state officer confronted with an unfamiliar form.

B. Execution on Behalf of a Corporation

Assuming that authority to sign has been established as residing in the individual who proposes to execute the agreement in the corporation's behalf,[7] the only object of formality going beyond the procurement of signature is to make the signature provable in the event of later denial of its authenticity by the signatory or his principal.

A device commonly relied upon in this connection is to require that there be coupled with the signature of the principal signing officer the signature of the corporation secretary or of an "attesting secretary" and the affixation of the corporate seal. Signatures following this plan may appear as follows:

XYZ Company

By _____

_____
    Date   Vice President

Attest:

_____
Secretary

                                 (SEAL)

or

XYZ Company

By _____

_____
    Date   General Manager,
                                     ABC Division

Attest:

_____
Attesting Secretary

                                 (SEAL)

An "attesting secretary" (so titled) is a person designated by the corporation to perform a witnessing function, and incidentally (in most instances) to apply the corporate seal when directed to do so by

---

[7]*See* Section 20.00 of this chapter.

appropriate authority. He is, in effect, an official "witness" to the signatures of company officers and, if called on in event of controversy, would appear primarily in a capacity differing little from that of any other subscribing witness. His attachment of the corporate seal is a ministerial act undertaken at the direction and under the authority of the primary signatory of the document. Other ground rules can, of course, be established by the corporate bylaws or board resolution creating the office of "Attesting Secretary," but there would seem to be nothing implicit in the title itself that goes beyond the limits suggested in the preceding sentences.

The corporate secretary, on the other hand, is ordinarily a recognized officer of the corporation, and his "attestation" may have both a witnessing and a countersigning function. That is to say, a document bearing the signature of both the president and secretary of the company may be considered executed upon the authority of both. Similarly, while legal sources are not uniform on the matter, the seal may probably be considered as applied on the authority of either of them.

It is the rule in most states that the impression of a corporate seal on a document is *prima facie* evidence that the person who signed the document on behalf of the corporation was duly authorized to do so.[8] The practical meaning and limitations of this proposition may be judged by brief reference to a few landmarks of New York law on the subject.

New York's General Corporation Law, Section 14 (as amended by L. 1941, c. 329, Section 3) reads in part as follows:

> Every corporation as such has power though not specified in the law under which it incorporated:
> 1. . . .
> 2. To have a common seal, and to alter the same at pleasure. The presence of the seal of a corporation on a written instrument purporting to be executed by authority of the corporation shall constitute a rebuttable presumption that the instrument was so executed.

The decisional law which undergirds that statute includes two illuminating cases. The first of these, *Quackenboss* v. *Globe and R. F. Insurance Co.*,[9] involved an action brought upon a contract which had been signed by the president and secretary of the defendant company, the corporate seal also being affixed. These facts having been proved by the plaintiff, the trial court nevertheless refused to accept the contract in evidence, on the ground that it did not appear that the contract had been authorized by the defendant's board of

---

[8]Note, however, that the authenticity of the seal and any accompanying signatures must be proved by conventional evidentiary procedures if these items are controverted before the court.

[9]177 N.Y. 71, 69 N.E. 223 (N.Y. 1903).

directors. At the final appellate level this ruling was held to be in error, the court stressing the *prima facie* evidentiary value of the seal and observing that—

> Whatever proof was given as to the regularity of the contract bore, not upon its admissibility, but upon its effect when received.

However, while, under the foregoing decision, the presence of an authenticated seal will normally serve to get a challenged contract before the court, it by no means determines the final outcome of the challenge. This is shown (in continuing reference to New York law) by the further decision of the New York Court of Appeals in *Gause v. Commonwealth Trust Co. of New York*.[10] Here a vice president of the defendant Trust Company had, with knowledge of its president, but without reference to its board of directors, executed a contract of guaranty and caused the contract to be sealed with the corporate seal and attested by the assistant secretary of the company. While the contract was blatantly improvident, and demonstrably outside the corporate powers of the Trust Company, the plaintiff nevertheless attempted to assert its enforceability on the basis of its sealed character. The court firmly rebuffed this attempt, saying:

> Although the presence of a seal upon an instrument is prima facie proof that it has been attached by proper authority (Quackenboss v. Globe and R. F. Insurance Co. . . .), it is only such proof as may be conclusively rebutted, and it has been conclusively rebutted in this case.[11]

One must conclude, then, that if authority of the acting officer is a matter of vital concern in a contracting situation, there is no real alternative to requiring certified corporate documents showing the existence of such authority. (See Section 20.00, above). Most corporations will be prepared to supply these.

The further formal step of requiring acknowledgment of execution of a corporate instrument before a state officer or notary will be useful only if one can imagine a possible denial of authenticity of signatures[12]—in which case the acknowledgment will facilitate proof.

---

[10]196 N.Y. 134, 89 N.E. 476 (N.Y. 1909).

[11]*See also* 13 AM. JUR. §945 (1938), as follows: "It is the universal rule that the use of the corporate seal is, at most, prima facie evidence of the authority of its officer or agent, and that if he in fact had no authority, express or apparent, to act for the corporation, his use of the seal cannot impart validity to the transaction." (Decisions cited.)

[12]An exception exists, of course, in respect to documents which will require recordation under a statute or regulation which specifies acknowledgment as a prerequisite to recording. Thus, where patents are being "assigned," as distinguished from "merely licensed," the assigning documents must be duly acknowledged to permit recordation in the assignment records of the U.S. Patent Office (35 U.S.C. 261). The title-protecting value of recordation of assigned patents makes this formality (and accordingly the prior formality of acknowledgment of the documents) highly desirable in such cases.

For symmetry with heading (A), above, however, it may be noted that the device of acknowledgment is just as available in the corporation case as it is in the case of the individual signatory, and that a form as the following may serve the former case:

STATE OF
COUNTY OF }ss

On this _____ day of _____, 19____, before me personally came _____, to me known, who, being duly sworn, did depose and say that he resides in _____, that he is _____ of _____, the corporation described in and which executed the above agreement, that he knows the seal of said corporation, that the seal affixed to said agreement is said corporate seal, that it was so affixed by authority of the Board of Directors of said corporation, and that he signed his name thereto by like authority.

(NOTARIAL)
(SEAL)
(APPLIED)

_____
Notary Public

In some foreign countries, the act of two directors signifies the act of the corporation, and it is in any event desirable in dealing with a foreign corporation to make appropriate inquiry (from sources other than the foreign party) concerning requisite authority in the country in question. Acknowledgments of assignments and agreements executed in foreign countries are ordinarily made before a United States Consular Officer, because United States statutes provide that acknowledgments so made are *prima facie* proof of their execution by the parties making the acknowledgments. The following is a typical form:

U.S. CONSULATE GENERAL:

:
:ss:
:
:

I, _____, Consul General of the United States of America, at Zurich, Switzerland, duly commissioned and qualified; and residing at Zurich, Switzerland, do hereby certify that on the _____ day of _____, 19__, before me personally appeared _____ _____ and _____, Directors of Aktiengesellschaft of Baden, Switzerland, to me personally known, and known to me to be the individuals whose names are subscribed to and who executed the foregoing instrument, who being affirmed did depose and say that they are Directors of Aktiengesellschaft, a firm of Baden, Switzerland, and that they executed the same by authority of said firm.

CONSUL GENERAL OF THE UNITED STATES OF AMERICA

21

Agreements Concerning the Sale or Other Transfer of Unpatented Technological Values[1]

There are numerous situations in which technological values other than patentable inventions become the objects of sale or other transfer. Such values may include, for example, materials variously described as "submitted ideas," "trade secrets," "know-how," "manufacturing information," etc. It is common to group all of these generically under the heading "proprietary information."

It will be the scheme of this chapter to suggest usable patterns of contracting for the several classes of subject matter connoted by the various terms used above. Analysis will proceed first by offering definitions for the more crucial terms and then by proposing contractual formulas in which the recommended treatment is progressively adjusted to the technical complexity of the subject matter dealt with. This development will be followed by commentary on the prob-

---

[1]The following assumptions are reflected in the tenor of the drafting suggestions embodied in the ensuing text material:

(1) The possibility of making reasonable contracts concerning the transfer and protection of valuable technical information is not likely to be destroyed.

(2) Court-imposed limitations on freedom of trade-secret contracting affect first and foremost the permissible scope of restrictions in respect to the use of the transferred information and products made using the transferred information.

(3) The contract-inhibiting impact of court decisions tends to be more severe as the trade-secret quality of the transferred information is found to be less.

(4) Forms of compensation for transferred information which appear to impose an unreasonable continuing burden on the affected commerce, may be seen as "restrictive" and hence subject to attack under (2) and (3), above. *But see* Aronson v. Quick Point Pencil Co., 440 U.S. 257, 201 USPQ 1 (1979).

lem of defining the technical values involved in any given information-transferring contract, and there will finally be added some suggestions concerning appropriate limitations on the responsibilities of the supplier and the recipient of transferred information.

21.00 Definitions

A. "Proprietary Information"

"Proprietary information" is a question-begging term used to describe any information in which the courts will recognize at least some exclusive rights. It necessarily includes all possible categories of communicable information within the limits to which these will be protected by law. But, as has been pointed out by Mr. Justice Holmes,[2] to call any aggregate of interests "property" (or to apply the derivative word, "proprietary") and then to afford them legal protection on this ground is in effect to insert in the premise of a syllogism the result proposed to be drawn out in the conclusion. While the courts themselves occasionally fall into this entrapment, the contract drafter must not indulge in the delusion that he can compel a favorable result by calling something "proprietary" which fails to meet, at least generally, the classical criteria established for legal protectibility. Some commonly encountered statements of these criteria are presented in section (C), below.

B. "Submitted Ideas"

This is a term widely applied in business circles to unsolicited suggestions of a technical or business nature which are offered "out of the blue" to an enterprise which, in the judgment of the submitter, might be interested in receiving and using them. Companies which advertise widely, particularly in respect to consumer products, may receive hundreds, and even thousands, of these submissions yearly.

Conceptually, a "submitted idea" may have any degree of technical content. However, because nearly all of them, as received on an unsolicited basis, come from persons without substantial technical background or much knowledge of the practical problems of marketing new products, only about one in a thousand is likely to have significant value. For this reason, the term "submitted ideas" as used in the present text will be considered to be limited to proposed disclosures of low technical content and of highly doubtful legal protectibility.

---

[2]E. I. du Pont de Nemours Powder Co. v. Masland, 244 U.S. 100 (1917).

C. "Trade Secrets" and "Know-How"

In a particular case, either of these two widely used terms can be made to mean whatever the contract drafter chooses for its meaning by a carefully designed definition. However, in searching for semi-established distinctions between them that may have legal significance worth drawing upon, it will be useful to consider frequently cited authorities.

The American Law Institute defines a "trade secret" in Section 757 of the Restatement of the Law of Torts, Comment (b), as follows:

> A trade secret may consist of any formula, pattern, device or compilation of information which is used in one's business, and which gives him an opportunity to obtain an advantage over competitors who do not know or use it. . . .

> . . . a substantial element of secrecy must exist, so that, except by the use of improper means, there would be difficulty in acquiring the information. . . . Some factors to be considered in determining whether given information is one's trade secret are: (1) the extent to which the information is known outside of his business; (2) the extent to which it is known by employees and others involved in his business; (3) the extent of measures taken by him to guard the secrecy of the information; (4) the value of the information to him and to his competitors; (5) the amount of effort or money expended by him in developing the information; (6) the ease or difficulty with which the information could be properly acquired or duplicated by others.

The expression "know-how" has frequently appeared in litigation involving assertion of property rights with respect to large masses of undifferentiated technical information. For example, in *Mycalex Corp. of America* v. *Pemco Corp.*,[3] the court said that "know-how" is

> factual knowledge not capable of precise, separate description, but which when used in an accumulated form, after being acquired as the result of trial and error, gives to the one acquiring it an ability to produce something which he otherwise would not have known how to produce with the same accuracy or precision found necessary for commercial success.

So used, "know-how" has been viewed as a broader term than "trade secret." Thus, in *United States* v. *Timken Roller Bearing Co.*[4] the court said:

> It must be noted at the outset of the discussion of the problem that the know-how furnished by defendant to the other companies was not a secret process for the manufacture of tapered roller bearings. Other manufacturers were admitted to the plants of British and French Timken, where they could observe all the know-how put into operation. In the extensive record of the testimony dealing with the assistance given by

---

[3] 64 F. Supp. 420, 68 USPQ 317 (D. Md. 1946), *aff'd*, 159 F.2d 907 (4th Cir. 1947).
[4] 83 F. Supp. 284, 81 USPQ 28 (N.D. Ohio 1949).

the officials and technical staff, there is no trace of any secret process which was imparted by them. The know-how consisted of designs, data showing how defendant manufactured its product, the advice of defendant's employees and help of like nature.

Consistent with observations previously made concerning the term "proprietary information," it must again be noted that the legal consequences flowing from contractual use of a particular description of technical information depend very little upon a dictionary viewpoint respecting the description itself. On the contrary, such consequences depend almost entirely upon the limitations given to the content of the descriptor by its specific definition, where there is one, or by context where no definition is provided. Regardless of the decisions cited above, nothing of legal value can be gained by labelling as "trade secret" or "know-how" subject matter which in fact is public information. Conversely, subject matter called simply "Licensor's Data" (for example) may be highly protectible if the "Data" referred to is limited by the contract to safeguarded information that is of esoteric quality and substantial business value.

21.01 Principal Drafting Problems in Contracts for the Transfer of Technological Information

In transactions involving subject matter which falls under any of the descriptive headings used in the preceding section of the chapter, it will ordinarily be found that the principal problems facing the contract negotiator and his legal drafter concern the following:

(1) Definition of the technical values to be dealt with;
(2) Description of the means of disclosure to be employed;
(3) Specification of the kind of payment, if any, to be made and the basis on which it is to be calculated;
(4) Delineation of the obligations of the recipient of the technical values with respect to their use and protection; and
(5) Determination of the duration and conditions of termination of such obligations.

Each of the sections which follow has been constructed with this checklist in mind and attempts to illustrate practical approaches to meeting the demands which the checklist poses. As suggested at the outset of the chapter, the cases dealt with proceed from the more elementary toward the more complex. The sections which conclude the chapter become specific with respect to treatment of items (1), (2), and (4) of the checklist.

21.02 Dealing With "Submitted Ideas" and Other Technical Proposals of Highly Contingent Value

Because of the highly contingent value of most "submitted ideas," some companies have adopted a policy of declining to receive them. This policy, where employed, is usually implemented by use of a polite but firm letter returning each attempted submission.

Other companies, concerned with the public relations implications of appearing unwilling to consider new ideas, accept their submission provided the submitter agrees to conditions designed to protect the receiving party from unintended and unwanted legal liability. Devices used for this purpose vary widely, depending mainly upon the prior experience of the particular company as to what is required to avoid misunderstanding and controversy with its submitters. One large company, presumably impelled by experience toward the conservative side, asks, as a prerequisite to its consideration of any informally submitted idea, that the submitter execute one or the other of the following forms:

Form A—For Use Where Compensation Is Not Expected

Submitted Ideas Department
XYZ Company
New York, New York

The suggestion concerning _____

_____

which I am submitting for your consideration is submitted gratuitously and without expectation of compensation. You are free to consider and use it without obligation to me for its consideration or use.

_____
Signature of Submitter

Date: _____

_____
Submitter's Address

_____

Form B—For Use Where Compensation Is Hoped For

ACCEPTANCE OF CONDITIONS

XYZ Company:

I have read your booklet on Policies Concerning Submitted Ideas. In consideration of the Company's being willing to examine certain ideas which I have submitted or propose to submit to, I agree to the Conditions of Submission set forth below. I further agree that such Conditions shall apply to all disclosures made incidental to the original material submitted and to all information previously or hereafter disclosed or submitted relating directly or indirectly to such material. The subject matter which I am submitting relates to the following:

_____
Signature of Submitter

Date: _____

_____
Submitter's Address

_____

CONDITIONS OF SUBMISSION

(1) No confidential relationship is to be established by such submission or implied from consideration of the submitted material, and the material is not to be considered to be submitted "in confidence."

(2) The Company makes no commitment that the idea or material submitted in connection with it shall be kept a secret.

(3) The Company does not agree to pay any compensation whatsoever for its use of ideas which have not been patented. If, despite the conditions herein contained to the contrary, it shall be alleged that the Company has incurred liability to the submitter with respect to any unpatented idea submitted to it, the submitter agrees that in no event shall he assert any claim for equitable relief or for damages in excess of $1,000, which sum the submitter agrees shall be the maximum damages for any and all liability of the Company with respect to such unpatented idea, including but not limited to the Company's use or disclosure thereof. If any such unpatented idea shall subsequently be covered by the claims of a patent granted to the submitter, the foregoing clause shall not apply to any rights under such patent.

(4) The reception and consideration by the Company of any submitted disclosure of an idea shall not in any way impair the Company's right to contest the validity or infringement of any patent that may have been or may thereafter be obtained on it. The submitter's sole remedy if he believes the Company to be infringing such patent shall be enforcement by him under the applicable patent laws of such exclusive rights as he may possess by virtue of his patent.

(5) The Company will give each submitted idea only such consideration as in the judgment of the Company it merits.

(6) The Company shall be under no obligation to return any material submitted or to reveal its acts in connection with the submitted idea.

(7) The Company shall be under no obligation to reveal any information regarding its activities in either the general or specific field to which the submitted idea pertains.

(8) If the Company decides not to offer compensation for a submitted idea, it assumes no obligation to give reasons for its decision—or to do other than to communicate its decision to the submitter.

(9) Entering into negotiations for the purchase of any idea submitted, or the making of any offer for its purchase, shall not in any way prejudice the Company, nor shall it be deemed an admission of the novelty of the idea, or of priority or originality on the part of the person submitting it or of any other person.

(10) Any and all prior negotiations or agreements by any agent or representative of the Company are merged into these Conditions of Submission and no such prior representations, negotiations, or agreements shall be binding on the Company or of any force or effect.

(11) The foregoing Conditions may not be modified or waived except in writing signed by an officer of the Company, or the General Manager of a Division of the Company, or the Company's General Patent Counsel.

For the most part, the provisions of a form such as that set forth immediately above are clear as to their legal objectives. Several of the numbered items, such as 6, 7, and 8, deal with matters as to which submitters tend to expect more information than the typical company can afford to provide—particularly if large numbers of submissions are being received.

In respect to numbered item 3, some companies handle the corresponding point by providing that any compensation to be paid shall be "determined entirely in the discretion of the Company" or equivalent wording. There are circumstances, however, in which the protective value of such language may prove illusory because of the disposition of some courts to hold that "discretion" is limited to the exercise of what the court thinks would represent "fairness and good faith" in the particular circumstances.[5] The uncertainty of outcome evidenced by these several decisions may well attach to any language whatever which could be used at this point, but the assignment of a specific monetary limit (as in paragraph 3 of the form given above)

---

[5]*See, e.g.,* Pillois v. Billingsley, 179 F.2d 205 (2d Cir. 1950). *See also* Deering Milliken Research Corp. v. Textured Fibres, Inc., 310 F. Supp. 491, 165 USPQ 56 (D. S.C. 1970) for an extended discussion of similar decisions in respect to such phrases as "in the judgment of" and "to the satisfaction of." *But see* Davis v. General Foods Corp., 21 F. Supp. 445 (S.D.N.Y. 1937) for a determination on particular facts that a provision that the "compensation, if any, to be paid therefore, are matters resting solely in our discretion" was to be literally construed.

should make it difficult for an arbitrary award to be made in excess of the stated amount.[6]

Forms of the kind under consideration are ordinarily transmitted to the prospective submitter with a booklet which undertakes to explain in acceptable public relations terms why the various provisions are thought necessary and how they serve the objective of avoiding painful misunderstanding with friends and customers of the company. While in a certain proportion of cases offered submissions are finally withheld by the submitter because of unwillingness to accept the company's conditions, in a much larger number of instances the forms are duly executed and consideration of the submitted idea proceeds.

21.03 Contracting for "Acceptance" of a "Submitted Idea"

For the reasons stated in the definitional discussion of the term "submitted ideas," only a very small percentage of submissions are found sufficiently useful to justify payment for their use. However, in the exceptional case in which value is found, the accepted submission form points the way toward an appropriate superseding agreement. Such an agreement, covering in this case a submission relating to an ice-cube tray, might, for example, have the following outline.[7]

RECITALS

1. SUBMITTER represents that he is the originator of the ice-cube tray design shown in drawing No. 17869 attached to this agreement and bearing date of February 1, 1983; that he has the right to grant the license included in this agreement and that he has not and will not execute any agreement in conflict with such grant.

2. Prior to any disclosure of his ice-cube tray design to COMPANY, SUBMITTER received from COMPANY a copy of COMPANY'S booklet identified as APC-1-C, and accepted the conditions specified therein by delivering a signed "Acceptance of Conditions" form to COMPANY on January 2, 1983. After such delivery, SUBMITTER disclosed to COMPANY an ice-cube tray design corresponding essentially to that shown in drawing No. 17869, above referred to. As a result of its consideration of this

---

[6]For the practical application of a liability-limiting clause similar in general intent to paragraph 3 of the subject form, *see* Sylvania Elec. Prods., Inc. v. Brainerd, 166 USPQ 387 (D. Mass. 1970).

[7]Introductory language, "boiler plate" provisions, and other obviously indicated provisions are omitted. The outline covers only those matters which are needed for an appropriate transition from the Submitted Ideas form to an agreement covering the acceptance and use of the submitted idea.

disclosure, COMPANY desires to obtain certain rights in respect to the ice-cube tray design of drawing No. 17869.

Accordingly, the parties agree as follows:

I

SUBMITTER will grant to COMPANY under any of SUBMITTER'S rights of proprietorship, including any patent that may be obtained by SUB-MITTER which contains claims applicable to an ice-cube tray of the type shown in drawing No. 17869 or any improved version of such tray, a license to make, use, and sell such trays. For a period of two years from the date of this agreement, SUBMITTER will not grant or agree to grant an equivalent or overlapping license to others than COMPANY, but at the end of that period shall be free to grant further licenses without limitation.

II

(a) For a period of two (2) years from the effective date of this Agreement, COMPANY will pay SUBMITTER as follows in respect to all ice-cube trays manufactured by or for COMPANY within the period which corresponds to the disclosure of drawing No. 17869:

(Here would be inserted whatever scheme of payment the parties agree upon.)

(b) Subject to the provisions of Article III of this agreement and to the further provisions respecting termination which appear in Article X, COMPANY will, for the period following two years from the effective date of this agreement, make payments to SUBMITTER at the rates specified in paragraph (a) of this Article II in respect to all ice-cube trays corresponding to or based upon the disclosure of drawing No. 17869 which are manufactured by or for COMPANY during the period and which at the time of manufacture are covered by a claim of a United States patent granted to SUBMITTER or by a claim allowed to SUBMITTER in an application pending before the United States Patent Office and not (at the time of such manufacture) involved in a contest as to priority of inventorship of the subject matter of such claim.

III

If, at the end of two (2) years from the effective date of this agreement, no claim which, in the judgment of COMPANY is applicable to ice-cube trays of the type disclosed in drawing No. 17869 has been allowed in any application for patent filed by SUBMITTER in the United States Patent Office, COMPANY shall have the right, exercisable by written notice at any time within one year after the end of the two year period, to terminate this agreement effective as of the date of notice. Any such termination shall terminate all obligations of COMPANY under the agreement except the obligation for payment (at the rates specified) in respect to ice-cube trays manufactured by or for COMPANY prior to the date of termination. Termination shall be without prejudice to the assertion by COMPANY, in respect to its operations subsequent to termination, of the limitations of liability provided for in Condition 3 of the "Acceptance of Conditions" form previously referred to in this agreement.

(Rights of termination by COMPANY *under conditions other than those referred to in Article III might in some circumstances be desirable and fair. Such rights would, of course, have to be provided for in subsequent paragraphs of the agreement.)*

IV, V, VI, ETC.

("Boiler plate" *provisions covering details of payment and accounting should, of course, be added to the basic provisions spelled out above. Provisions concerning the rights of manufacture in or export to foreign countries may be included if appropriate. Insofar as the granting of additional licenses by* "SUBMITTER" *are contemplated (See Article I), a* "more favored nations" *clause may be required by* "COMPANY."*)*

It should be obvious that nothing precludes the waiver by "COMPANY" of the $1,000 limitation imposed by Condition 3 of the "Acceptance of Conditions" form on payments to be made to submitter in the absence of valid patent protection. Whether such a waiver would be equitable depends, of course, on objective evaluation of the worth to company if the disclosed submission is unpatented. In any such evaluation, one factor to be weighed would be the extent to which any payment above $1,000 would put company at an economic disadvantage with respect to its competitors, who in the situation postulated, would be free to copy company's ice-cube tray (once marketed) without liability either to submitter or to company.

21.04 Contracting in Respect to a "Confidential Disclosure" of Unevaluated Information Presumed to Be Valuable

An especially interesting challenge is presented to the negotiator and contract drafter in the case in which one of the prospective contracting parties possesses technical information which the other party has some reason to believe may be valuable to it,[8] but which has initially been disclosed only in general terms and in broad outline. The problem in such a situation is to devise a procedure which avoids: (a) compelling the owner of the information to disclose it without reasonable protection of his proprietary values; or (b) obliging the other party to make commitments which could prove improvident when the dimensions and limitations of the information are disclosed

---

[8]On this premise, the sort of information here involved differs significantly from that presented in the typical "Submitted Idea" situation discussed in the preceding section. The difference arises at least in part from the fact that the originator of the "valuable" information now being discussed is likely to be a technical specialist or experienced manufacturer in the field to which the information pertains. Because of the difference, more elaborate methods of treatment may be called for.

in their ultimate detail. The solution of the dilemma is frequently to be found in the development of a step-by-step approach to disclosure. The number and nature of the steps required will obviously depend upon the character of the parties and the complexity of the subject matter to be dealt with. The following several outlines will illustrate particular possibilities and should suggest others.

Illustration 1

Factual Background. This illustration assumes that Party 1 is known to have in use in its European factory a successful process for the production of tubing made of a refractory material not yet satisfactorily adapted to this use in the United States. Details of the process are considered to be trade secrets. The commercial success of the tubing has been sufficient tentatively to establish the value of the process from the viewpoint of Party 2, a U.S. manufacturer of generally related products. After initial discussions have indicated the willingness of Party 1 to work toward a mutually acceptable licensing arrangement, the following kind of two-step agreement[9] is entered into:

AGREEMENT

I. DEFINITIONS

(As appropriate to the subject matter involved)

II. RIGHT TO INSPECT

Party 1 will allow representatives of Party 2 to visit the plants of Party 1 in which the process and/or equipment are in operation and in the course of such inspection to obtain general technical and manufacturing information in respect to said process and equipment for the purpose of determining whether or not it wishes to exercise the option hereinafter defined. The duration of such inspection shall not exceed five (5) days and shall come within the period from June 15 to September 15, 1984. Inspection shall take place during regular working days and hours and at times mutually convenient to the parties.

III. USE OF INFORMATION

Party 2 shall be under no confidential relationship in respect to the process or equipment to be inspected, whether it does or does not acquire subsequent rights or exercise the option specified in Article IV of this agreement, except that Party 2 shall not disclose to third parties during a period of _____years following the inspection, any information obtained during the inspection. Party 2 shall have the right to use any features of the process or equipment which Party 2 learns about during the inspection and which are not or do not become the claimed subject matter of an issued patent owned by Party 1. For any such use, Party

---

[9]Only key aspects of the agreement are outlined, it being assumed that the more conventional parts of the agreement can readily be prepared by the contract drafter.

2 shall be under no obligation to pay Party 1 any consideration beyond that stipulated in Article V, below.

IV. OPTION

Party 2 shall have the option to acquire, within six months from the date of this agreement, the license set forth in the agreement starting at Article VI and continuing to the end of the agreement. This option shall be considered as exercised if Party 2 places in the mail a notice to that effect addressed to Party 1 at its above address not later than six (6) months from the date of this agreement.

V. CONSIDERATION

In consideration of the covenants made and the option granted by Party 1 in Articles I to IV, inclusive, of this agreement, Party 2 will pay to Party 1 the sum of _____thousand dollars at the time of execution of this agreement as follows:

(1) _____ thousand dollars by check to the order of Party 1, and

(2) _____ thousand dollars to Black, Smith, and Jones as escrow agents with the understanding that said escrow agents shall deliver the said amount of _____thousand dollars to Party 1 immediately upon receipt of a signed confirmation from the representatives of Party 2 making the inspection mentioned in Article II to the effect that adequate opportunity to inspect has been provided and that inspection has been completed.

In the event there is disagreement as to the adequacy of the opportunity to inspect, the matter shall be submitted to and resolved by arbitration as stipulated in Article XV of this agreement. Any determination by the arbitrators shall include instructions to the escrow agents for the disposition of the funds held by them.

VI. LICENSE AND RIGHTS OF FURTHER INSPECTION

In the event Party 1 exercises the option stated in Article IV, above, and in consideration of the royalty provisions set forth in Article VIII, Party 1 hereby grants to Party 2:

(a) The right, at any time or times within a period of one (1) year from the date of exercise of the option, to inspect further and to study, analyze, examine, and record all technical and manufacturing information, including cost data and drawings, relating to the process and equipment which is the subject of this agreement.

(*Here would be included also a description of the patent licenses and rights to use and disclose information which are intended to exist following exercise of the option.*)

VII. TECHNICAL ASSISTANCE

(*Here would be included a specification of the technical assistance, if any, which Party 1 is to give to Party 2 in placing the license process and equipment in operation.*)

VIII. Payments by Party 1

(Here would be stated the royalties or other payment intended to be made by Party 1 in consideration of the licenses and other rights resulting from the exercise of its option.)

IX, X, XI, etc.

(Under these additional Articles would be included customary or necessary provisions on record keeping, termination, etc.)

Illustration 2

Factual Background. An established manufacturing company (Party 1) has developed a molding process found to be advantageous in producing the special products of that company. It seems possible (but not certain) that the process will have value in connection with the entirely different products of Party 2. At least some aspects of the process are of trade secret quality. The parties seek a solution to their mutual problems of confidentiality by entering first into a relatively informal exploratory letter agreement and, following successful implementation of that agreement, by execution of a superseding license agreement. Prototypes for such agreements follow:

Letter Agreement

ABC Company
New York, New York

Gentlemen:

In accordance with the recent discussion between our Mr. White and your Mr. Conway regarding your Glensmith process and apparatus, we should be glad to visit your Detroit plant to determine the possible application of this process and apparatus to our manufacture of grommets and our possible interest in acquiring patent licenses and know-how which would permit such application. To facilitate such a visit and in order that there may be an understanding between us with respect to any disclosures which may be made to our representatives in connection with the visit, we propose the following:

1. This agreement shall become effective upon your acceptance of this letter.

2. You will permit up to four (4) of our employees, who will be designated in advance by us, to visit your Detroit plant for the purpose of observing the Glensmith process and apparatus, and you will disclose to these employees the details of the process and apparatus to the extent necessary to permit us to determine (i) their applicability to the operations of our Company, (ii) our interest in negotiating for rights under your patents Nos. ____, ____, and ____(which patents we understand cover certain aspects of such process and apparatus), and (iii) our interest in acquiring such "know-how" as may be necessary to practice the Glensmith process.

3. We understand that in making the disclosure referred to in paragraph 2, you may be revealing information of a trade secret nature.

Therefore, any information which we receive that is designated "confidential" by you at the time of disclosure will be received and accepted in confidence. We will not disclose such information to anyone except officers and employees in our organization, who shall be informed by us of the confidential nature of the information, and subject only to the provisions of paragraph 4, below, we will use the information only for the purpose of evaluating our interest in the process and apparatus.

4. Notwithstanding the provisions of paragraph 3—

(a) Our obligation with respect to keeping information confidential and with respect to use of information shall terminate with respect to any part of such information which appears in issued patents or printed publications or which ceases to be confidential through no fault of ours;

(b) We shall not be precluded from disclosing or making any use whatsoever of any information which we can show by written records was in our possession prior to the disclosure made by you or subsequently came into our possession through channels independent of your company;

(c) For the purpose of keeping confidential information derived from your company, we shall use efforts fully commensurate with those which we employ for the protection of corresponding information of this company, but we shall not be liable for unauthorized revelations of information which occur in spite of such efforts.

(d) In any event, the obligation of paragraph 3 with respect to disclosure and use of information shall terminate three (3) years from the date of this letter.

5. The visit and disclosure referred to in paragraph 3 will be made within sixty (60) days after the effective date of this agreement. We agree within sixty (60) days from the date of completion of disclosure to notify you whether we are interested in negotiating a license agreement, and you agree to take no action within such sixty-day period which would preclude you from concluding a nonexclusive license agreement with us. Any license agreement thereafter entered into shall contain such provisions and be in such form as we shall mutually determine.

If the foregoing arrangement is acceptable to you, please indicate your acceptance by signing the duplicate copy of this letter which is enclosed herewith and returning that copy to us.

> Very truly yours,
>
> XYZ Company
>
> By _____
> 　　　　(Title)

Accepted and agreed to this
day of 　　, 19

ABC Company

By _____
　　　(Title)

The arrangement covered by the proposed letter agreement just outlined differs in effect from the plan covered under Illustration 1, above, in a number of respects.

First, it does not undertake to define the agreement to be entered into in the event the evaluation by XYZ Company is favorable. As to this, it may be observed that advance visualization of a complete licensing plan is apt to be possible only where the business to be engaged in by the prospective licensee (if it proceeds with the transaction) will resemble the present business of the prospective licensor, in which case the commercial values involved are already reasonably evident to both parties. This would not necessarily be true in the circumstances postulated in Illustration 2.

Second, the letter does not provide complete freedom from obligations of confidentiality as does the more formal agreement of Illustration 1. As an offset, however, the letter does provide a series of escape clauses from the obligations which are assumed. Of these, the most important may be the last, which limits obligation to a short period of years. From the licensee's standpoint, the inclusion of such a limitation is highly desirable. Assuming a licensor sufficiently experienced to be aware of the fleeting character of most so-called confidential information, it should ordinarily be negotiable.

Whether an informal exploratory arrangement of the sort defined by Illustration 2 will lead to a definitive licensing agreement depends, of course, on the results of the evaluation process. If these results are favorable, a license designed to meet the mutual interests of the parties can be prepared, drawing, for example, on the details of Illustration 1 and other materials set forth in earlier chapters of this book.

Illustration 3

Factual Background. An unaffiliated scientist, Steinmuir, of national reknown, approaches the ABC Company with a proposal to disclose to it an unpatented invention relating to an improved electronic device (hereafter called "THE ELECTRONIC DEVICE"). The device is within the field of interest of the company, and Steinmuir's reputation is such as to dispose the company to depart from the "Submitted Ideas" policies to which it ordinarily adheres in such cases, provided this can be done without excessive financial risk. Steinmuir is cooperative, but wishes at least some compensation for initial disclosure of his ideas. In such a case, the following outline of agreement may be found mutually acceptable:

1. The Term THE ELECTRONIC DEVICE means—(*here would follow as precise a definition of subject matter as the present posture of the parties permits*).

2. Within ten (10) days after final execution of this agreement, the Company will pay Steinmuir the sum of Ten Thousand Dollars ($10,000). The sum shall represent consideration for (i) the disclosure of full information with respect to THE ELECTRONIC DEVICE and (ii) the option to enter into a license agreement which is specified in paragraph 5, below. Moreover, if the option specified in paragraph 5 is exercised, so that a license agreement comes into effect, all of the Ten Thousand Dollars ($10,000) referred to above shall be applied as prepayment against royalties coming due under the license agreement. Such prepaid royalties shall be offset against one half of the royalties due to Steinmuir in each of the reporting periods specified in the license agreement until the entire Ten Thousand Dollars ($10,000) shall be so offset.

3. Steinmuir will, upon execution of this agreement, promptly disclose to the Company any and all information (including any pending patent applications) which he then possesses relevant to THE ELECTRONIC DEVICE. The Company, upon such disclosure, shall be entitled

without further obligation to Steinmuir to make any use it may choose of this information except to the extent that the information may be the subject of patent claims based upon inventions made by Steinmuir prior to the date of this agreement. As to such information and inventions, Steinmuir's rights shall be solely those accruing under the patent statutes and under any license agreement which may result from the exercise of the option specified in paragraph 5.

4. (a) As soon as reasonably practicable after the date of this agreement, Steinmuir will arrange for filing and continuing the prosecution of an application or applications for Letters Patent of the United States covering patentable inventions embodied in THE ELECTRONIC DEVICE. Steinmuir agrees to promptly supply to the Company copies of all applications so filed and of all communications between himself or his patent attorney and the United States Patent Office relating to such patent applications, once they are filed.

(b) The Company will reimburse Steinmuir for costs up to the sum of Two Thousand Dollars ($2,000) incurred by him in connection with the filing and prosecution of patent applications under the provisions of paragraph 4(a), above.

5. With respect to patent applications to be filed by Steinmuir under the provisions of paragraph 4 of this agreement, the Company shall have an option, exercisable by written notice to Steinmuir deposited in the United States mail and addressed to him at _____ to enter into an agreement in the form attached hereto and marked "Exhibit A." Steinmuir covenants that he has full right to grant this option and the license specified in Exhibit A and that he has not executed and will not execute any agreement in conflict therewith. In the event the Company fails to exercise the option, the Company retains any defenses with respect to such applications and the inventions covered thereby which it would have been free to assert had this agreement not been entered into.

The license agreement to eventuate upon exercise of the option provided for in the preliminary agreement sketched above would, of course, be in any form thought appropriate by the parties. The reference of "prepayment of royalties" contained in the preliminary agreement is obviously appropriate only if the "Exhibit A" license establishes a scale of royalties based on production—as it might very well do.

It would not be unusual and might in some cases be highly desirable to include in the license agreement provisions for consultation by the party Steinmuir in respect to the exploration and development of his invention.

Such provisions might, for example, include the following:

6. (a) Steinmuir shall act as consultant and advisor to the Company on such matters pertaining to THE ELECTRONIC DEVICE as may be referred to him by the Director of Research of the Company, or his designated representative, making himself available for such purpose for a total of not more than forty (40) days during the two-year period immediately following the date of execution of this agreement.

(b) Steinmuir shall in no sense be considered an employee of the Company nor shall he be entitled to or eligible to participate in any benefits or privileges given or extended by the Company to its employees.

(c) The Company will, for two (2) years, pay Steinmuir a fee of _____ Thousand Dollars per year, the fee to be payable in equal quarterly-yearly installments at the end of each quarter, the first such payment to be made on _____, 19___, for consulting services rendered under this paragraph 6. The Company will also reimburse Steinmuir for reasonable traveling expenses incurred by him in discharging his obligations under this agreement and for the cost of materials which Steinmuir may purchase from time to time for the necessary purposes of this agreement.

7. In view of the confidential relations contemplated between Steinmuir and the officers and employees of the Company, and the payments to be made him under paragraph 6, above, Steinmuir will disclose to the Company all inventions made or conceived by him during the life of this agreement which relate to THE ELECTRONIC DEVICE or its improvement. Steinmuir will and does grant to the Company a nonexclusive, irrevocable, fully paid license to make, use, and sell products embodying all such inventions, but the Company shall have an option, exercisable prior to _____, 19___ by written notice to Steinmuir, mailed and addressed to him at _____, to make such license exclusive by agreeing to pay to Steinmuir royalties in addition to and at one half the rate set forth in Exhibit A on any apparatus covered by one or more claims of a patent obtained by Steinmuir or any such invention. Steinmuir shall have the right to determine whether or not to file patent applications on his inventions and shall pay the full costs of filing and prosecuting such patent applications, except as may otherwise be agreed between him and the Company in a particular case.

It will be obvious that the kind of transaction outlined above is capable of variation in any and all of its details. The "Exhibit A" license agreement which would result from the exercise of the option of paragraph 5 is intentionally left undescribed because its specifics would be so utterly dependent on the nature and importance of the technological development involved.

The real point of the "Illustration" is that it offers an approach to negotiation for the company which feels that it has finally encountered the rare case in which a "black box" offer has some attractiveness. The virtue of the program presented is that, while it calls for substantial payment for a look into the "black box," the commitment made is strictly limited, and once the look has been taken, the company is left free of all claims except those which may arise from the discovered presence of patentable subject matter. These are ordinarily capable of reasonably accurate dollars-and-cents evaluation, while those which spring from less guarded acceptance of a "confidential disclosure" ordinarily are not.

Illustration 4

An even more complex situation than any of those so far considered may be presented in a case in which Party 1, as an offshoot of its normal research activity, has originated and made substantial investment in a promising new development, which, however, is finally seen to lie outside the company's projected field of business interest. The values which Party 1 holds at this point may include, for example, a stock of semideveloped equipment, considerable process technology, relevant computer programs, etc. In such a case, the indicated procedure may well be to offer the project in its then state of development to another company (Party 2) whose lines of specialization it seems to fit.

If this is the course of action decided upon, all the problems of tentative evaluation explored in Illustrations 1 through 3 will be present, but others will be added by (1) the substantial investment which Party 1 must seek to recoup and (2) the still contingent issue of the development's real value to Party 2. Because of factor (1) in particular, there may be a need to visualize more fully than in the earlier illustrations the situation which will exist if, after initial evaluation and possible development effort under an agreement entered into by Party 2, that party becomes discouraged and wishes to bring its commitments to an end. At this point, there may still be substantial residual values to be disposed of, and any agreements to be entered into with Party 2 should, therefore, make contingent provision for their disposition. In such a context, the negotiators for Parties 1 and 2 may usefully consider a three-part program having the following ingredients:

(1) A Preliminary Evaluation Agreement involving a skeletal disclosure only;

(2) A Second Stage Evaluation Agreement which will permit Party 2 to receive access to all technical information of Party 1, with an associated option, exercisable upon suitable consideration to acquire possession of (or at least complete access to) equipment and accumulated records of Party 1 for purposes of secondary testing; and

(3) A Final Evaluation Agreement specifying the options whose existence is desired if the secondary testing provided for under (2) persuades Party 2 that it wishes to attempt commercial development of the subject process or project.

Parts (1) and (2) of the suggested program could easily be developed from details of Illustration 1 of this section, substituting an option to acquire possession of equipment and records for the licensing option which that illustration provides. The elements of commercial testing are not covered in Illustration 1, however, nor are the problems connected with the reversionary interests which will arise if the ultimate results of such testing are unfavorable. These matters would become the crucial elements of the Final Evaluation Agreement and might well include items such as the following:[10]

FINAL EVALUATION AGREEMENT

ARTICLE I

"AFORESAID INVENTIONS" means the inventions identified by this term in the Second Stage Evaluation Agreement.

ARTICLE IV

For a period of three years following exercise of the option provided for in the Second Stage Evaluation Agreement, Party 2 will continuously assign at least _____ men to study and evaluate the XYZ

---

[10]It will be recognized that key provisions only are set forth. "Boiler plate" and other conventional paragraphs are omitted in order to highlight the less commonly encountered aspects of a complex technological transaction of the type being dealt with.

Process and will commit not less than _____ Hundred Thousand Dollars a year to the evaluation process.

ARTICLE VII

At any time prior to termination of the three year period specified in Article IV, Party 1 will, upon payment to it by Party 2 of the sum of _____ Hundred Thousand Dollars, assign to Party 2 full right, title, and interest in and to the AFORESAID INVENTIONS, including patents and applications thereon, subject to terms and conditions hereafter set forth.

Following the assignment by Party 1 to Party 2 of the AFORESAID INVENTIONS in accordance with this Article VII, Party 2 will be considered released from the provisions of the Second Stage Evaluation Agreement with respect to holding in confidence technical information of Party 1.

There would, of course, be included in the Final Evaluation Agreement any desired provisions for royalty and other payments to Party 1—beyond the payment specified in Article VII—for the rights acquired by Party 2. In addition, if it is an underlying objective of the total arrangement that Party 1 shall receive the financial benefits from its original development which would result from its widest possible use in the industry to which it pertains, provisions of the following type might also be appropriate:

ARTICLE XII

LICENSES TO OTHERS

Party 2 represents that it intends to establish and maintain an effective program of licensing others to manufacture products of the XYZ process with the objective of achieving maximum financial return under the AFORESAID INVENTIONS. As further consideration for the assignment of the AFORESAID INVENTIONS, Party 2 agrees to make payments to Party 1 in respect to products manufactured in accordance with the XYZ process under licenses granted by Party 2, either at the rate of one half of one percent (½ of 1%) of the licensee's net selling price, or in the amount of fifty percent (50%) of all royalties and other sums collected from licensees, whichever shall assure Party 1 of the larger payment. As used in this Article XII, the "net selling price" shall be defined as in Article _____ of this agreement. Any payment due Party 1 in accordance with this Article XII shall be reported to Party 1 concurrently with the report provided for in Article _____.

ARTICLE XIII

REASSIGNMENT UNDER A CONDITION SUBSEQUENT

If, by a date four (4) years from the date of assignment to it of the AFORESAID INVENTIONS, Party 2 shall have failed to establish an effective licensing program with respect to the patents on such INVENTIONS, Party 1 shall have the right at any time during the continuance of such failure, at its election, to require reassignment of such patents to it.

Establishment of an effective licensing program may be demonstrated by Party 2 by its showing (1) that licenses have in fact been granted to one (1) major company in the U.S.A. other than Party 2 which is qualified to produce products of the XYZ process, or (2) that licenses have been generally offered to the appropriate industry in the U.S.A. at terms designed to encourage the widespread use of the AFORESAID INVENTIONS throughout such industry.

In the event Party 1 shall, under the circumstances stated in the first paragraph of this Article XIII require reassignment to it of the AFORESAID INVENTIONS, Party 2 shall be granted as an incident to such reassignment a nonexclusive license to continue its manufacture of contract products, subject to continuance of payment in respect thereto as specified in Article _____ hereof. In addition Party 1 shall, at the time of such reassignment and in recognition of the investment in development of processes and apparatus to which Party 2 is committed under this agreement, pay to Party 2 the sum of _____ Dollars.

ARTICLE XIV

SALE TO OTHERS

Any assignment, sale, or license by Party 2 of the AFORESAID INVENTIONS to a third party shall be on terms which preserve the right of Party 1 to receive payments and other benefits as provided in this agreement. Any purported assignment, sale, or license in violation of the terms of the preceding sentence shall be void and of no effect.

The agreement provisions set out in the several articles above are patently fragmentary and incomplete. They are offered solely on the ground that the basic pattern which they introduce can be varied and expanded with the aid of other materials in this book to meet the needs of a contracting situation which arises from premises broadly resembling those of this Illustration 4.

21.05 Definition of the Field of Technical Values to Be Dealt With

In all preceding parts of this chapter, it has been assumed that the subject matter to be bought or sold was well defined within the minds of the respective negotiators. This is an unrealistic assumption, and it is important for the contract drafter to recognize it as such when he approaches the task of specifying the metes and bounds of unpatented technology which is to be sold or otherwise transferred. Everything which is to be said on this subject has retroactive application to the final literary resolution of the patterns of contracting described under Section 21.04.

In an agreement providing for transfer of technical information, it is easy to produce a statement of scope which is adequately broad (e.g., "The Universe and Other Things"). It will be found, however, that a scope definition which is unduly extensive serves neither the interests of the supplier of information nor those of its recipient.

From the standpoint of the supplier, the vice of an excessive scope of wording is that it commits him indefinitely, that is, without adequate delineation of the limits of his obligation to deliver. From the recipient's viewpoint, there is a similar problem of uncertainty as to what he is going to receive, plus an even more serious uncertainty as to the magnitude of the obligations he may be assuming with respect to protection of the received information.

To analyze this problem more concretely, let us postulate an overly simplified agreement drawn generally in the following terms. (Such agreements *have* been entered into.)

AGREEMENT

1. A agrees to furnish to B all information in his possession relating to A's refrigeration cycle apparatus.

2. B agrees to pay royalties to A at the rate of X percent on all apparatus manufactured by him which is based on the information received from A.

3. B will under no circumstances disclose to others any of the aforesaid information nor will he use such information for purposes other than the manufacture of refrigeration cycle apparatus for heavy duty commercial applications.

When A undertakes compliance with an agreement such as that of paragraph 1, he will obviously find considerable difficulty in deciding when he has reached the limit of his commitment. What about background materials accumulated by A in the course of his development efforts related to refrigeration cycle apparatus? Or what about informal records as distinguished from finished work pieces? Clearly, from A's standpoint paragraph 1 cannot really mean exactly what it says.

But from B's standpoint, is the matter in any more satisfactory position? Suppose he receives from A, in purported full discharge of A's obligations, a small packet of informal documents describing A's theoretical work on refrigeration cycle apparatus in general terms but containing little if any data on manufacturing specifications. Shall he sue for specific performance and, if so, in what terms? Or, alternatively, if he accepts what he receives, and undertakes design engineering which leads him to a production model differing widely from A's proposed constructions, how far is he still bound by the provisions of paragraph 2? Or of paragraph 3?

The real problems of the parties have obviously not been satisfactorily anticipated by the contract drafter (or negotiator) responsible for our hypothetical agreement. It is an object of this section to point out possibilities for doing a more complete job.

It may first be observed, of course, that the obligations of paragraphs 2 and 3 need not be predicated upon the same information base as is established in paragraph 1. Indeed, each of the three paragraphs may require its own set of antecedent definitions. The several sides of the problem will be looked at in what follows.

The approach to be taken naturally depends upon the subject matter with which the contract negotiation is concerned. If the matter in discussion is a fully developed product (for example, an apparatus already being marketed by Party 1), the parameters may be quite definite and specific. On the other hand, if the situation under consideration involves an embryonic development, not yet ready for the market place, exact and complete description will naturally be more difficult. It will facilitate a logical development of the subject to consider this last problem first.

Illustration 1

Assume that Party 1 is an independent inventor who represents that he has developed an FM stereo receiver of greatly improved stability and who has demonstrated to Party 2 on a "black box" basis a prototype which satisfies Party 2 of the substantial accuracy of the inventor's claims. Patentability is an unknown quantity, so that initial discussions must proceed on the basis of purchase of "technical information" with patent rights to be included on a when, as, and if basis. The following paragraphs outline the principal provisions of a type of agreement arguably suitable in this situation.

1. The term "Glensmith Receiver" means an FM stereo receiver which (i) has performance characteristics matching those of the prototype receiver demonstrated by Party 1 to Party 2 at the meeting of the parties held at the Claridge Hotel in Detroit, Michigan, on January 20, 1981 (as such characteristics are recorded in the mutually accepted "Memorandum" of that meeting dated January 21, 1981) and (ii) is based upon designs originated by Party 1 and incorporated in the prototype receiver.

2. Party 1 represents that he is in position to supply:

(a) A complete written explanation of the design and operation theory of the Glensmith Receiver,

(b) Drawings and specifications of all parts of the Glensmith Receiver, including materials and tolerances, of such nature as to permit an accurate manufacturing cost analysis to be made,

(c) Assembly drawings and description of assembly techniques of Glensmith Receivers, and

(d) Drawings and written descriptions of any special machinery, jigs, fixtures, molds, and machine tools, insofar as developed to the date of this agreement, for making or assembling parts for the Glensmith Receiver or for testing such Receivers.

3. "Technical Information" means the items specified in subparagraphs (a) through (d) of paragraph 2 of this agreement.

4. "Proprietary Information of Party 1" means that content of Technical Information furnished by Party 1 which has been originated by or is peculiarly within the knowledge of Party 1 and is subject to protection under recognized legal principles, provided that no element of

Technical Information shall be considered Proprietary Information after any date on which

(a) It appears in issued patents or printed publications or is shown to be in the public domain for reasons other than breach of this agreement by Party 2,

(b) Party 2 can show by written records that such Information was in its possession prior to disclosure to it by Party 1 under this agreement or has legally come into its possession through channels independent of Party 1, or

(c) It has been in the hands of Party 2 for more than five (5) years without becoming the claimed subject matter of a United States Patent taken out in the name of Party 1.

5. Party 1 agrees to furnish Party 2, with certification of completeness, all Technical Information (as defined) of Party 1 within sixty (60) days of the date of this agreement.

6. Party 2 agrees to pay Party 1 the sum of _____ Thousand Dollars within thirty (30) days after receipt by it of all Technical Information to be furnished by Party 1 under paragraph 5 of this agreement.

7. Party 2 further agrees to pay to Party 1 the royalties hereinafter specified on each Glensmith Receiver manufactured by it during the period terminating ten (10) years from the date of this agreement, provided that no such payments shall be made in respect to receivers manufactured after two years from the date of this agreement which as of the time of manufacture, do not either

(a) Embody significant elements of Proprietary Information as defined, or

(b) Infringe claims of an issued but unexpired patent taken out in the name of Party 1.

8. In respect to Proprietary Information of Party I, Party 2 will use every reasonable effort to keep such information confidential, but shall not be liable for unauthorized disclosures of such information by its employees.

9. *(Other provisions of the agreement would specify the exclusivity of the rights extended to Party 2 (insofar as exclusivity is intended), consulting services of Party 1, if desired, and conventional provisions respecting royalties, accounting, termination, etc.)*

It is not the authors' intention to recommend the "black box" disclosure approach as a suitable basis for negotiation (except in the most extraordinary case) nor to suggest that the agreement outline given above provides an escape from all the pitfalls of such a negotiation. The outline is offered merely to show that the most skeletal negotiating base can be given considerable specificity in its documentation if a close look is taken at the probable interests of the parties. Certainly, with all its defects, the expanded outline under discussion gives the parties a more reliable definition of their commitments than the elementary provisions postulated on page 193. To argue whether the particular outline is too heavily weighted on one side or the other would be beside the point.

We are, of course, on sounder ground when we come to consider the case in which the subject matter of a proposed information transfer is already well defined by the existence of a marketable product to which the information pertains. In this case we have only to consider alternatives among many available treatments. The following illustrations will serve better than a textual exegesis.

Illustration 2

Factual Background. Party 1 is an established manufacturer of small engines, which it produces in a variety of types. Party 2 wishes to purchase information sufficient to enable it to produce a corresponding line of engines. The business posture is such that Party 1 is willing to sell this information. The parties agree on the following contract provisions as establishing the scope of the information and other technical values to be transferred.

AGREEMENT

1. The term "engine models" as used hereinafter in this agreement shall mean engines of the types identified as of the date of this agreement, by the model designations set forth below:

5BBY9, 5BA10, 5BBY13, 5BN14, 5PD14, 5PY14, 5PG18, 5PY18, 5BBY18 and 5BBY10 (but excluding 5BBY10GJP and 5BBY10FJ19).

2. Party 1 will, within thirty (30) days of the date of this agreement, supply Party 2 with one reproducible copy of all model lists, outline specifications, winding specifications, related drawings, parts lists, and planning cards which relate to engine models within the designations set forth in paragraph 1 to the extent that such lists, specifications, drawings, and planning cards are available to Party 1 on the date of this Agreement, and in the condition that they then exist and to the extent only that they relate to engines which have been manufactured during the year preceding the date of the Agreement in the Detroit plant of Party 1. Party 1 shall also furnish detailed material specifications in those instances in which the satisfactory performance of the engine is dependent upon the use of special materials manufactured by or for Party 1. Party 1 need not furnish detailed specifications for noncritical materials which are referred to on lists and drawings, but if it elects not to do so, it will furnish the closest equivalent commercial specification or sufficient information to enable Party 2 to order such materials.

3. Party 1 will sell to Party 2 certain special dies, fixtures, and patterns in its possession on the date of this Agreement which are utilized in the manufacture of said engine types and which cannot be applied to the production of any engines other than said engine types. Such special dies, fixtures, and patterns and the prices to be charged for them are set forth in Appendix A attached hereto and made a part hereof.

4. With respect to the items set forth in paragraph 3 hereof, which are to be sold by Party 1 to Party 2, Party 1 makes no representations of any kind as to the condition, or suitability for use, of any of such items, it being expressly understood that all such items are sold on an

"as-is" basis, and that Party 2 will undertake to inspect and use such items only in reliance on its own inspection.

5. (*The agreement includes further provisions as required to cover any patent rights involved and the compensation to be paid to Party 1 for the values conveyed.*)

Illustration 3

The degree of elaboration in describing the information to be transferred and the means to be employed in its transfer obviously depend heavily upon the complexity of the technology to which the agreement pertains. For example, in connection with an agreement covering a complete electrical power generating system the following "checklist" type of outline might be appropriate.

I. For purposes of the Agreement, POWER SYSTEMS TECHNICAL INFORMATION includes:

1. POWER SYSTEM scope and arrangement drawings prepared by Party 1.

2. Outline drawings, procurement specifications and quality standards for COMPONENTS procured by Party 1 from its outside suppliers.

3. Procedures used and results obtained in final acceptance tests of COMPONENTS coming within the scope of subsection 2, above.

4. Engineering specifications and drawings, including assembly drawings and detailed drawings of individual parts and quality standards for any COMPONENTS manufactured by Party 1.

5. Procedures used and results obtained in final acceptance tests of COMPONENTS coming within the scope of subsection 4, above.

6. Specifications for materials specified by Party 1 in procurement or used by Party 1 in manufacture of COMPONENTS referred to in subsections 2 and 4, above.   ———

7. POWER SYSTEMS operator training procedures.

8. Operating and maintenance manuals for POWER SYSTEMS.

9. Procedures for and results of preoperations tests, proceeding-to-power tests and warranty tests of COMPONENTS and POWER SYSTEMS.

II. In addition to the information specified in Section I, above, POWER SYSTEMS TECHNICAL INFORMATION further includes:

1. Design and analytical engineering criteria, procedures, practices, and techniques other than computer information; the design calculations; the physics, thermodynamic and hydrodynamic data; and results of development tests; all to the extent embodied as of the date of this agreement in formal Technical Reports of Party 1 and directly used by Party 1 in the design, construction, or startup of a POWER SYSTEM of a type within the scope of this agreement.

2. Computer information in the form of programs in application programming language and the user's manual for such programs, directly used by Party 1 in the design, construction, or startup of a POWER SYSTEM within the scope of this agreement.

III. For purposes of this agreement, POWER SYSTEMS TECHNICAL INFORMATION still further includes SPECIAL MANUFACTURING INFORMATION, as follows:

1. Descriptions of manufacturing methods, inspection procedures, quality control plans, manufacturing equipment, and production test equipment, which INFORMATION is in actual use by Party 1 in its own manufacturing operations in respect to POWER SYSTEMS within the scope of this agreement.

IV.

1. POWER SYSTEMS TECHNICAL INFORMATION to be furnished by Party 2 under this agreement shall be supplied as two (2) typewritten or printed copies or reproductions thereof of each report, specification, drawing procedure, or any other documentary and graphic materials incorporating such TECHNICAL INFORMATION.

2. Party 1 shall not be obligated either to

(a) Modify any POWER SYSTEMS TECHNICAL INFORMATION in any way from the form in which it was produced by and used by Party 1 in its production of POWER SYSTEMS

or

(b) Reduce to documentary or graphic form technical information not already in such form when used by Party 1 in its work on POWER SYSTEMS.

Party 1 will, however, furnish Party 2 technical information falling under subparagraph (b) of this paragraph 2 as "CONSULTING SERVICES" under and subject to the terms and conditions of Article X.

An agreement of this degree of complexity obviously requires clear provisions concerning the time of supply of information, the mechanism of transmission, and if not covered in the broader compensation provisions of the agreement, an indication how the costs of preparing information-conveying materials are to be borne. An exemplary provision covering the methodology of supplying information is as follows:

X. Within _____days after final execution of this agreement, Party 1 will furnish Party 2 all TECHNICAL INFORMATION required under the terms of Articles I through V. With the delivery of such INFORMATION, Party 1 will furnish in duplicate to Party 2 a list completely identifying the INFORMATION furnished. Within _____days after receiving such list, Party 2 will return one copy of the list to Party 1, on which it will have written an acknowledgment of receipt of items actually received, with appropriate indication of items, if any, which may have been inadvertently omitted.

21.06 Responsibility of the Supplier of Information; Disclaimers and Reservations

While the outcome is largely a negotiating matter, it is in the interest of both parties that there be no misunderstanding concerning the responsibility (or lack of it) on the part of the supplier for the adequacy of the supplied information for the purposes for which it is intended.[11] The following rather broad disclaimer of responsibility may serve as a useful starting point for determining exactly how the

---

[11]For an extended comment on "Implied Warranties in Patent, Know-How and Technical Assistance Licensing Agreements," *see* 56 CAL. L. REV. 168 (1969).

burdens of responsibility should be split between the supplier and acquirer of information in a particular case.

> X. PARTY 1 REPRESENTS THAT THE MATERIAL LISTS, DRAWINGS, SPECIFI-
> CATIONS, INSTRUCTIONS, AND OTHER ELEMENTS OF "TECHNICAL INFOR-
> MATION" TO BE SUPPLIED BY IT UNDER THIS AGREEMENT HAVE BEEN USED
> BY IT IN THE MANUFACTURE OF POWER SYSTEMS, BUT DOES NOT OTHER-
> WISE WARRANT THE ACCURACY OF THIS INFORMATION; NOR DOES PARTY
> 1 WARRANT THAT POWER SYSTEMS PRODUCED IN ACCORDANCE WITH SUCH
> INFORMATION WILL BE FREE FROM CLAIMS OF INFRINGEMENT OF THE PAT-
> ENTS OR COPYRIGHTS OF ANY THIRD PARTY. PARTY 1 SHALL NOT, EXCEPT
> AS PROVIDED IN THIS ARTICLE X, BE UNDER ANY LIABILITY ARISING OUT
> OF THE SUPPLYING OF INFORMATION UNDER, IN CONNECTION WITH, OR AS
> A RESULT OF THIS CONTRACT, WHETHER ON WARRANTY, CONTRACT, NEG-
> LIGENCE, OR OTHERWISE.

An alternative approach to a disclaimer of liability is provided by the following in a situation in which goods (COMPONENTS) are being transferred to the licensee:

> X. PARTY 1 WARRANTS THAT THE "TECHNICAL INFORMATION" FURNISHED
> OR TO BE FURNISHED UNDER THIS AGREEMENT WILL BE THE SAME AS THAT
> USED IN THE DESIGN, PRODUCTION, INSTALLATION, AND MAINTENANCE OF
> POWER SYSTEMS PRODUCED IN ITS OWN FACTORIES AND THAT ANY "COM-
> PONENTS" SOLD BY PARTY 1 TO PARTY 2 UNDER THE PROVISIONS OF ARTICLE
> _____ WILL CARRY THE SAME WARRANTY AS TO MATERIAL AND WORKMAN-
> SHIP AS WHEN SOLD BY PARTY 1 TO OTHER COMMERCIAL CUSTOMERS. THE
> FOREGOING WARRANTIES ARE IN LIEU OF ALL OTHER WARRANTIES, EX-
> PRESSED OR IMPLIED, AND IT IS EXPRESSLY AGREED THAT PARTY 1 SHALL
> NOT BE LIABLE, NOR IN ANY WAY RESPONSIBLE FOR, AND MAKES NO REP-
> RESENTATIONS OR WARRANTIES WHATSOEVER IN RESPECT TO OPERATION,
> PERFORMANCE, SERVICEABILITY, QUALITY OF PERFORMANCE OF MATERIAL
> IN CONNECTION WITH POWER SYSTEMS MANUFACTURED BY PARTY 2. UNDER
> NO CIRCUMSTANCES SHALL PARTY 2 BE LIABLE FOR CONSEQUENTIAL DAM-
> AGES.[12]

In a case in which the subject matter of contract is viewed as developmental by both parties (as when, for example, the objective of the contract is to enable Party 2 to evaluate, from the standpoint of its interest in acquiring further rights, technical values which are being offered for such evaluation by Party 1), a provision of the following kind might be useful and in accordance with the intention of the parties.

> X. The information and consultation to be furnished to Party 2 under
> this agreement are for the use of Party 2 in conducting its own devel-

---

[12]Disclaimers of the implied warranty of merchantability or fitness for a particular use, in any way connected to the sale of goods, should be conspicuous (preferably in all capital letters) to be effective. U.C.C. §2–316 (1978). Also, to disclaim the implied warranty of merchantability, merchantability must be specifically mentioned. This example does not attempt to disclaim the implied warranty of merchantability with respect to COMPONENTS.

opment and production programs. Party 1 makes no representations, and assumes no responsibilities whatever with respect to the use, sale, or other disposition by Party 2 or any other person of products or processes employing INFORMATION furnished under this agreement or with respect to any infringement of patents of third parties by use of such INFORMATION. Party 2 agrees to hold Party 1 harmless against all liabilities, demands, damages, expenses, or losses arising out of use by Party 2, or by third parties acquiring through Party 2, of any materials or INFORMATION furnished under this agreement, and, if requested, to defend Party 1 against any and all claims arising out of such use.

It is occasionally desirable (or necessary) that the prospective supplier of information avoid obligating himself with respect to information which he himself may hold subject to restrictions on its use. In this connection, the need for reservations such as the following should be considered:

> XI. Party I shall not be required to furnish information in any case in which such action would be contrary to
>   (a) Any law, rule, or regulation of any agency or branch of the United States Government;
>   (b) Any legal obligation to a third party.

21.07 Limitations and Restrictions on the Conduct of the Recipient of Transferred Information; Abnegation of Restrictions

Consistent with the viewpoint stated in footnote 1 of this chapter, this writing takes no position concerning the propriety, under present or future law, of limitations or restrictions imposed by the transferor of "proprietary information" on the use of such information by the transferee. The classical doctrine has been that limitations which are "ancillary" to the purposes of the covering agreement are supportable. Under the aegis of that doctrine, specific limitations have been supported and indeed have been construed as implying negative covenants to avoid their breach.[13]

---

[13]*See, e.g.*, Aktiebolaget Bofors v. United States, 153 F. Supp. 397, 114 USPQ 243 (Ct. Cl. 1957). In this case, the U.S. government obtained the drawings of the Bofors gun under a contract which licensed the government to have the gun manufactured in the United States "for the United States' use." Subsequent to execution of the agreement, Bofors guns manufactured in the United States were exported for use by our foreign allies. Bofors sued for breach of contract. The court held that under the language of the contract and considering the circumstances and statements of the parties during the course of the negotiations, the government had not obtained a license to export, but, on the contrary, *had "by necessary implication," agreed that it would not export*. On this basis it found liability for the exportation that had actually occurred.

In a patent license agreement in which the license is for a limited purpose and the parties wish to deny any obligation of the licensee to avoid activity outside the scope of the license (subject only to assumption of the risk of suit for patent infringement in respect to such activity), this may be done in one way by language such as the following:

> X. This agreement imposes on Licensee no obligation, express or implied, of forbearance from activities outside the scope of the license granted, provided, however, that no rights are granted by this Article X or otherwise in respect to such activities under any patents of Licensor.

Where there are no patent values, however, and where all rights of limitation, if any arise from the proprietary technical values transferred, the proviso of the above clause would obviously be useless to the licensor. He must, therefore, rely on affirmative limitation of the use rights granted if he is to avoid the possibility that a particular transaction will in all respects destroy his property values in the technology in question.

Where this is the case and where the parties agree that use limitation is reasonably ancillary to the purposes of this agreement, a clause such as the following may be considered:

> Licensee shall not at any time prior to _____ years from _____, without the written consent of Licensor, use for any purpose other than the manufacture of widgets, or in any place other than its plant in Detroit, proprietary information supplied to it hereunder, or communicate such proprietary information to persons other than its employees. After said _____ years shall have elapsed, nothing in this agreement shall be deemed to prevent the use or communication by Licensee for any purpose of such proprietary information which it then lawfully possesses.

As is suggested by footnote 1 of this chapter, the supportability against legal attack of a provision such as that just offered very possibly will depend, among other things, upon the provable existence of classically proprietary content in the information involved and upon the reasonableness, in context, of the duration of the restrictions imposed.

In respect to both these matters, the position of the supplier of the information might be improved (and the position of the user of the information be made more comfortable) by the inclusion in the agreement (with intentions of good-faith administration by the supplier) of a supplementary provision of the following type:

> XI. At the end of one year from the date of this agreement, and at the end of each year thereafter, the Licensor will review its files of proprietary information supplied to Licensee under this agreement and within ninety (90) days after the end of such year notify Licensee in writing of the items of information no longer to be regarded as proprietary after the date of the notice.

From the licensee's standpoint, annual notification of items *still considered proprietary* might be preferable, but commitment to a notification in this form would obviously increase the licensor's burdens very materially.

21.08 Consequences of Early Termination of a Know-How Agreement

Termination of a patent license agreement by the licensor as a consequence of some default by the licensee ordinarily invokes provisions of the agreement which revoke the licenses granted. Such termination thus tends to restore the licensor to his original position with regard to his power to exclude the licensee from practice of the licensed inventions.

The case is not as simple, however, in respect to an agreement in which the rights conveyed pertain wholly or mainly to the use of information (trade secrets or know-how) disclosed to the licensee. In such a situation, nothing can wholly restore the grantor to a condition of exclusive possession of the once-disclosed information. In addition, both practical and legal considerations militate against too extravagant an attempt to prohibit all further use of the information by the terminated licensee. On the one hand, to the extent the information is capable of retention in the memory of individuals, their possession of it is realistically ineradicable. On the other hand, the presumption that most information, unless of highly esoteric quality, can be privately recreated by reasonable effort and investment argues against any long term preclusion of the terminated licensee from the field of activity to which the information pertains.

The facts of each particular case will determine what is logically possible and legally expedient in that case. Nevertheless, consideration of the following hypothetical fact situation and the suggested treatment of it may assist the drafter of a know-how agreement in framing provisions appropriate to the particular termination problem which he has in hand.

ASSUMED FACTUAL BACKGROUND

The licensor has extensive know-how concerning the manufacture of a precision-built widget in respect to which, prior to licensing, he occupied an essentially exclusive market position. It is doubtful that any aspects of the know-how are of absolute trade-secret quality in the sense of being essentially undiscoverable by independent investigation. On the other hand, many aspects involve material specifications, dimensional tolerances, and the like which, although theoretically discoverable, could be duplicated only at considerable expense. Communication of know-how to the licensee is to be primarily by delivery of detailed drawings, material specifications, manufacturing instructions, etc. It has already been decided that the opening paragraphs of the licensing agreement will include a definition of "Technical Information" corresponding to paragraph 2 of Illustration 1, Section 21.05 of this chapter, and that "Proprietary Information" will be defined as follows:

3. "Proprietary Information of Party 1" means that content of Technical Information furnished by Party 1 which has been originated by or is peculiarly within the knowledge of Party 1 and is subject to protection under recognized legal principles, provided that no element of Technical Information shall be considered Proprietary Information after any date on which

(a) It appears in issued patents or printed publications or is shown to be in the public domain for reasons other than breach of this agreement by Party 2, or

(b) Party 2 can show by written records that such information was in its possession prior to disclosure to it by Party 1 under this agreement or has legally come into its possession through channels independent of Party 1.

Payment obligations of the licensee are specified to terminate in any event 10 years after the effective date of the agreement. The remaining question is as to the position of the parties if the agreement terminates through withdrawal or default of the licensee (or, indeed, on any other contingency recognized by the agreement) prior to the date on which the obligations of the licensee are to be considered as fully paid.

(ILLUSTRATIVE PROVISIONS RESPECTING THE CONSEQUENCES OF
AGREEMENT TERMINATION)

1. If this agreement shall be terminated under the provisions of either Article X or XI of the agreement prior to ten (10) years from its effective date, Party 2 will:

(a) Return

(i) All drawings, specifications, instructions, and other documents pertaining to the manufacture of widgets which it has received from Party 1 under the agreement, and

(ii) All copies, elaborations, modifications, and adaptations which it has made of the documents identified in clause (i) of this subparagraph (a), and

(b) For a period of two years from the date of such termination, refrain from any manufacture of widgets involving use of Proprietary Information of Party 1, as defined in this agreement.

It may be added that subsequent events, including changing legal doctrines, may dictate reevaluation of the usefulness or suitability of insisting upon compliance with termination provisions such as the foregoing when the time for their invocation arrives.

22

Foreign Patent License Agreements

On many points the format and terms of an international patent (or know-how) agreement will track those of a corresponding agreement between U.S. nationals. As to these points, the recommendations of earlier chapters of this work will, of course, apply.

On the other hand, it is likely that any country outside the United States will have at least some special legal requirements in respect to the granting or acceptance of licenses by its nationals. For this reason, it would be beyond the scope of this work to try to treat the subject of foreign licensing extensively.[1] There are, however, certain considerations which frequently present themselves in agreements for extension by a U.S. entity of patent or related rights in a foreign country. These include the following:

(1) Place of payment of royalties and determination of rates of exchange between currencies;

(2) Allocation of tax burdens;

(3) Problems of governmental approval;

(4) Requirements in respect to registration or recordation of the transaction;

(5) Observance of export laws and regulations in the United States;

(6) Terminability in the event of change in

    (a) Status of one of the parties because of governmental action, or

    (b) Exchange control regulations;

(7) Choice of applicable law;

(8) The availability of arbitration;

---

[1]For up-to-date, brief discussions of legal and practical considerations in foreign licensing on a country-by-country basis, see "Investing Licensing & Trading Abroad," a looseleaf, regularly updated publication of Business International Corporation.

(9) Applicable language.

Each of these matters requires resolution in light of the facts of the particular situation and the existing relationships (financial and otherwise) between the United States and the foreign country involved. The following brief analysis and exemplary forms are offered, therefore, only to illustrate the problems presented and to suggest directions for their treatment. It is assumed that appropriate legal, financial, and governmental counsel will be sought in respect to the disposition of problems confronted in specific cases.

22.00 Place of Payment; Rate of Exchange; Tax Burdens

The licensing party will ordinarily (but not inevitably) desire payment to be made in his home country and in the currency of that country. Moreover, where the amount to be paid is to be calculated initially in the currency of the other country, as would be true, for example, if the payments are to be royalties computed on sales in that country, then there will need to be a method prescribed for determining the equivalent amount in the currency of the licensor's country. The licensor will also want to guard against diminution of his returns by tax burdens imposed on the transaction by the country of the other party. The following are approaches to these matters found helpful in particular cases:

Alternative 1

All payments specified by this agreement shall be made in the City of New York, State of New York, in United States currency. The United States currency payments hereunder shall be determined on the basis of the official rate of exchange as determined by the _____ Bank, or equivalent governmental agency of _____, in effect on the date such payments are due. All payments due shall be made without deduction for taxes, assessments, or other charges of any kind which may be imposed on LICENSOR by the Government of _____ or any political subdivision thereof with respect to any amounts payable to LICENSOR pursuant to this agreement, and such taxes, assessments, or other charges shall be assumed by LICENSEE.

Alternative 2

Payments shall be due on the last day of each calendar quarter and shall be paid within ninety (90) days thereafter by LICENSEE to LICENSOR in New York, New York, United States of America, in United States currency without deduction for taxes, assessments, or other charges of any kind or description, except that income taxes imposed by the Government of _____ on amounts payable to LICENSOR hereunder may be deducted to the extent that such taxes are allowable as a direct credit to LICENSOR against United States income taxes levied on such amounts. The United States currency amounts payable hereunder shall be determined on the basis of the official rate of exchange applicable to each such payment on the payment date thereof, or ninety (90) days after the due date, whichever is earlier.

22.01 Problems of Governmental Approval

In some countries, balance of payment problems and other considerations of national policy lead to a requirement that any transaction involving cross-boundary payments shall receive governmental approval before it can become legally effective. Such requirements will obviously apply to any license arrangement which calls for royalty or other disbursement by a national of the affected country to a national of the United States.[2]

This problem of preliminary approval, where it exists, needs to be appropriately recognized in the covering agreement. Specifically, from the standpoint of a U.S. licensor, there should be assurance either that the required approval will be forthcoming in a reasonable time or that the offer to license shall be considered as withdrawn. This point may be covered variously as follows:

Alternative 1

This agreement shall become effective as of the date first written above provided it has been formally approved prior to that date by the competent authorities of the Government of _____. Otherwise it shall become effective as of the date of such approval. If the specified approval shall not have been obtained by _____, 19___, this agreement shall become void and of no effect.

Alternative 2

The effective date of this agreement shall be the date when the agreement, including its payment provisions, is finally validated by the Japanese Government or its appropriate agency, or when a validated li-

---

[2]In the postwar period, and until about 1980, Japan was the outstanding example of a country in which licensing practices were fully regulated by a governmental agency—in this case, the Ministry of International Trade and Industry (MITI). No Japanese patent and know-how contract, at least where significant Japanese commitments were involved, could become operative without concurrence of this agency. The Japanese model has been adapted by many developing countries.

cense is issued by the United States Government, or its appropriate agency, with respect to the export of Manufacturing Data, whichever date is later. LICENSEE shall use its best efforts to obtain validation by the Japanese Government, and LICENSOR shall use its best efforts to obtain a validated license from the United States Government, but if both validations have not been obtained by _____, 19____, this agreement shall on that date become void and of no effect.

The second of the above alternatives—with its requirement of U.S. validation—might be called for if the agreement provides for furnishing technical information of a class which requires government approval for its transmission from this country. The first alternative assumes that only a license under patents is involved or that the information to be supplied is already covered by a general export license.

22.02 Registration, Notification, or Recordation of the Transaction

The question of "registration" or of "notification" of international agreements has been brought to the fore by the adoption of new antitrust concepts, particularly in the European countries. The desire to control unduly restrictive practices has now attained powerful statutory force, especially in the 1957 Law Against Restraints of Competition in Germany and in the Common Market Antitrust Law of 1962. One mechanism of control involves an invitation for "notification" to an appropriate agent (in the case of the European Economic Community, its "Commission") of any agreement respecting which it is desired to obtain an opinion concerning validity under the applicable antitrust law. A simple patent license agreement presumably raises no questions which would make such "notification" desirable, but the inclusion in the agreement of price, territorial, or other significant restrictions on the licensee's freedom of action might well make expedient an attempt at advance clearance.

The variability of the demands of the various countries and the changeability of the applicable law are so great that standardized treatment of the notification problem is hardly possible. Subject to the advice of appropriately specialized counsel obtained at the time of contracting, however, it may be useful to consider including in any agreement which raises questions of the need for notification a provision of the following sort:

If the terms of this agreement are such as to require or make it appropriate that the agreement or any part of it be registered with or reported to a national or supranational agency of any area in which LICENSEE will do business under the agreement, LICENSEE will, within _____ days of the effective date of the agreement, and at LICEN-

SEE'S expense, undertake such registration or report. Prompt notice and appropriate verification of the act of registration or report of any agency ruling resulting from it will be supplied by LICENSEE to LICENSOR.

Of somewhat similar concern is the requirement for recordation of certain agreements. In some cases, recording is beneficial to the licensee (e.g., as notice to third parties of the licensee's rights). Where this is all that is involved, it may be assumed, even without treatment in the contract, that all will be done that needs to be done in respect to recordation. In other cases, however (and apparently in Brazil, for example), recording may be a prerequisite to the validity and enforceability in local courts of a patent license agreement. In such a case, it might be prudent for the licensor to require that there be added to the clause previously offered in this Section 22.02 a provision such as the following:

> Any formal recordation of this agreement required by the law of _____ as a prerequisite to enforceability of the agreement in the courts of _____ or for other reasons shall also be carried out by LICENSEE at its expense, and appropriately verified proof of recordation shall be promptly furnished to LICENSOR.

22.03 Export Laws and Regulations of the United States

The export of any goods or technical data from the United States requires some form of license from the U.S. government. Although many such licenses are issued as a matter of law, other licenses, depending on the nature of the goods or technical data and on the country of import, must be specifically applied for.

The Export Administration Act of 1979,[3] as amended by the Export Administration Amendments Acts of 1981 and 1985 and the Multilateral Export Control Enhancement Amendments Act,[4] creates formidable powers in the executive agencies through which the Act is administered to control the export and the application after export of most nonmilitary goods and technical data from the United States. The object of such control is to limit the flow of such goods and data: (1) which would be detrimental to the national security of the United States; (2) which would be detrimental to the foreign policy of the United States; or (3) which, in the case of scarce materials, are in short supply in the United States.

The export of other goods and technical data is regulated by other U.S. agencies through different acts and implementing regulations.

---

[3]50 App. U.S.C. §§2401–2420 (1989).

[4]*Id.*

For example, the export of goods and technical data considered by the U.S. government to be inherently military in nature is regulated by the Department of State pursuant to the Arms Export Control Act[5] and the International Traffic in Arms Regulations.[6]

Insofar as the matter is of interest to parties engaged in licensing patents and know-how, the Export Administration Act is administered primarily by the Bureau of Export Administration of the Department of Commerce and more specifically by its Office of Export Licensing (OEL). The regulations[7] issued by OEL apply to:

(1) Export of goods and technical data from the United States;

(2) Reexports of goods which were previously exported from the United States and of U.S.-origin technical data from a foreign destination to another foreign destination;

(3) U.S.-origin parts and components used in a foreign country to manufacture a foreign end-product for export; and, in some instances,

(4) The foreign-produced direct product of U.S.-origin technical data.

As a generalization, the mere granting of licenses under issued patents requires no special clearance, nor does it require inclusion in the licensing agreement of special restrictions on the foreign licensee. Where the agreement includes technical data, however, the terms of existing U.S. regulations must be considered. Specifically, the regulations may require either: (1) a special license for transmission of the licensed information to the licensee; (2) restriction against retransmission to specified countries of the information itself or products of it; or (3) both of the foregoing. In the case of licensing agreements pertaining to goods or technology considered to be inherently military in nature, the actual agreement may be required to be submitted to the Department of State for prior approval.

Point (1), where it is relevant, will, of course, be taken care of by obtaining (in prescribed form) advance governmental approval of the proposed commitment to transmit information to the licensee. Point (2), however, will involve inclusion in the agreement itself of appropriate commitments by the licensee. As of the date of this writing, the following alternative provisions may be considered illustrative of the commitments which are required under the Export Administration Act:

---

[5]22 U.S.C. §2778 (1989).

[6]22 C.F.R. §§120–130 (1989).

[7]15 C.F.R. §§768–799.2 (1989).

Alternative 1

Regulations of the United States Department of Commerce prohibit, except under an individual validated license, the exportation from the United States of technical data relating to certain commodities unless the exporter (Licensor) has received certain written assurances from the foreign importer. So that Licensor can fulfill the requirements of these regulations, Licensee hereby gives its assurance that Licensee will not, without prior authorization of the United States Office of Export Licensing, knowingly:

1. With respect to any technical data received from Licensor relating to commodities identified by the symbol "W" in the corresponding entry of the Export Administration Regulations ("EAR") Commodity Control List (15 C.F.R. §799.1, Supplement 1) under the paragraph titled "Validated License Required," reexport such technical data, directly or indirectly, to Country Group Q, S, W, Y, or Z as defined in the EAR (15 C.F.R. §770, Supplement 1) or to Afghanistan or the People's Republic of China without prior authorization from the Office of Export Licensing, United States Department of Commerce. Licensee will not knowingly export, directly or indirectly, any "direct product" of such technical data to Country Group Z as defined in the EAR without prior authorization from the Office of Export Licensing, United States Department of Commerce; or

2. With respect to the "direct products" as defined in the EAR of any technical data received from Licensor, which "direct products" are identified by the code letter "A" following the Export Commodity Control Number for those "direct products" in the EAR Commodity Control List, export, directly or indirectly, any such direct products of such technical data to Country Groups Q, S, W, or Y, as defined in the EAR, or Afghanistan or the People's Republic of China, without prior authorization from the Office of Export Licensing, United States Department of Commerce.

Alternative 2

1. The Export Administration Regulations of the United States Department of Commerce prohibit, except under an individual validated license, the exportation from the United States of technical data relating to certain commodities (listed in the Export Administration Regulations), unless the exporter (Licensor) has received certain written assurances from the foreign importer. Licensee has advised Licensor that it has received a copy of the current Export Administration Regulations of the United States Department of Commerce and has arranged for a subscription under which it will receive Supplementary Bulletins from the United States Department of Commerce upon their issuance. Licensee hereby agrees to comply with the Export Administration Regulations of the United States Department of Commerce and hereby gives to Licensor the assurances called for in Part 779.4 of the Export Administration Regulations.

2. This Agreement shall be subject to all United States Government laws and regulations now or hereafter applicable to the subject matter of the Agreement.

The policy of the United States is constantly changing with respect to the matters dealt with in this section and each situation must be carefully considered to determine exactly which regulations apply. For this reason, neither of the alternatives stated above is recommended for unchecked application in a particular contract. Their form will, however, indicate the nature of the problems involved and should be helpful in guiding the drafter to the kind of updating inquiry which ought to be addressed to the Office of Export Licensing of the Department of Commerce.[8]

22.04 Termination Because of Change of Status of One Party or Because of Modified Exchange Regulations

An agreement between nationals of different countries which is seen as mutually advantageous to both parties at the time of execution may be relatively less advantageous to one party if the government of the other party takes certain actions. Such actions might, for example, (i) change the ownership or basic character of the other party or (ii) modify exchange regulations in a way which adversely affects the financial interests of the first party.

These possibilities, where they are foreseen as such, can be at least partially guarded against by provisions such as the following:

A. Either party may, immediately upon notice, terminate this agreement in its entirety or with respect to any patent license granted under the agreement if:
    (1) Such termination is necessary to comply with an order or official request of the government of the terminating party, or
    (2) Normal conduct of the business of the other party as a private enterprise ceases or is substantially altered as a consequence of action taken by governmental or other authority.
B. LICENSOR may, immediately upon notice, terminate this agreement in its entirety or with respect to any license or right granted by it under the agreement if by law or regulation of the government of _____, LICENSEE is disabled from making the payments to LICENSOR which it is required to make under the agreement, and such disability continues for more than ninety (90) days.

It will be apparent that protective provisions of the kind outlined above cannot, against hostile action of the government of the licensee's home country, make the licensor whole in all respects. That is to say, technical information already imported can hardly be reclaimed or its further use precluded, and the continued practice of

---

[8]The authors acknowledge with appreciation the assistance of John M. Romary and William H. Pratt in updating Section 22.03.

licensed inventions may not be preventable in the face of contrary governmental pressure on the licensee. Termination under the circumstances visualized in this Section 22.04 will, therefore, be effective primarily to end the licensor's obligation to supply continuing technical information or other services where these are called for by the agreement.

22.05 Choice of Applicable Law

Selection of applicable law in connection with an agreement between U.S. nationals has been discussed in Section 16.02 of Chapter 16. Some of the considerations mentioned in that section are directly relevant to international agreements, but some differentiating considerations also apply.

There is perhaps even less certainty in respect to foreign licenses than in respect to domestic licenses that the forum in which litigation eventually occurs will permit itself to be bound by the choice of the parties in respect to the law to be applied. Moreover, while the U.S. licensor will probably instinctively favor recourse to the law of his home country, it is by no means certain that this will be most advantageous to him if litigation actually arises. Particularly where the assets available for paying a claim of the licensor are located exclusively in the home country of the other party, there may be value in choosing to rely on the law of that country. Indeed, because of the uncertainty of the context in which a legal issue will arise, an argument can be made in many cases for letting the agreement remain silent both as to applicable law and choice of forum.[9] Under such a choice, the forum for adjudication of a specific issue can be selected on the basis of logical (and available) jurisdiction at the time, and the applicable law will be determined by "conflict of law" principles which that forum conventionally applies. However the forum is selected, it is broadly true, as one writer has remarked, that the practical rule concerning applicable law is that "if the particular forum likes the law selected by the parties, it is enforced, otherwise the forum finds a legal basis for not applying it."

Where, in spite of the doubts concerning effectiveness expressed immediately above, an "applicable law" clause is to be included, it may be generally in the following form:

> This agreement and the relationships between the parties shall be governed in all respects by the law of the State of _____, United States of America, except that questions affecting the construc-

---

[9] 58 TRADE-MARK REP. 13, 15 (1968).

tion and effect of any patent shall be determined by the law of the country in which the patent has been granted.

22.06 Arbitration

Because of the applicable law difficulties suggested in the preceding section, it is relatively common in international agreements to provide for arbitration of all issues or of predefined issues that may arise. Section 16.03 of Chapter 16 suggests recourse to the International Chamber of Commerce in such matters and provides a contract clause usable for this purpose.

The United Nations Convention of June 10, 1958 on the Recognition and Enforcement of Foreign Arbitral Awards was ratified by the United States in 1968. The instrument of ratification was deposited at the United Nations on September 30, 1970, after an implementing statute[10] (Public Law 91-368) had been enacted on July 31, 1970. The Convention and the U.S. statute just referred to establish the enforceability of agreements to arbitrate (as between citizens of countries which are adherents to the Convention) and provide for court confirmation of awards which result from such arbitrations.

22.07 Applicable Language

Where agreements are reached as the result of negotiations between nationals who speak different languages, drafts will ordinarily have been prepared in both languages and such drafts may in some cases both be formally executed. Unless these have been prepared with extraordinary care in respect to mutual translatability, it is likely that there will be differences, minor or otherwise, in their legal effects. For this reason it is customary to provide that the "official" or legally binding version shall be that execution copy which is in a particular language. The following type of clause may serve this purpose:

> In the event of controversy between the parties respecting the interpretation or application of the terms of this agreement, the English language version of the agreement shall be controlling.

If an agreement containing such a provision were later to be litigated in the country of the non-English-speaking party, there would, of course, be need to produce an agreed or appropriately certified translation of the English version. In recognition of the prob-

---

[10]9 U.S.C. §§201–208.

lems which such a situation might present, parties occasionally agree that *both* language versions shall be formally executed and that *each* shall have official status. In this event, a clause such as the following may be employed:

> This instrument of agreement has been executed by the parties in counterpart originals, one in the English language and one in the French language. Either the English or the French version may be offered in evidence by either party without objection by the other party as comprising the true and complete agreement of the parties.

Adoption of the mode of contract execution represented by the preceding clause will, of course, require that each party assure itself in advance of execution, presumably by recourse to skilled bilingual counsel, that the two agreement versions are in fact identical in meaning and effect. This may be difficult, but is probably no more difficult than the task of obtaining a judicially acceptable translation of a single language instrument which has to be litigated in the language of the other party. Indeed, it may be easier to obtain agreement as to effective identity of the two versions before controversy has arisen than to settle the accuracy of a translation prepared when the parties are in process of litigation.

22.08 Definition of Included Patent Rights

One further point that deserves attention in relation to licenses granted under foreign patents is that of appropriate definition of the patent rights intended to be included in the license grant. Particularly where the intention of the parties is to provide rights under all patent values which may pertain to a specified field of technology, thought will need to be given to the terminology by which these values are described.

A problem arises in this connection because of the differing names and conditions under which statutory protection of inventions is extended in various countries. Thus, in the United States, the term "patents" ordinarily refers to 17-year patents obtained on any "new and useful process, machine, manufacture or composition of matter, or any new and useful improvement thereof."[11] The term may, however, unless context prevents this, refer also to "design patents" (i.e., any patent on a "new, original and ornamental design for an article of manufacture"),[12] or to "plant patents."[13] In some foreign countries,

---

[11]35 U.S.C. §101.
[12]35 U.S.C. §171.
[13]35 U.S.C. §161.

on the other hand, one may additionally encounter "utility model patents" (usually short-term protection for innovations of a low level of inventiveness) and "patents of addition," which are in the nature of improvement patents limited to expire on the same date as the dominant patent to which they pertain. Russian law provides for "patents" and "inventors certificates" as alternative modes of invention protection. There are also various possibilities of renewal, reissue, and extension of patents that may need to be recognized.

For these reasons, in connection with any patent license which is to be taken or extended in a foreign country and which is intended to be comprehensive in its coverage, it may be useful to make "patents" a defined term and to provide definitions such as the following:

> PATENTS means any and all letters patent (including but not limited to patents of implementation, improvement, or addition, utility model and appearance design patents and inventors certificates, as well as divisions, reissues, continuations, renewals, and extensions of any of these), applications for letters patent, and letters patent which may issue on such applications.
>
> LICENSED PATENTS means PATENTS (as defined) which relate to inventions in or applicable to _____ and which are owned or controlled by LICENSOR during the term of this agreement, or in respect to which LICENSOR has or may acquire during the term of this agreement the right to grant licenses of the scope to be granted in Article _____ of the agreement.

This proposed definition set is obviously aimed at omnibus coverage, and the drafter must consider whether such comprehensive licensing is really intended by the parties in a given case. In particular, the inclusion of reference to "appearance design patents" might well be inappropriate where it is not intended to encourage the licensee to adopt the appearance as well as the functional features of the licensor's products. Other references may be omitted if they are inappropriate to the countries dealt with.

If the intent of the parties is to limit the patent rights to be transferred to a specific territory defined in the license agreement, express language and a schedule of licensed patents should be used to negate implications that otherwise arise. For example, in *Kabushiki Kaisha Hattori Seiko* v. *Refac Technology Development Corp.*,[14] the court held that an authorized first sale abroad by a licensee who also has the right to sell in the United States bars the licensor from obtaining an injunction or collecting royalty when a foreign customer of the licensee resells product in the United States.

---

[14]9 USPQ2d 1046 (S.D.N.Y. 1988).

APPENDIX A

Some Fundamentals of U.S. Patent Law and Practice

I. The Constitution and the Patent Statutes

Article I, Section 8, of the U.S. Constitution contains the following:

> Congress shall have power . . . To promote the Progress of Science and useful Arts, by securing for limited Times to Authors and Inventors the exclusive Right to their respective Writings and Discoveries.

Under the above constitutional provision, the Congress has from time to time passed various patent statutes, of which the most recent, enacted in 1952, has the following crucial provisions:[1]

> Whoever invents or discovers any new and useful process, machine, manufacture, or composition of matter, or any new and useful improvement thereof, may obtain a patent therefor. . . .

> Every patent shall contain . . . a grant to the patentee, his heirs or assigns, for the term of seventeen years, of the right to exclude others from making, using, or selling the invention throughout the United States. . . .

Other clauses of the law provide for the granting of "design patents" covering purely ornamental features of articles of manufacture and of "plant patents" on new and distinct varieties of plant life.

II. Basic Principles

A. A patent gives no affirmative right to practice the invention which it covers, but only the negative right to exclude others from

---

[1]35 U.S.C. §101.

practicing the invention. A patent owner's right to use the patented invention is subject at all times to possible dominant conflicting rights of others. (See IV, below.)

B. A patent can be obtained only on a specific process, machine, manufacture, or composition of matter shown to be capable of practical use. Theoretical concepts, such as the theory of relativity, and business ideas, such as the "self-service" retail concept, cannot be patented.

C. A patent is effective only for 17 years from the date of its issue. It may be extended only by special act of Congress, and, after expiration, its subject matter is freely available for use by the public (as far as that particular patent is concerned).

D. To be patentable, an invention must be sufficiently unobvious that it would not readily have occurred to the man having ordinary skill in the art to which it pertains. Mere newness is not enough.

E. A patent may not be obtained by an inventor on something patented or described in a printed publication anywhere in the world prior to his discovery of it.

F. An invention may not be patented if it has been in public use or on sale in this country or published by the inventor (or anyone else) anywhere more than one year prior to the date when an application for patent was filed.

G. A patent may not be obtained on something previously invented in this country by another who has not abandoned or suppressed his invention, as by failing to apply it usefully or by deliberately withholding its benefit from the public.

H. A patent obtained in the United States affords no rights in foreign countries. To protect the foreign situation, patents must be acquired in each country desired to be covered. Under an existing International Convention, patents may be applied for in all principal foreign countries with valuable priority benefits, if application is made within one year of the filing date of the U.S. application.

I. In most foreign countries a patent may not be obtained unless the foreign application (or the corresponding U.S. application) was filed before any public use, sale, or publication of the invention anywhere.

III. The Nature of the Patent Document; "Disclosure" and "Claims"

A. A patent is required to contain
    1. A complete disclosure of the construction and mode of use of the invention proposed to be covered; and

2. A set of claims which specifically define the particular elements of the invention believed to be new and unobvious.

B. The right to exclude others given by a patent applies only to matters within the scope of its claims and does not extend to disclosed subject matter not covered by any claim contained in the patent.

C. If all elements of a patent claim are found in an earlier existing disclosure (that is, if the claim "reads on" the disclosure), the claim is "unpatentable" or "invalid." Thus, a sufficiently early issued patent to the same or some other inventor may, by its disclosure (and without regard to its claims), bar the obtaining of desired claims in a later patent or invalidate such claims if obtained. The same is true of a sufficiently early publication (i.e., other than in a patent) or a sufficiently early public use of the invention.

D. If a claim "reads on" a construction or process originated after the claimed invention, such later construction or process infringes the claim, and, if the claim is valid, unlicensed use of the construction or process may be enjoined by court order.

E. In testing an earlier patent or publication for its invalidating effect on a later patent, compare the disclosure of the earlier with the claims of the later.

F. In testing a patent for infringement by a later construction, compare the claims of the patent with the details of the construction.

IV. Relationship of "Dominant" and "Improvement" Patents

A. A "dominant patent" is one which covers the invention of more or less basic character. An "improvement patent" is one which covers an improved way of practicing a basic invention.

B. The owner of a "dominant patent" may freely practice the unimproved version of his basic idea (unless a still more basic and "dominant" patent exists), but may not practice a version covered by an "improvement patent" owned by another without the consent of its owner.

C. The owner of an "improvement patent" may not practice his improvement without a license from the owner of the "dominant patent"—provided the latter has not reached the end of its 17-year term.

V. Procedure in Obtaining a Patent

A. A U.S. patent may be obtained only by filing a formal application in the U.S. Patent Office and only after a finding by the

Patent Office that the application discloses something which is new, useful, and unobvious.

B. A period in excess of three years may be required between the date when an application is filed and the date when a patent issues. This period is occupied by correspondence between the Patent Office and the applicant's attorney trying to reach agreement as to the proper limits of the patent. Until an application is actually "allowed" and issued as a patent, the Patent Office is obliged to keep its contents confidential. Also, until the application becomes a patent, it cannot be used to prevent use of the claimed invention by others.

VI. Use and Enforcement of Patents

A. A patent granted by the Patent Office will not necessarily be enforced by the courts. The courts have power to declare a patent invalid (and hence unenforceable) when they conclude that a mistake has been made by the Patent Office in issuing it.

B. Because of the inability of the Patent Office to make a completely exhaustive investigation concerning the novelty of a given invention, a substantial proportion of the patents which it issues and which are tested in court are found by the court to be invalid. The enforcement of every patent, therefore, requires consideration of the possibility of this result.

C. The owner of a valid patent can, for the 17 years of its life, enjoin competitors from using the patented invention or collect damages for unlicensed use of the invention.

D. As an alternative to preventing use of his patented invention by others, the patentee may, entirely at his option, license others to use the invention for an appropriate consideration.

E. Licenses may be
    a. Exclusive—which means that only one licensee is permitted to practice the invention, or
    b. Nonexclusive—which means that a number of licensees may be authorized to practice the invention concurrently.

F. Ownership of patents may be assigned in accordance with the following statutory provision:[2]

Applications for patent, patents, or any interest therein, shall be assignable in law by an instrument in writing. The applicant, patentee, or his assigns or legal representatives may in like manner grant and convey an exclusive right under his application for patent, or patents to the whole or any specified part of the United States.

---

[2]35 U.S.C. §261.

G. Joint ownership of patents is recognized and is made subject to the following statutory provision:[3]

> In the absence of any agreement to the contrary, each of the joint owners of a patent may make, use or sell the patented invention without the consent of and accounting to the other owners.

Inventors who apply for and obtain a joint patent on a jointly made invention are, in the absence of assignment of their rights, "joint owners" within the meaning of the statute.

VIII. "Do's" and "Don'ts" Concerning Patents

A. *Do* arrange to have important developments reviewed for patentable features before publication of the results and before advertising for sale the resulting product.

B. *Do not* place undue reliance upon the protective value of patents obtained on inventions not known to be of outstanding technical merit—they may be held invalid if ever sued upon.

C. *Do* arrange to have new developments going into use reviewed for possible infringement of the patents of others before investment has reached a point at which a change of direction will be unduly costly.

D. *Do not* permit new products or product modifications to be released for production without prior investigation to determine whether licenses are needed under patents of other persons or companies.

---

[3]35 U.S.C. §262.

APPENDIX B

Assignments

I. Of an Issued Patent by a Corporation

In consideration of One Dollar and other good and valuable consideration, of which receipt is acknowledged, ABC Company, a corporation of Massachusetts, owner of the entire right, title, and interest in United States Letters Patent No. _____, granted in the name of _____, on _____, 19____, hereby sells and assigns to XYZ Company, a corporation of Delaware, its entire right, title, and interest in the said Letters Patent, to be held and enjoyed by the XYZ Company, its successors, and assigns, as fully and entirely as the same would have been held and enjoyed by the ABC Company had this assignment and sale not been made.

In testimony whereof, the ABC Corporation has caused this assignment to be signed by its duly authorized officers and its seal to be attached this _____ day of _____, 19____.

_____
ABC Corporation

Attest

_____
by
(CORPORATE SEAL)

_____
Secretary

State of Massachusetts
Country of Berkshire   ss

On this the _____ day of _____, 19____, before me personally appeared _____, who acknowledged himself to be the _____ of _____, a corporation, that he knows the seal of said corporation, that the seal affixed to the foregoing instrument is that seal, that it was so affixed by authority of the Board of Directors of the corporation, and that, by like authority, he executed the instrument for the purposes stated in it by signing the name of the corporation by himself as _____.

In witness whereof I hereunto set my hand and the seal of my office.

_____

(SEAL)

II. Of a Pending Previously Assigned Application—By an Owner Other Than the Inventor

By assignment recorded in the United States Patent Office on Reel _____, Frame _____, I, John A. Doe of Pittsfield, Massachusetts, am owner of all right, title, and interest in United States Patent Application Serial No. _____, filed _____, 19____, in the name of _____ for improvements in _____.

In consideration of One Dollar and other good and valuable consideration, receipt of which is acknowledged, I hereby sell and assign to ABC Company, a corporation of Delaware, its successors, and assigns, the entire right, title, and interest in the aforesaid Patent Application Serial No. _____ and the invention described and claimed in it to be held and enjoyed by the ABC company as fully and entirely as the same would have been held and enjoyed by me if this assignment and sale had not been made.

_____, 19____

(Acknowledgment)

III. Of an Invention, With Ensuing Patent Rights—By the Inventor to a Corporation

In consideration of One Dollar and other good and valuable consideration, of which receipt is acknowledged, I _____ of _____, sell and assign to ABC Company, a Delaware corporation, the entire right, title, and interest in and to the improvements in _____ invented by me as described in the application for United States patent executed by me concurrently herewith, and any and all applications for patent and patents in any and all countries, including all divisions, continuations, reissues, and extensions thereof and all rights of priority resulting from the filing of said United States application and authorize and request any official whose duty it is to issue patents to issue any patent on said improvements or resulting therefrom to said ABC Company, or its successors, assigns, or nominees and agree that on request and without further consideration, but at the expense of the ABC Company, I will communicate to the Company or its representatives or nominees any facts known to me respecting said improvements and testify in any legal proceedings, sign all lawful papers, execute all divisional, continuing, and reissue applications, make all rightful oaths and generally aid said Company, its successors, assigns, and nominees to obtain and enforce proper patent protection for said invention in all countries.

——————, 19——

(Acknowledgment)

APPENDIX C

Simple License Agreement

ABC Company, a New York corporation, with a principal place of business at _____, and XYZ Company, a New Jersey corporation with a principal place of business at _____, agree as follows:

1. ABC Company is the owner of United States Patent No. _____, granted _____, 1983, for fuses. Effective upon execution of this agreement, and for the consideration stated in paragraph 2 of this agreement, ABC Company grants to XYZ Company a fully paid nonexclusive license under this patent to make, use, and sell fuses embodying the invention of the patent throughout the United States and its territories. The license so granted shall run for the life of the patent and shall be assignable at any time with the business and goodwill of XYZ Company in fuses.

2. At the time of execution of this agreement, XYZ Company will pay to ABC Company, the sum of Ten Thousand Dollars ($10,000).

ABC Company

By _____
President

_____, 19____
XYZ Company

By_____
President

_____, 19____

APPENDIX D

A More Complex License Agreement*

Effective January 1, 1983, ABC Company, a corporation of New York (hereafter ABC), having a principal place of business at _____, and XYZ Company, a corporation of Delaware (hereafter XYZ), having a principal place of business at _____, agree as follows:

ARTICLE I

GENERAL[1]

1.01 ABC and XYZ are hereafter occasionally referred to as "parties" (in singular or plural usage, as indicated by the context).

1.02 Terms in this agreement (other than names of parties and Article headings) which are set forth in upper case letters have the meanings established for such terms in Article II of the agreement, or, as to certain terms, in Article IV of the agreement.

1.03 ABC has numerous patents and maintains extensive continuing development in respect to:

(a) SIGNAL CONTROLLED TRACTION EQUIPMENT, and

---

*The agreement here presented has been constructed to illustrate a generous number of the drafting practices discussed in the text of this work, and in this way to serve as a rough checklist of drafting points to be considered. It should, therefore, not be considered as representing a "typical" licensing transaction or as implying the suitability of its dollars-and-cents aspects for any substantial number of negotiating situations likely to be encountered in practice.

The numbered footnotes in this appendix are intended to lead the user to the most relevant parts of the expository text.

[1]*See* Chapter 2, Sections 2.03 and 2.04, for arguments supporting this kind of agreement opening.

(b) COMPONENTS for equipment falling under (a), above.

1.04 ABC represents that it is prepared in respect to its United States patents applicable to products named in Section 1.03, above, to grant to any financially responsible applicant a nonexclusive license on proportionately reasonable terms.

1.05 XYZ has certain patents relating to equipment and components of the classes identified in Section 1.03, above, and proposes additional developments in this field. It desires assurance of a license under the applicable patents of ABC.

1.06 The parties, having examined the relative value to one another of their respective relevant patent holdings and their respective levels of technological effort, have found a present balance of value in favor of ABC. In view of this finding, they have jointly concluded that their respective needs and interests will be served by an exchange of licenses supplemented by payment of certain royalties by XYZ to ABC, all under the conditions stated in the remaining Articles of this agreement.

ARTICLE II

DEFINITIONS[2]

2.01 SIGNAL CONTROLLED TRACTION EQUIPMENT means equipment for moving loads under the control of remotely generated signals propagated through space. The term includes equipment which is alternatively responsive to local control means provided such equipment also has the remote control capability specified in the preceding sentence. Where load-moving equipment incorporates a number of completely separable load-carrying or traction units, some of which do and some of which do not have the specified remote control capability, the term SIGNAL CONTROLLED TRACTION EQUIPMENT applies only to those units of the complete equipment which have the specified capability.

2.02 COMPONENTS means subassemblies and parts specifically designed and adapted for use in SIGNAL CONTROLLED TRACTION EQUIPMENT. It excludes subassemblies and parts which, although usable in equipment of the named class, are developed or designed for general use or for uses other than in equipment of the named class. It specifically excludes materials, including, but not limited to, plastics, metals, alloys, paints, lubricants, and wire.

2.03 PATENT means any United States patent, other than an appearance design patent, which contains a claim or claims applicable to

(a) SIGNAL CONTROLLED TRACTION EQUIPMENT, or

---

[2]*See* Chapter 3 for general discussion of definition practice.

(b) COMPONENTS, or

(c) a machine, instrumentality, or process specifically designed for the development, manufacture, installation, testing, repair, or maintenance of items identified in (a) or (b) of this Section 2.03.

2.04 LICENSED PATENTS[3] of a granting party means all PATENTS issued or issuing on patent applications filed prior to January 1, 1988, or filed subsequent thereto but receiving, or entitled to receive, the benefit of a filing date prior to January 1, 1988, and as to which the granting party has the right at any time during the term of this agreement to grant licenses or releases of the scope or within the scope of the licenses and releases granted in this agreement. If the grant or exercise of rights under a patent which would otherwise be a LICENSED PATENT requires or results in the payment of a royalty or penalty or other consideration by a grantor to another (except for payments for inventions made by such other while employed by the grantor), then that patent shall not be a LICENSED PATENT until and unless the party receiving rights under the patent undertakes to reimburse the grantor for the payment so made.

The term LICENSED PATENTS does not include any patent on an invention with respect to which:

(a) By law, regulation, or contract, the exclusive power of licensing is passed to a governmental agency;

(b) A party grants, or agrees to grant to a customer of that party, prior to the conception of such invention and as the result of a bona fide negotiation for the customer's business, rights which negate the power to grant to others licenses of the scope proposed to be granted in this agreement.

ARTICLE III

LICENSE GRANTS[4]

3.01 Each party grants to the other party under the granting party's LICENSED PATENTS a nonexclusive license to make, use, sell, or otherwise dispose of SIGNAL CONTROLLED TRACTION EQUIPMENT and COMPONENTS throughout the United States, its territories, and possessions.

3.02 The term of license as to each LICENSED PATENT shall be for the full life of the PATENT.[5]

---

[3]For considerations affecting the definition of LICENSED PATENTS, *see* Section 7.01(C) of Chapter 7 and Section 3.01(B) of Chapter 3.

[4]*See* Chapter 7 for general discussion of this subject.

[5]For reasons applicable in some contexts for defining the life of a patent, *see* Section 7.01(D), Chapter 7.

3.03 Nothing in this agreement is intended to preclude the export or sale for export of products licensed in Section 3.01 of this Article III to be sold or otherwise disposed of (and on which, in the case of XYZ, royalties shall have been paid to the extent required by Section 4.01 of Article IV), but no rights are granted or implied in respect to such exported products under any foreign patent of either party to this agreement or of any other person.[6]

3.04 Each party releases the other party and all purchasers and users of SIGNAL CONTROLLED TRACTION EQUIPMENT and COMPONENTS acquired, mediately or immediately, from the released party from any and all claims, demands, and rights of action which the releasing party may have on account of any infringement or alleged infringement of any LICENSED PATENT by the manufacture, use, sale, or other disposition of SIGNAL CONTROLLED TRACTION EQUIPMENT or COMPONENTS which, prior to the effective date of this agreement, were manufactured, used, sold, or otherwise disposed of by the released party.[7]

ARTICLE IV

ROYALTIES, REPORTS, AND PAYMENTS[8]

4.01 XYZ will pay royalties to ABC on ROYALTY-BEARING PRODUCTS at the rate of two percent (2%) of the NET SELLING PRICE of all such PRODUCTS sold or otherwise disposed of subsequent to the date of this agreement and prior to the expiration of the five-year period beginning on the date of the agreement.

4.02 ROYALTY-BEARING PRODUCTS means:

(a) SIGNAL CONTROLLED TRACTION EQUIPMENT and
(b) COMPONENTS sold or otherwise disposed of other than as incorporated parts of SIGNAL CONTROLLED TRACTION EQUIPMENT

which, as sold or otherwise disposed of, (i) come within any claim of an unexpired LICENSED PATENT of ABC or (ii) are made by use of a process or machine which, at the time of such making, comes within any claim of an unexpired LICENSED PATENT of ABC.

4.03 The expression "ROYALTY-BEARING PRODUCTS . . . otherwise disposed of" means and includes (i) ROYALTY-BEARING PRODUCTS not sold but delivered by XYZ to others (including deliveries for export), regardless of the basis of compensation, if any; (ii) ROYALTY-BEARING PRODUCTS not sold as such but sold by XYZ as components or constituents of other products and (iii) ROYALTY-BEARING PRODUCTS put into use by XYZ for any purpose other than routine testing.

----

[6]For the rationale of this paragraph, *see* Section 7.01(G).

[7]On "releases," *see* Section 8.01, Chapter 8.

[8]Careful review of Chapter 9 is recommended in connection with the design of provisions falling under this heading.

4.04 NET SELLING PRICE in respect to ROYALTY-BEARING PRODUCTS sold means invoice price, f.o.b. factory, after deduction of regular trade and quantity discounts, but before deduction of any other items, including but not limited to freight allowances, cash discounts, and agents' commissions.[9]

Where ROYALTY-BEARING PRODUCTS are not sold, but are otherwise disposed of, NET SELLING PRICE for the purpose of computing royalties shall be the NET SELLING PRICE at which products of similar kind and quality, sold in similar quantities, are currently being offered for sale by XYZ. Where such products are not currently being separately offered for sale by XYZ, the NET SELLING PRICE of ROYALTY-BEARING PRODUCTS otherwise disposed of shall be XYZ's cost of manufacture, determined by XYZ's customary accounting procedures, increased by _____ percent (_____%).

4.05 In order to assure ABC the full royalty payments contemplated in this agreement, in the event any ROYALTY-BEARING PRODUCTS shall be sold for resale either (i) to a corporation, firm, or association which, or individual who, owns a controlling interest by stock ownership or otherwise, or (ii) to a corporation, firm, or association in which XYZ or its stockholders own a controlling interest by stock ownership or otherwise, the royalties to be paid in respect to such ROYALTY-BEARING PRODUCTS shall be computed upon the NET SELLING PRICE at which the purchaser for resale resells such products rather than upon the NET SELLING PRICE of XYZ.[10]

4.06 XYZ will make written reports to ABC quarterly within thirty (30) days after the first days of each January, April, July, and October through, and including January 1988, and as of such dates, stating in each such report the number, description, and aggregate NET SELLING PRICES of ROYALTY-BEARING PRODUCTS sold or otherwise disposed of during the preceding three (3) calendar months and upon which royalty is payable as provided in this Article IV. The first such report shall include all ROYALTY-BEARING PRODUCTS so sold or otherwise disposed of between the date of this agreement and the date of such report.

XYZ will make a written report to ABC within thirty (30) days after the date of any termination by XYZ prior to January 1, 1988, of any license under a PATENT of ABC received by XYZ under this agreement, stating in such report the number, description, and NET SELLING PRICES of all ROYALTY-BEARING PRODUCTS sold or otherwise disposed of and upon which royalty not previously reported to ABC is payable solely in consequence of such PATENT.

---

[9]*See* Section 9.01(B), Chapter 9.

[10]For alternative treatments of the problem to which this paragraph is addressed, *see* Section 9.01(B) of Chapter 9.

Concurrently with the making of each report, XYZ will pay to ABC royalties at the rate specified in this Article IV on the ROYALTY-BEARING PRODUCTS included in the report.

Under this Agreement, ROYALTY-BEARING PRODUCTS shall be considered to be sold when billed out, except that upon expiration of any patent covering such ROYALTY-BEARING PRODUCTS, or upon any termination of license, all shipments made on or prior to the date of such expiration or termination which have not been billed out prior thereto shall be considered as sold (and therefore subject to royalty). Royalties paid on ROYALTY-BEARING PRODUCTS which are not accepted by the customer shall be credited to XYZ.

4.07 In case the royalties otherwise payable to ABC under this agreement fail to aggregate a minimum of Ten Thousand Dollars ($10,000) for each calendar year during the life of this agreement (and prior to January 1, 1988), XYZ will, within thirty (30) days of the end of the year in which the failure occurs, pay ABC such additional sum as may be necessary to bring the payment for such year up to Ten Thousand Dollars ($10,000).[11]

4.08 XYZ will keep records showing the ROYALTY-BEARING PRODUCTS sold or otherwise disposed of by it prior to January 1, 1988, under the license granted in Article III, such records to be in sufficient detail to enable the royalties payable to ABC to be determined. XYZ will also permit its books and records to be examined from time to time to the extent necessary to verify the reports provided for in Section 4.06, such examination to be made at the expense of ABC by an independent auditor appointed by ABC who shall report to ABC only the amount of royalty payable for the period under audit. Upon termination of this agreement for any reason, ABC shall have the right to have a final audit conducted by an independent auditor appointed by ABC and paid by ABC.

ARTICLE V

REPRESENTATIONS AND WARRANTIES; LIMITATIONS[12]

5.01 Subject to limitations on the meaning of LICENSED PATENTS established by Section 2.05 of this agreement, each of the parties represents and warrants that:

(a) It has accepted and will accept no commitments or restrictions in respect to its right to grant licenses which will materially affect the value of the rights granted by it in this agreement.

---

[11]For alternative treatments of the subject matter of Sections 4.07 and 4.08, *see* Sections 9.04 and 9.05 of Chapter 9.

[12]*See* Chapter 14.

(b) It will, as far as it is reasonably practicable for it to do so, cause its employees who are employed to do research, development, or other inventive work to disclose to it inventions within the scope of this agreement and to assign to it rights in such inventions such that the other party shall receive, by virtue of this agreement, the licenses agreed to be granted to it.

5.02 Nothing in this agreement shall be construed as:

(a) A warranty or representation by either party as to the validity or scope of any LICENSED PATENT; or

(b) A warranty or representation that anything made, used, sold, or otherwise disposed of under any license granted in this agreement is or will be free from infringement of patents of third persons; or

(c) A requirement that either party shall file any patent application, secure any patent, or maintain any patent in force; or

(d) An obligation to bring or prosecute actions or suits against third parties for infringement of any patent; or

(e) An obligation to furnish any manufacturing or technical information, or any information concerning pending patent applications; or

(f) Conferring a right to use in advertising, publicity, or otherwise any trademark or tradename of the party from which a license is received under the agreement; or

(g) Granting by implication, estoppel, or otherwise, any licenses or rights under patents other than LICENSED PATENTS.[13]

5.03 Neither party makes any representations, extends any warranties of any kind, either express or implied, or assumes any responsibilities whatever with respect to use, sale, or other disposition by the other party or its vendees or transferees of products incorporating or made by use of inventions licensed under this agreement.

ARTICLE VI[14]

TRANSFERABILITY OF RIGHTS AND OBLIGATIONS

6.01 Any license or release granted in this agreement by a party in respect to a LICENSED PATENT shall be binding upon any successor of the party in ownership or control of the LICENSED PATENT.

6.02 The obligations of XYZ to make reports, pay royalties, and maintain records in respect to any subsisting license under this agree-

---

[13]For a stronger wording of this provision applicable in some circumstances, *see* Section 14.01 of Chapter 14.

[14]*See* Chapter 12.

ment shall run in favor of any person or legal entity which is a successor or assignee of ABC in respect to ABC's benefits under the agreement.

6.03 The licenses received by any party under this agreement shall pass to any assigns for the benefit of creditors of the licensed party, and to any receiver of its assets, or to any person or corporation succeeding to its entire business in LICENSED PRODUCTS as a resuilt of sale, consolidation, reorganization, or otherwise, provided such assignee, receiver, person, or legal entity shall, without delay, accept in writing the provisions of this agreement and agree to become in all respects bound thereby in the place and stead of the licensed party, but may not otherwise be transferred without the written consent of the licensing party.

ARTICLE VII[15]

TERM AND TERMINATION

7.01 The word "termination" and cognate words, such as "term" and "terminate," used in this Article VII are to be read, except where the contrary is specifically indicated, as omitting from their effect the following rights and obligations, all of which shall survive any termination to the degree necessary to permit their complete fulfillment or discharge:

(a) XYZ's obligation to supply a terminal report in respect to terminated licenses as specified in Section 4.06 of Article IV of this agreement;

(b) ABC's right to receive or recover and XYZ's obligation to pay royalties (including minimum royalties) accrued or accruable for payment at the time of any termination;

(c) XYZ's obligation to maintain records and ABC's right to conduct a final audit as provided in Section 4.08 of Article IV of this agreement;

(d) Licenses and releases running in favor of customers or transferees of either party in respect to products sold or transferred by that party prior to termination of this agreement or of any license arising under this agreement (subject, in the case of XYZ, to payment of any royalties payable in respect to such products);

(e) Any cause of action or claim of either party, accrued or to accrue, because of any breach or default by the other party.

7.02 Unless otherwise terminated as provided in Section 7.03 or 7.04 of this Article VII, this agreement shall run to the end of the

---

[15]For considerations affecting termination provisions, *see* Chapter 17.

life of the last to expire of the LICENSED PATENTS and shall thereupon terminate.[16]

7.03 XYZ may prospectively terminate this agreement or its license and concomitant future obligations in respect to any LICENSED PATENT upon thirty (30) days written notice to ABC. Assertion by XYZ, subsequent to the date of its execution of this agreement, of the invalidity of any claim of any LICENSED PATENT, if coupled with or followed by

(a) Withholding, or notice of intention to withhold, or denial of obligation to pay, royalties otherwise payable under this agreement in respect to XYZ's operations under such claim, or

(b) Initiation or participation in a suit challenging or denying the validity of such claim in reference to XYZ's operations under this agreement,

may, at the option of ABC, be conclusively presumed to constitute XYZ's termination, as of the earliest provable date of such withholding, notice, denial, initiation, or participation, of its license in respect to such claim and of its obligation under this agreement for payment of royalties in respect to XYZ's future operations under the claim (but not under any other claim).[17]

7.04 With respect to acts of XYZ other than those set forth in Section 7.02 of this Article VII, ABC may terminate this agreement at any time in the event of a default by XYZ in the due observance or performance of any covenant, condition, or limitation of this License Agreement required to be performed by XYZ, but only if XYZ shall not have remedied its default within thirty (30) days after receipt from ABC of written notice of such default.

7.05 If, in any proceeding in which the validity, infringement, or priority of invention of any claim of any LICENSED PATENT licensed to XYZ is in issue, a judgment or decree is entered which becomes not further reviewable through the exhaustion of all permissible applications for rehearing or review by a superior tribunal, or through the expiration of the time permitted for such applications (hereinafter referred to as an "irrevocable judgment"), the construction placed upon any such claim by such irrevocable judgment shall thereafter be followed, not only as to such claim but as to all claims to which such construction applies, with respect to acts occurring thereafter; and, if such irrevocable judgment holds any claim invalid or is adverse to the patent as to inventorship, XYZ shall be relieved thereafter from including in its reports apparatus sold or otherwise dis-

---

[16]For a note on the possible desirability of defining the "life" of a patent, *see* the concluding part of Section 7.01(D) of Chapter 7.

[17]For the rationale of this paragraph, *see* Chapter 13.

posed of thereafter covered only by such claim or by any broader claim to which such irrevocable judgment is applicable, and from the performance of those other acts which may be required by this agreement only because of any such claim: provided, however, that if there are two or more conflicting irrevocable judgments with respect to the same claim, the decision of the higher tribunal shall be followed thereafter, but if the tribunals be of equal dignity, then the decision more favorable to the claim shall be followed until the less favorable decision has been followed by the irrevocable judgment of another tribunal of at least equal dignity. In the event of conflicting irrevocable judgments of the Supreme Court of the United States, the latest shall control.[18]

ARTICLE VIII[19]

NOTICES; APPLICABLE LAW; ARBITRATION

8.01 Any notice, report, or payment provided for in this agreement shall be deemed sufficiently given when sent by certified or registered mail addressed to the party for whom intended at the address given at the outset of this agreement or at such changed address as the party shall have specified by written notice.

8.02 This agreement shall be construed, interpreted, and applied in accordance with the laws of the State of New York.

8.03 Any controversy or claim arising under or related to this contract insofar as it involves or is limited to a question of infringement of any claim or claims of a LICENSED PATENT shall be settled by arbitration in accordance with the Patent Arbitration Rules of the American Arbitration Association before a single arbitrator selected in accordance with those rules, and judgment upon the award rendered by the arbitrator may be entered in any court having jurisdiction thereof.

ARTICLE IX[20]

INTEGRATION

9.01 This instrument contains the entire and only agreement between the parties and supersedes all preexisting agreements between them respecting its subject matter. Any representation, prom-

---

[18]For the rationale of this paragraph, *see* Chapter 13.

[19]For discussion of the matters dealt with in this article, *see* Chapter 16. Note also that the subject of "Patent Marking" (treated in Chapter 16) is not covered in this agreement. Where a policy of systematic marking is followed by either party, appropriate covering language will need to be negotiated. (See Section 16.01.)

[20]For the theory and limitations of an article of this kind, *see* Chapter 18, particularly Sections 18.01 and 18.02.

ise, or condition in connection with such subject matter which is not incorporated in this agreement shall not be binding upon either party. No modification, renewal, extension, waiver, and (except as provided in Article VII hereof) no termination of this agreement or any of its provisions shall be binding upon the party against whom enforcement of such modification, renewal, extension, waiver, or termination is sought, unless made in writing and signed on behalf of such party by one of its executive officers, or in the case of ABC, by the Manager of its Licensing Operation. As used herein, the word "termination" includes any and all means of bringing to an end prior to its expiration by its own terms this agreement, or any provision thereof, whether by release, discharge, abandonment, or otherwise.

IN WITNESS WHEREOF,[21] each of the parties has caused this agreement to be executed and duly sealed in duplicate originals by its duly authorized representative.

ABC Company
by

_____
Manager, Licensing Operation

Attest:

_____   (SEAL)
Secretary

XYZ Company
by

_____
President

Attest:

_____   (SEAL)
Secretary

---

[21]For notes on the formalities of execution and considerations affecting them, *see* Chapter 20.

APPENDIX E

Defined Field Patent License Agreement (Exclusive)

THIS AGREEMENT, effective _____, is entered into by _____, a corporation of _____, having its principal place of business at _____(herein called LICENSEE), and _____, a corporation of _____, having its principal place of business at _____ (herein called LICENSOR).[1]

I. Background of Agreement[2]

1.00 LICENSOR represents that it has certain patents pertaining to _____ in respect to which it is prepared to grant an exclusive license to LICENSEE.

1.01 LICENSEE wishes to acquire an exclusive license under selected patents of LICENSOR for purposes of _____.[3]

II. Definitions[4]

As used herein, the following terms shall have the meanings set forth below:

---

[1]*See* Chapter 2, The Opening Part of the Agreement.

[2]*See* Chapter 2.

[3]Sections 1.00 and 1.01 as drafted provide for a prima facie defense to an allegation of misuse based on coercive package licensing. (*See* Chapter 10). The blank space is present to show the LICENSEE's acceptance of a defined field (limited in subject matter scope) license.

[4]*See* Chapter 3.

2.00 PATENT or PATENTS means the following listed patents and/ or patent applications, patents to be issued pursuant thereto, and all divisions, continuations, reissues, substitutes, and extensions thereof:

Applications

U.S.　　　　　　Application No.　　　　　　Date Filed

Letters Patent

U.S.　　　　　　Patent No.　　　　　　Expiration Date

2.01 LICENSED TERRITORY means the United States of America, its territories, and its possessions.

2.02 IMPROVEMENT or IMPROVEMENTS means any patented modification of a device, method, or product described in a PATENT provided such a modification, if unlicensed, would infringe one or more claims of issued PATENTS.[5]

2.03 LICENSED FIELD means, and is limited to, the practice of the PATENTS and IMPROVEMENTS to _____
_____.[6]

2.04 LICENSED PRODUCTS means any and all products which fall within the LICENSED FIELD and which are covered by or are produced using a process or method covered by a claim of a PATENT or IMPROVEMENT.[7]

2.05 EFFECTIVE DATE shall be _____, 199___.

2.06 NET SALES PRICE for the purpose of computing royalties, means LICENSEE'S invoice price, f.o.b. factory, after deduction of regular trade and quantity discounts, but before deduction of any other items, including but not limited to freight allowances, cash discounts, and agents' commissions. Where products are not sold, but are otherwise disposed of, the NET SALES PRICE of such products for the purposes of computing royalties shall be the selling price at which products of similar kind and quality, sold in similar quantities, are currently being offered for sale by LICENSEE. Where such products are not currently being offered for sale by LICENSEE, the NET SALES PRICE of

---

[5]*See* Chapter 8, Section 8.00.

[6]*See* Chapter 7, Section 7.02.

[7]*See* Chapter 9, Section 9.01A.

products otherwise disposed of, for the purpose of computing royalties, shall be the average selling price at which products of similar kind and quality, sold in similar quantities, are then currently being offered for sale by other manufacturers. Where such products are not currently sold or offered for sale by LICENSEE or others, then the NET SALES PRICE, for the purposes of computing royalties, shall be LICENSEE'S cost of manufacture, determined by LICENSEE'S customary accounting procedures, plus _____ percent (__%). In order to assure to the LICENSOR the full royalty payments contemplated in this agreement, LICENSEE agrees that in the event any LICENSED PRODUCTS shall be sold for purposes of resale either (1) to a corporation, firm, or association which, or individual who, owns a controlling interest in LICENSEE by stock ownership or otherwise, or (2) to a corporation, firm, or association in which the LICENSEE or its stockholders own a controlling interest by stock ownership or otherwise, the royalties to be paid in respect to such LICENSED PRODUCTS shall be computed upon the net selling price at which the purchaser for resale sells such PRODUCTS rather than upon the net selling price of the LICENSEE.[8]

III. License Grant[9]

3.00 LICENSOR hereby grants to LICENSEE, to the extent of the LICENSED FIELD and LICENSED TERRITORY, a license under PATENTS and IMPROVEMENTS to make, use, and sell LICENSED PRODUCTS. No license under PATENTS and IMPROVEMENTS is granted, and no license should be implied, with respect to activities of LICENSEE outside the LICENSED FIELD and LICENSED TERRITORY.

3.01 The license granted pursuant to paragraph 3.00 hereof shall be exclusive, with the right to grant sublicenses, until _____, and nonexclusive with no right to grant sublicenses thereafter for the term of this Agreement.[10]

IV. License Fees and Royalty[11]

4.00 LICENSEE shall, as a license fee, pay to LICENSOR, within 10 days after the EFFECTIVE DATE _____ dollars ($_____) which

---

[8]*See* Chapter 9, Section 9.01B for drafting techniques for defining "net selling price."

[9]*See* Chapters 6 and 7.

[10]*See* Section 6.03B for techniques to protect the licensor from a nonperforming licensee.

[11]*See* Chapter 9.

shall be nonrefundable and not creditable against the royalty called for under Section 4.01.

4.01 LICENSEE shall pay to LICENSOR a royalty of _____ percent (_____%) of the NET SALES PRICE of all LICENSED PRODUCTS sold or otherwise disposed of under the license granted under paragraph 3.00 of this License Agreement.

V. Minimum Royalties[12]

5.00 LICENSEE shall pay to LICENSOR royalties as stated in paragraph 4.01, but in no event shall royalties for a calendar year for practice of the PATENTS and IMPROVEMENTS in the LICENSED FIELD and LICENSED TERRITORY be less than the following minimum royalties during each of the calendar years indicated:

Calendar Year	Minimum Royalty, U.S. $ per Calendar Year*
199__	$
199__	
199__	
199__ and each calendar year thereafter during the term of this Agreement	

* Net to LICENSOR after taxes, if any, withheld at the source.

5.01 LICENSOR may, by written notice to LICENSEE, terminate this Agreement during any February subsequent to the year 19__, if LICENSEE has not practiced the PATENTS during the calendar year that precedes each such February to the extent of generating earned royalties as provided by paragraph 4.01 of this Agreement in the amount of _____ ($_____).

VI. Sublicensing[13]

6.00 Sublicensing in the LICENSED FIELD and LICENSED TERRITORY shall be the responsibility of LICENSEE so long as this license remains exclusive and it is the intent of the parties that sublicenses shall be available to qualified third parties on fair and reasonable terms. Sublicenses shall be nonexclusive licenses that are transferable only

---

[12]*See* Chapter 9, Section 9.04.
[13]*See* Chapter 6, Section 6.01.

from LICENSEE to LICENSOR. LICENSEE shall supply LICENSOR with a copy of each such sublicense agreement within thirty (30) days of the execution of the sublicense agreement.

6.01 The royalty for sublicensees shall be no less than that set forth for LICENSEE in paragraph 4.01, above.

6.02 LICENSEE shall pay to LICENSOR _____ percent (__%) of any and all income received by LICENSEE from sublicensing. Payment of LICENSOR's share of sublicensing income shall be made to LICENSOR semiannually as provided in Section 7.00.

6.03 If this Agreement becomes nonexclusive or if it is terminated for any reason, LICENSEE shall immediately assign all of its right, title, and interest to all sublicenses to LICENSOR including the right to receive all income from sublicensees. LICENSEE shall prior to execution of each sublicense make the sublicensee aware of this contingency.

6.04 Income received by LICENSEE from sublicensees shall not apply to the minimum royalty provisions of paragraph 5.00 or the earned royalty provisions of paragraph 5.01.

VII. Payments[14]

7.00 Not later than the last day of each January and July, LICENSEE shall furnish to LICENSOR a written statement in such detail as LICENSOR may reasonably require of all amounts due pursuant to paragraphs 4.01 and 6.02 for the semiannual periods ended the last days of the preceding December and June, respectively, and shall pay to LICENSOR all amounts due to LICENSOR. In the event that the amounts due at the end of any calendar year do not equal the minimum royalties specified in paragraph 5.00 for said calendar year, LICENSEE shall pay to LICENSOR on the last day of the following January, the amount required to satisfy the minimum royalty obligation for the preceding calendar year. Such amounts are due at the dates the statements are due. If no amount is accrued during any semiannual period, a written statement to that effect shall be furnished.

7.01 Payments provided for in this Agreement, when overdue, shall bear interest at a rate per annum equal to one percent (1%) in excess of the "PRIME RATE" published by "The Wall Street Journal" at the time such payment is due, and for the time period until payment is received by LICENSOR.

7.02 If this Agreement is for any reason terminated before all of the payments herein provided for have been made (including minimum royalties for the year in which the agreement is terminated),

---

[14]*See* Chapter 9, Section 9.02.

LICENSEE shall immediately submit a terminal report and pay to LICENSOR any remaining unpaid balance even though the due date as above provided has not been reached.

VIII. Representations and Disclaimer of Warranties[15]

8.00 NOTHING IN THIS AGREEMENT SHALL BE DEEMED TO BE A REPRESENTATION OR WARRANTY BY LICENSOR OF THE VALIDITY OF ANY OF THE PATENTS OR IMPROVEMENTS. LICENSOR SHALL HAVE NO LIABILITY WHATSOEVER TO LICENSEE OR ANY OTHER PERSON FOR OR ON ACCOUNT OF ANY INJURY, LOSS, OR DAMAGE, OF ANY KIND OR NATURE, SUSTAINED BY, OR ANY DAMAGE ASSESSED OR ASSERTED AGAINST, OR ANY OTHER LIABILITY INCURRED BY OR IMPOSED UPON LICENSEE OR ANY OTHER PERSON, ARISING OUT OF OR IN CONNECTION WITH OR RESULTING FROM (a) THE PRODUCTION, USE, OR SALE OF ANY APPARATUS OR PRODUCT, OR THE PRACTICE OF THE PATENTS OR IMPROVEMENTS; OR (b) ANY ADVERTISING OR OTHER PROMOTIONAL ACTIVITIES WITH RESPECT TO ANY OF THE FOREGOING, AND LICENSEE SHALL HOLD LICENSOR, AND ITS OFFICERS, AGENTS, OR EMPLOYEES, HARMLESS IN THE EVENT LICENSOR, OR ITS OFFICERS, AGENTS, OR EMPLOYEES, IS HELD LIABLE.

8.01 LICENSOR shall have the sole right to file, prosecute, and maintain all of the PATENTS that are the property of LICENSOR and shall have the right to determine whether or not, and where, to file a patent application, to abandon the prosecution of any patent or patent application, or to discontinue the maintenance of any patent or patent applications.

IX. Termination[16]

9.00 This Agreement shall terminate upon the expiration of the last to expire of the PATENTS and IMPROVEMENTS included herein, or upon the abandonment of the last to be abandoned of any patent applications included herein, whichever is later, unless the Agreement is sooner terminated.

9.01 LICENSEE may terminate this Agreement at any time upon sixty (60) days' written notice in advance to LICENSOR.

9.02 If either party shall be in default of any obligation hereunder, or shall be adjudged bankrupt, or become insolvent, or make an assignment for the benefit of creditors, or be placed in the hands of

---

[15]*See* Chapter 14, Section 14.01.
[16]*See* Chapter 17.

a receiver or a trustee in bankruptcy, the other party may terminate this Agreement by giving sixty (60) days' notice by Registered Mail to the other party, specifying the basis for termination. If within sixty (60) days after the receipt of such notice, the party receiving notice shall remedy the condition forming the basis for termination, such notice shall cease to be operative, and this Agreement shall continue in full force.

9.03 The word "termination" and cognate words, such as "term" and "terminate," used in this Article IX and elsewhere in this agreement are to be read, except where the contrary is specifically indicated, as omitting from their effect the following rights and obligations, all of which survive any termination to the degree necessary to permit their complete fulfillment or discharge:

(a) LICENSEE'S obligation to supply a terminal report as specified in paragraph 7.02 of this agreement.

(b) LICENSOR'S right to receive or recover and LICENSEE'S obligation to pay royalties (including minimum royalties) accrued or accruable for payment at the time of any termination.

(c) LICENSEE'S obligation to maintain records under paragraph 11.00 of this agreement.

(d) Licenses, releases, and agreements of nonassertion running in favor of customers or transferees of LICENSEE in respect to products sold or transferred by LICENSEE prior to any termination and on which royalties shall have been paid as provided in paragraph 4.01 of this agreement.

(e) Any cause of action or claim of LICENSOR accrued or to accrue, because of any breach or default by LICENSEE.

(f) The representation and disclaimer of warranties of Section 8.00.

X. Litigation[17]

10.00 Each party shall notify the other party in writing of any suspected infringement(s) of the PATENTS and IMPROVEMENTS in the LICENSED TERRITORY and shall inform the other party of any evidence of such infringement(s).

10.01 LICENSEE shall have the first right to institute suit for infringement(s) in the LICENSED FIELD and the LICENSED TERRITORY so long as this Agreement remains exclusive. LICENSOR agrees to join as a party plaintiff in any such lawsuit initiated by LICENSEE, if

---

[17]*See* Chapter 6, Section 6.04.

requested by LICENSEE, with all costs, attorney fees, and expenses to be paid by LICENSEE. However, if LICENSEE does not institute suit for infringement(s) within ninety (90) days of receipt of written notice from LICENSOR of LICENSOR'S desire to bring suit for infringement in its own name and on its own behalf, then LICENSOR may, at its own expense, bring suit or take any other appropriate action.

10.02 If this Agreement is nonexclusive at the time of infringement(s), the sole right to institute suit for infringement and to recover damages shall rest with LICENSOR.

10.03 LICENSEE shall be entitled to any recovery of damages resulting from a lawsuit brought by it pursuant to paragraph 10.01. LICENSOR shall be entitled to recovery of damages resulting from any lawsuit brought by LICENSOR to enforce any PATENT or IMPROVEMENT, pursuant to paragraph 10.01.

10.04 Neither party may settle with an infringer without the prior approval of the other party if such settlement would affect the rights of the other party under the PATENTS and IMPROVEMENTS.

XI. Records

11.00 LICENSEE shall keep accurate records of all operations affecting payments hereunder, and shall permit LICENSOR or its duly authorized agent to inspect all such records and to make copies of or extracts from such records during regular business hours throughout the term of this Agreement and for a reasonable period of not less than three (3) years thereafter.

XII. Nonassignability[18]

12.00 The parties agree this agreement imposes personal obligations on LICENSEE. LICENSEE shall not assign any rights under this Agreement not specifically transferable by its terms without the written consent of LICENSOR. LICENSOR may assign its rights hereunder.

XIII. Severability

13.00 The parties agree that if any part, term, or provision of this Agreement shall be found illegal or in conflict with any valid

---

[18]*See* Chapter 12, Sections 12.01 and 12.02.

controlling law, the validity of the remaining provisions shall not be affected thereby.

13.01 In the event the legality of any provision of this Agreement is brought into question because of a decision by a court of competent jurisdiction, LICENSOR, by written notice to LICENSEE, may revise the provision in question or may delete it entirely so as to comply with the decision of said court.

XIV. Nonuse of Licensor's Name[19]

14.00 In publicizing anything made, used, or sold under this Agreement, LICENSEE shall not use the name of LICENSOR or otherwise refer to any organization related to LICENSOR, except with the written approval of LICENSOR.

XV. Waiver, Integration, Alteration

15.00 The waiver of a breach hereunder may be effected only by a writing signed by the waiving party and shall not constitute a waiver of any other breach.

15.01 This Agreement represents the entire understanding between the parties, and supersedes all other agreements, express or implied, between the parties concerning PATENTS and IMPROVEMENTS.

15.02 A provision of this Agreement may be altered only by a writing signed by both parties, except as provided in paragraphs 13.00 and 13.01, above.

XVI. Marking[20]

16.00 LICENSEE shall place in a conspicuous location on LICENSED PRODUCTS, a patent notice in accordance with 35 U.S.C. §282. LICENSEE agrees to mark any products made using a process covered by any PATENT or IMPROVEMENT with the number of each such patent and, with respect to such PATENTS and IMPROVEMENTS, to respond to any request for disclosure under 35 U.S.C. §287(b)(4)(B) by only notifying LICENSOR of the request for disclosure.

---

[19]*See* Chapter 14, Section 14.02B for other techniques for a licensor to avoid potential tort liability due to acts of the licensee.

[20]*See* Chapter 16, Section 16.01.

XVII. Applicable Law[21]

17.00 This Agreement shall be construed in accordance with the substantive laws of the State of _____ of the United States of America.

XVIII. Notices Under the Agreement[22]

18.00 For the purpose of all written communications and notices between the parties, their addresses shall be:

LICENSOR: _____
　　　　　 _____
　　　　　 _____
　　　　　 _____
　　　　　　　　　　　　　　　　and
LICENSEE: _____
　　　　　 _____
　　　　　 _____
　　　　　 _____

or any other addresses of which either party shall notify the other party in writing.

IN WITNESS WHEREOF the parties have caused this Agreement to be executed by their duly authorized officers on the respective dates and at the respective places hereinafter set forth.[23]

LICENSEE
(COMPANY NAME)

ATTEST:
By: _____　　By: _____
　　　　　　　　　　　　　　　　　　Title: _____
Signed at: _____　　Date: _____

LICENSOR
(COMPANY NAME)

ATTEST:

----

[21]*See* Chapter 6, Section 16.02.
[22]*See* Chapter 16, Section 16.00.
[23]*See* Chapter 20.

APPENDIX F

Patent and Technical Information License Agreement (Nonexclusive)

THIS AGREEMENT is entered into by _____, a corporation of _____, having its principal place of business at _____(herein called LICENSEE), and by _____, a corporation of _____, having its principal place of business at _____(herein called LICENSOR).[1]

I. Background of Agreement[2]

1.00 LICENSOR is the owner of certain PATENTS and TECHNICAL information relating to _____
_____.

1.01 LICENSEE wishes to acquire the right to use such PATENTS and TECHNICAL INFORMATION.[3]

II. Definitions[4]

As used herein, the following terms shall have the meanings set forth below:

2.00 PATENT or PATENTS means the following United States patents and/or patent applications, patents to be issued pursuant thereto,

---

[1]*See* Chapter 2, The Opening Part of the Agreement.

[2]*See* Chapter 2.

[3]Sections 1.00 and 1.01, as drafted, help establish a prima facie defense to an allegation of misuse based on coercive package licensing. (*See* Chapter 10.)

[4]*See* Chapter 3.

251

and all divisions, continuations, reissues, substitutes, and extensions thereof:

Applications

Application No.   Date Filed

Letters Patent

Patent No.   Expiration Date

2.01 TECHNICAL INFORMATION means unpublished research and development information, unpatented inventions, know-how, trade secrets, and technical data in the possession of LICENSOR at the effective date of this Agreement which are needed to produce LICENSED PRODUCTS and which LICENSOR has the right to provide to LICENSEE.[5] A list of documents containing TECHNICAL INFORMATION to be transferred to LICENSEE is attached hereto as Appendix __.

2.02 LICENSED TERRITORY means the United States, its territories, and possessions.[6]

2.03 LICENSED PRODUCTS means products which in the absence of this license agreement would infringe at least one claim of a PATENT or products which are made using a process or machine covered by a claim of a PATENT, or products made, at least in part, using TECHNICAL INFORMATION.

2.04 NET SALES PRICE for the purpose of computing royalties, means LICENSEE'S invoice price, f.o.b. factory, after deduction of regular trade and quantity discounts, but before deduction of any other items, including but not limited to freight allowances, cash discounts, and agents' commissions. Where products are not sold, but are otherwise disposed of, the NET SALES PRICE of such products for the purposes of computing royalties shall be the selling price at which products of similar kind and quality, sold in similar quantities, are currently being offered for sale by LICENSEE. Where such products are not currently being offered for sale by LICENSEE, the NET SALES PRICE of products otherwise disposed of, for the purpose of computing royalties, shall be the average selling price at which products of similar kind and quality, sold in similar quantities, are then currently being offered for sale by other manufacturers. Where such products are not

---

[5]*See* Chapter 21, Section 21.05.
[6]*See* Chapter 7, Section 7.01G.

currently sold or offered for sale by LICENSEE or others, then the NET SALES PRICE, for the purposes of computing royalties, shall be LICENSEE'S cost of manufacture, determined by LICENSEE's customary accounting procedures, plus ____ percent (__%). In order to assure to the LICENSOR the full royalty payments contemplated in this agreement, LICENSEE agrees that in the event any LICENSED PRODUCTS shall be sold for purposes of resale either (1) to a corporation, firm or association which, or individual who, owns a controlling interest in LICENSEE by stock ownership or otherwise, or (2) to a corporation, firm, or association in which the LICENSEE or its stockholders own a controlling interest by stock ownership or otherwise, the royalties to be paid in respect to such LICENSED PRODUCTS shall be computed upon the net selling price at which the purchaser for resale sells such PRODUCTS rather than upon the net selling price of the LICENSEE.[7]

2.05 EFFECTIVE DATE means _____, 199__.

III. Patent License[8]

3.00 LICENSOR hereby grants to LICENSEE, to the extent of LICENSED TERRITORY, a nonexclusive license under PATENTS to make, use, and sell LICENSED PRODUCTS. Nothing in this Agreement is intended to preclude the export or sale for export of products licensed in the Agreement to be sold or otherwise disposed of and on which royalties shall have been paid as provided in Sections 5.01, 5.02, and 5.03 of this Agreement, subject, however, to the understanding that no rights are granted or implied in respect to such exported products under any patent of LICENSOR or any other person in any foreign country.

IV. Technical Information License

4.00 LICENSOR hereby grants to LICENSEE, to the extent of LICENSED TERRITORY, a nonexclusive license to use the TECHNICAL INFORMATION to make LICENSED PRODUCTS.

4.01 LICENSOR shall within sixty (60) days of the EFFECTIVE DATE of this agreement make available to LICENSEE for its use TECHNICAL INFORMATION in LICENSOR'S possession needed to make LICENSED PRODUCTS. LICENSOR agrees to disclose to LICENSEE, upon execution of this

---

[7]*See* Chapter 9, Section 9.01B for drafting techniques for defining "net selling price."

[8]*See* Chapter 7, Section 7.02, Definition of Licensed Subject Matter.

Agreement, LICENSOR'S pending United States Patent Applications identified in Section 2.00 of this Agreement.[9]

4.03 LICENSEE shall not disclose any unpublished TECHNICAL INFORMATION furnished by LICENSOR pursuant to Section 4.01 above to third parties during the term of this Agreement, or any time thereafter, provided, however, that disclosure may be made of any such TECHNICAL INFORMATION at any time: (1) with the prior written consent of LICENSOR, or (2) to the extent necessary to purchasers of LICENSEE'S products or services, or (3) after the same shall have become public through no fault of LICENSEE or purchasers of LICENSEE'S products or services. To the extent that any such TECHNICAL INFORMATION is disclosed to purchasers of LICENSEE'S products or services, the agreements contained in this Article shall be made by LICENSEE to apply to and be made binding upon all such parties.

4.04 LICENSEE shall not use any TECHNICAL INFORMATION furnished by LICENSOR other than in the manufacture of LICENSED PRODUCTS and only during the term of this Agreement, provided, however, that other use of such TECHNICAL INFORMATION may be made: (1) with the prior written consent of LICENSOR, or (2) after the same shall have become public through no fault of LICENSEE or purchasers of LICENSEE'S products or services.

4.05 LICENSOR represents that the material lists, drawings, specifications, instructions, and other elements of TECHNICAL INFORMATION to be supplied by it under this Agreement have been used by it in the manufacture of LICENSED PRODUCTS, but does not otherwise warrant the accuracy of this information; nor does LICENSOR warrant that LICENSED PRODUCTS produced in accordance with such information will be free from claims of infringement of the patents or copyrights of any third party. LICENSOR shall not, except as provided in this Article IV, be under any liability arising out of the supplying of information under, in connection with, or as a result of this contract, whether on warranty, contract, negligence, or otherwise.

V. Royalties[10]

5.00 LICENSEE shall pay as a license execution fee the sum of $_____ which shall be nonrefundable and not creditable against the royalty called for under Sections 5.01, 5.02, or 5.03.

5.01 LICENSEE shall pay to LICENSOR a continuing royalty of _____ percent (____%) of the NET SALES PRICE of LICENSED PRODUCTS

---

[9]*See* Chapter 21, Section 21.05 for techniques for drafting a supply of information clause in a more complex situation.

[10]*See* Chapter 9.

used, sold, or otherwise disposed of under the license to PATENTS granted under Section 3.00.

   5.02 LICENSEE shall pay to LICENSOR a continuing royalty of _____ percent (____%) of the NET SALES PRICE of all LICENSED PRODUCTS used, sold, or otherwise disposed of under the TECHNICAL INFORMATION license granted under Article III.

   5.03 During the term of this Agreement the combined royalty rate of Sections 5.00 and 5.01 for any given LICENSED PRODUCTS shall not exceed _____ percent (____%) of NET SALES PRICE.

VI. Minimum Royalties[11]

   6.00 LICENSEE shall pay to LICENSOR royalties as stated in Section V, but in no event shall royalties for a calendar year for practice of the PATENTS and TECHNICAL INFORMATION in the LICENSED TERRITORY be less than the following minimum royalties during each of the calendar years indicated:

Calendar Year	Minimum Royalty, U.S. $ per Calendar Year* Nonexclusive License
199__	$
199__	
199__	
199__ and each calendar year thereafter during the term of this Agreement	

*Net to LICENSOR after taxes, if any, withheld at the source.

   6.01 LICENSOR may, by written notice to LICENSEE, terminate this Agreement during any February subsequent to the year 199__, if LICENSEE has not used, sold, or otherwise disposed of LICENSED PRODUCT sufficient to generate earned royalties as provided by Sections 5.01, 5.02, and 5.03 of this Agreement in the amount of _____ ($_____).

VII. Sublicensing

   7.00 LICENSEE shall not have the right to sublicense.

---

[11]*See* Chapter 9, Section 9.04.

VIII. Payments[12]

8.00 Not later than the last day of each January and July, LI-CENSEE shall furnish to LICENSOR a written statement in such detail as LICENSOR may reasonably require of all amounts due pursuant to Sections 5.01, 5.02, and 5.03 for the semiannual periods ended the last days of the preceding December and June, respectively, and shall pay to LICENSOR all amounts due to LICENSOR. In the event that the amounts due at the end of any calendar year do not equal the minimum royalties specified in Section VI for said calendar year, LICEN-SEE shall pay to LICENSOR on the last day of the following January, the amount required to satisfy the minimum royalty obligation for the preceding calendar year. Such amounts are due at the dates the statements are due. If no amount is accrued during any semiannual period, a written statement to that effect shall be furnished.

8.01 Payments provided for in this Agreement, when overdue, shall bear interest at a rate per annum equal to one percent (1%) in excess of the "PRIME RATE" published by "The Wall Street Journal" at the time such payment is due, and for the time period until payment is received by LICENSOR.

8.02 If this Agreement is for any reason terminated before all of the payments herein provided for have been made (including minimum royalties for the year in which the agreement is terminated), LICENSEE shall immediately submit a terminal report and pay to LICENSOR any remaining unpaid balance even though the due date as above provided has not been reached.

IX. Representations and Disclaimer of Warranties[13]

9.00 NOTHING IN THIS AGREEMENT SHALL BE DEEMED TO BE A REPRESENTATION OR WARRANTY BY LICENSOR OF THE VALIDITY OF ANY OF THE PATENTS OR THE ACCURACY, SAFETY, OR USEFULNESS FOR ANY PURPOSE, OF ANY TECHNICAL INFORMATION, TECHNIQUES, OR PRACTICES AT ANY TIME MADE AVAILABLE BY LICENSOR. LICENSOR SHALL HAVE NO LIABILITY WHATSOEVER TO LICENSEE OR ANY OTHER PERSON FOR OR ON ACCOUNT OF ANY INJURY, LOSS, OR DAMAGE, OF ANY KIND OR NATURE, SUSTAINED BY, OR ANY DAMAGE ASSESSED OR ASSERTED AGAINST, OR ANY OTHER LIABILITY INCURRED BY OR IMPOSED UPON LICENSEE OR ANY OTHER PERSON, ARISING OUT OF OR IN CONNECTION WITH OR RESULTING FROM (a)

---

[12]*See* Chapter 9, Section 9.02.

[13]*See* Chapter 14, Section 14.01. Note that under the Uniform Commercial Code §2-316, disclaimers of certain warranties related to sales of goods must be "conspicuous" to be effective, which suggests use of all capital letters in such disclaimers.

THE PRODUCTION, USE, OR SALE OF ANY APPARATUS OR PRODUCT, OR THE
PRACTICE OF THE PATENTS; (b) THE USE OF ANY TECHNICAL INFORMATION,
TECHNIQUES, OR PRACTICES DISCLOSED BY LICENSOR; OR (c) ANY ADVER-
TISING OR OTHER PROMOTIONAL ACTIVITIES WITH RESPECT TO ANY OF THE
FOREGOING, AND LICENSEE SHALL HOLD LICENSOR, ITS OFFICERS, EMPLOY-
EES, OR AGENTS, HARMLESS IN THE EVENT LICENSOR, OR ITS OFFICERS,
EMPLOYEES, OR AGENTS, IS HELD LIABLE.

X. Termination[14]

10.00 LICENSEE'S obligations under this Agreement relating to
an individual PATENT including the obligation to pay royalties for the
practice of the invention under any of the PATENTS licensed herein
shall end upon the expiration of the PATENT, unless the Agreement
is sooner terminated.

10.01 LICENSEE'S obligations under certain Sections of this Agreement relating to the TECHNICAL INFORMATION including the obligation
to pay royalties for the use of the TECHNICAL INFORMATION as specified
in Section 5.02 shall terminate ten (10) years from the date of the
first commercial use or sale of products or services utilizing the TECH-
NICAL INFORMATION, unless sooner terminated, but obligations under
Sections 4.03, 4.04, and 4.05 of this Agreement shall survive termination and continue until such time that LICENSOR elects to abandon such terms. LICENSEE shall notify LICENSOR of the date of first
commercial use or sale promptly thereafter.

10.02 LICENSEE may terminate this Agreement in part (Article
III or Article IV) or in whole at any time upon sixty (60) days' written
notice in advance to LICENSOR. If in part, such notice shall specify if
the Agreement shall be terminated in respect to the patent licenses
of Article III or the TECHNICAL INFORMATION license of Article IV and
shall state the reasons for such termination.

10.03 Termination of part of this Agreement in accordance with
Sections 10.01 and 10.02 above, or otherwise, shall not excuse LI-
CENSEE from the payment of a royalty in accordance with the royalty
provisions of Article 5 applicable to the surviving part. Survival of
this Agreement in part shall not deprive LICENSOR of the right to
enforce its proprietary rights against LICENSEE that are applicable to
the terminated part of the agreement.

10.04 If either party shall be in default of any obligation hereunder, or shall be adjudged bankrupt, or become insolvent, or make
an assignment for the benefit of creditors, or be placed in the hands
of a receiver or a trustee in bankruptcy, the other party may ter-

---

[14]*See* Chapter 17.

minate this Agreement by giving sixty (60) days' notice by Registered Mail to the other party, specifying the basis for termination. If within sixty (60) days after the receipt of such notice, the party who received notice shall remedy the condition forming the basis for termination, such notice shall cease to be operative, and this Agreement shall continue in full force.

10.05 Notwithstanding the provisions of Section 4.03 and 4.04, in the event this Agreement terminates prior to ten (10) years from the date of the first commercial use or sale of products or services utilizing the TECHNICAL INFORMATION, LICENSEE agrees: (1) that it will not use or sell LICENSED PRODUCT incorporating or made using TECHNICAL INFORMATION for a period of ten (10) years subsequent to the date of first commercial use of TECHNICAL INFORMATION if such use has occurred, or the EFFECTIVE DATE of this agreement; and (2) that it will promptly transfer to LICENSOR all written copies of unpublished TECHNICAL INFORMATION in its possession and delete all TECHNICAL INFORMATION from all computer data bases.

XI. Litigation[15]

11.00 LICENSEE shall notify LICENSOR of any suspected infringement of the PATENTS in the LICENSED TERRITORY. The sole right to institute a suit for infringement rests with LICENSOR. LICENSEE agrees to cooperate with LICENSOR in all respects, to have any of LICENSEE'S employees testify when requested by LICENSOR, and to make available any records, papers, information, specimens, and the like. Any recovery received pursuant to such suit shall be retained by LICENSOR.

11.01 During the term of this Agreement, LICENSEE shall bring to LICENSOR'S attention any prior art or other information known to LICENSEE which is relevant to the patentability or validity of any of the PATENTS and which might cause a court to deem any of the PATENTS wholly or partly inoperative or invalid. LICENSEE shall particularly specify such prior art or other information to LICENSOR at the time it learns thereof and not less than ninety (90) days prior to bringing any action against LICENSOR asserting the invalidity of any of the PATENTS.

XII. Patents

12.00 LICENSOR shall have the sole right to file, prosecute, and maintain all of the PATENTS covering the INVENTIONS that are the

---

[15]*See* Chapter 6, Section 6.04.

property of LICENSOR and shall have the right to determine whether or not, and where, to file a patent application, to abandon the prosecution of any patent or patent application, or to discontinue the maintenance of any patent or patent applications.

12.01 Improvement inventions made by LICENSEE shall be the exclusive property of LICENSEE.

XIII. Records

13.00 LICENSEE shall keep accurate records of all operations affecting payments hereunder, and shall permit LICENSOR or its duly authorized agent to inspect all such records and to make copies of or extracts from such records during regular business hours throughout the term of this Agreement and for a reasonable period of not less than three (3) years thereafter.

XIV. Nonassignability

14.00 This agreement imposes personal obligations on LICENSEE. LICENSEE shall not assign any rights under this Agreement not specifically transferable by its terms without the written consent of LICENSOR. LICENSOR may assign its rights hereunder.[16]

XV. Severability

15.00 The parties agree that if any part, term, or provision of this Agreement shall be found illegal or in conflict with any valid controlling law, the validity of the remaining provisions shall not be affected thereby.

15.01 In the event the legality of any provision of this Agreement is brought into question because of a decision by a court of competent jurisdiction of any country in which this Agreement applies, LICENSOR, by written notice to LICENSEE, may revise the provision in question or may delete it entirely so as to comply with the decision of said court.

XVI. Publicity

16.00 In publicizing anything made, used, or sold under this Agreement, LICENSEE shall not use the name of LICENSOR or otherwise

---

[16]*See* Chapter 12, Sections 12.01 and 12.02.

refer to any organization related to LICENSOR, except with the written approval of LICENSOR.

XVII. Waiver, Integration, Alteration

17.00 The waiver of a breach hereunder may be effected only by a writing signed by the waiving party and shall not constitute a waiver of any other breach.

17.01 This Agreement represents the entire understanding between the parties, and supersedes all other agreements, express or implied, between the parties concerning the PATENTS and TECHNICAL INFORMATION.

17.02 A provision of this Agreement may be altered only by a writing signed by both parties, except as provided in Section 15.01, above.

XVIII. Marking[17]

18.00 LICENSEE shall place in a conspicuous location on any product made or sold under any PATENT, a patent notice in accordance with 35 U.S.C. §287. LICENSEE agrees to mark any products made using a process covered by any PATENT with the number of each such patent and, with respect to PATENTS, to respond to any request for disclosure under 35 U.S.C. §287(b)(4)(B) by only notifying LICENSOR of the request for disclosure.

XIX. Cooperation

19.00 Each party shall execute any instruments reasonably believed by the other party to be necessary to implement the provisions of this Agreement.

XX. Construction

20.00 This Agreement shall be construed in accordance with the substantive laws of the State of _____ of the United States of America.

---

[17]*See* Chapter 16, Section 16.01.

XXI. Exportation of Technical Information

21.00 LICENSEE agrees to comply with the laws and rules of the United States Government regarding prohibition of exportation of TECHNICAL INFORMATION furnished to LICENSEE either directly or indirectly by LICENSOR.[18]

XXII. Notices Under the Agreement[19]

22.00 For the purpose of all written communications and notices between the parties, their addresses shall be:

LICENSOR: _____

_____

_____

_____

and

LICENSEE: _____

_____

_____

_____

or any other addresses of which either party shall notify the other party in writing.

IN WITNESS WHEREOF the parties have caused this Agreement to be executed by their duly authorized officers on the respective dates and at the respective places hereinafter set forth.[20]

LICENSEE
(COMPANY NAME)

ATTEST:

By: _____   By: _____

Title: _____

Signed at: _____   Date: _____

LICENSOR
(COMPANY NAME)

ATTEST:

By: _____   By: _____

Title: _____

Signed at: _____   Date: _____

---

[18]*See* Chapter 22, Section 22.03.

[19]*See* Chapter 16, Section 16.00.

[20]*See* Chapter 20.

Table of Authorities

Cases

Statutes, Rules, Regulations, and Codes

Other Publications

Topical Index

G.P. factors for R.R.

1. Royalties recieved by P.O. for patent
   - not full b/c litigation should be considered

2. Rates paided by licensee for comp. product

3. Nature of license
   - restrictions, exclusivity, teritory

4. P.O. Interest in maintaining monopoly

5. Commercial relationship
   - competitors

6. Convoyed Sales
   - Have to show higher per. of castoners purchase other items.

7. Length left on Patent

*8. Commercial Success of Product
   - Popularity - very imp

9. Utility of patent as an advance over old methods

10. Nature of patented invention
    - Benefits given, character

11. Extent to which infringer made use of invention
    - Used to directly compete?

12. Portion of profit or selling price that may be customary in the particular business

13. Portion of product att. to pat. product

14. Export test.

15. Amount reasonable licensee and licensor would have agreed upon
    - willing seller/buyer
    - presuming patent is valid.

Price Erosion
   - Decreasing of market price because of infr. products presence

*1. Lost Profits based on lost sales (show Panduit factors)

$$Dam = \left(ft. \text{ of cable sold by inf}\right)\left[\left(\frac{Pre\ inf\ price\ (P.O.\ price)}{ft\ sold\ by\ P.O}\right) - \left(Patent\ owners\ var.\ cost\ (overhead)\right)\right]$$

INCRIMENTAL profit margin

2. Price erosion

$$Dam = [Preinfringement\ price - price\ aft. infrm] * \left(\begin{array}{c}sales\ in\ ft\ by\\ P\text{i}O\ @\ reduced\ price\end{array}\right)$$

R.R. can only come into play aft validity and infring. have been determined
   - forcast statements are important

ENTIRE MARKET Rule
   - Is patented invention crucial in selling the whole machine
If yes, then may get "entire market value of machine.

Lost profits in a two supplier market
lost sales, increased expenses
diverted sales eroded prices

Burden:

Panduit Factors for damages Lost profits on L. Sales

1. Demand for patented product
2. Absence of acceptable sub.
   - At the time of infr.
   - Copying by others in industry - licensing
   - eliminate fact other products may be substituted
3. Manufacturing and mark. Capability to meet the demand.
4. Amount of profit that would have been made.

Implied License

1. Patent must be necessary to carry out expressed license
   - Implied in Law
2. P.O. must have knowledge of necessity
3. Language and/or conduct exhibited sufficient to constitute implication.

Metcoil
1. Eq. does not have a non-infr. use
2. Do circumstances at time of sale indicate implied license

Burden
Must prove losses by reasonable probility that A would have made the sales -

Implied in fact
- from surronding circumst.

Implied in Law (Equitable Est)
- facts make it inequitable to withhold license.

Shopright
- Employee, non royalty, nonexclusive, non-terminating license give to employer if made on co. time

Representations and Warranties

Exclusive
- Licensor will not grant any other licenses
- Will not practice

Non-Exc
- Will not sue

Licensee wants
  rep. of validity and scope

Licensor wants to say nothing
- any scope or validity statements may be used against him
- could say "not aware of any infrin or invalidity"

Indemnification
Should disclaim use of T.M. or TradeName

Marking Provision
Licensee should be required to mark

'Licensee may want "Best Efforts" disclaimer

Grant Back Disclosure
- Rep. that all employees will assign future inventions

Termination
- Define term who, How and When agreemnt will end
- Put in continuation provision for remaining activities
- Distinguish b/t material breach and other

"In the event of any breach of any provision party may terminate within 60 days unless notice of remedy is given".

Notice, Cure, notice

Effects of Termination
- Maintenence of conf., return of documents, pay for product made
  (know how transfer)
Sublicences continuation
    - licensee is agent of licensor

Resolution - Arbitration
  Where, What Issues, What Rules
  Nature of Award

Bankruptcy
- Licensor wants to anticipate choice of assignee.
- Ipso facto clause could be used to terminate int total
    but no longer enforceable

Licensee
- Can have option of treating agree. as terminated

Licensor
Security as no 1. creditor
- choice of rejecting or accepting assignee
1) must make license personal
2) Non-assignability w/o written notice

Intergration
This is the entire understanding b/w parties

Reasons to Licence (considerations)

1. Cross License – exchange of tech
2. Royalty/Monies
3. Interest in Co Stock
4. Lumpsum payments

Li.

Licensing fee cons:

1. Cost of neg.
2. Warranties & Guarantees given to licenses
3. Defense of licensee in potential lawsuit
4. Should not be more than licensee will pay to invent around.
5. Max price licensor will pay to litigate infring case

Avoid for Royalty Base

1) Anyway licensee may avoid reasonable royalty.
2) Payments based on profits – can be controlled be licensor
3) Net selling price if licensee controls also Inflation may be influencial

Pg 77-79

Prevent Infring - Clause

1) Should have some measuring level at which obligation kicks in
2) Another provision would prevent licensor from going after more than one infringer at a time
3) Notice of infringement should be given to licensor
4) Outside opinion on infringement

3rd Party indem

Licensees wants indem clause
Licensor wants limits – cond precedents
1. Notice of infringe
2. Limit the dates of covered patents
3. Should limit control the product to be made under agreement
   – too much control may be problematic
4. Licensor would be in control of lawsuit and settlement